BORDERS, MOBILITY AND TECHNOLOGIES OF CONTROL

Borders, Mobility and Technologies of Control

Edited by

Sharon Pickering,
Monash University, Melbourne, VIC, Australia

and

Leanne Weber
University of New South Wales, NSW, Australia

 Springer

A C.I.P. Catalogue record for this book is available from the Library of Congress.

ISBN-10 1-4020-4898-X (HB)
ISBN-13 978-1-4020-4898-2 (HB)
ISBN-10 1-4020-4899-8 (e-book)
ISBN-13 978-1-4020-4899-9 (e-book)

Published by Springer,
P.O. Box 17, 3300 AA Dordrecht, The Netherlands.

www.springer.com

Printed on acid-free paper

Printed in the Netherlands

This book is dedicated to the world's vagabonds:

for Stephen, who made it, and others who didn't.

Contents

Contributing Authors

Jan Carpenter is a PhD student in history at Northern Arizona University, studying immigration, race and gender in the United States–Mexico borderlands. Her first doctorate, in which she investigated motivations for corporate lobbying behaviour, is from Texas A&M University.

Professor Kerry Carrington Chair in Sociology in the School of Social Sciences at University of New England in northern New South Wales, has a wide variety of research interests in criminology, sociology, social policy and gender studies. She is author of *Offending Girls: Sex Youth & Justice* (1993) and *Who Killed Leigh Leigh?* (1998); co-author of *Policing the Rural Crisis* (2006) and co-editor of *Critical Criminology: Issues, Debates & Challenge (2002), Travesty! Miscarriages of Justice (1991)* and *Cultures of Crime and Violence (1995)*. In 2003, she worked as a senior researcher for the Australian Parliament and wrote a number of social policy briefs about immigration crime, border control, trafficking and the sex industry.

Mona J.E. Danner is Associate Professor of Sociology and Criminal Justice at Old Dominion University in Norfolk, Virginia. Social inequalities, justice policy and globalisation comprise her primary research interests.

Penny Green is Professor of Law and Criminology at the University of Westminster, London. She has written widely on the subject of state crime, Turkish criminal justice; state organisational deviance and 'natural' disasters; European asylum policy and drug trafficking. Her publications include *State Crime: Governments, Violence and Corruption, Criminal Policy in Transition, Drugs, Trafficking and Criminal Policy* and *The Enemy Without*. She is currently researching the market in looted antiquities, and the role of civil society in controlling state crime, particularly illegal logging.

Alice Hills is a senior lecturer at the University of Leeds where she directs the program in conflict, development and security. The core of her research focus is to develop a comparative framework for analysing why police forces evolve as they do, and what explains their interaction with governments, militaries and civil society in fragile states. Relevant publications include *Border Security in the Balkans: Europe's Gatekeepers*, (Adelphi paper No. 371).

Sharon Pickering is a senior lecturer in Criminology at Monash University, Melbourne. Her previous titles include *Refugees and State Crime* (2005); *Global Issues, Women and Justice* (2004 edited with Lambert) *Critical Chatter: Women and Human Rights in South East Asia* (2003 with Lambert and Alder); and *Women, Policing and Resistance* (2002).

Leanne Weber teaches in the School of Social Science and Policy at the University of New South Wales, and previously coordinated a Bachelor of Policing program at the University of Western Sydney. She has an interest in the intersection between criminal justice practice and human rights and has researched and written about the detention of asylum seekers and the policing of migration.

Dean Wilson lectures in Criminal Justice and Criminology in the School of Political and Social Inquiry, Monash University, Melbourne. His research interests include surveillance and social control, media representations of crime, and histories and cultures of policing. His current research is focused upon discourses of security in the Australian media and the socio-political significance of contemporary surveillance technologies.

Dr. Nancy A. Wonders is Professor of Criminal Justice at Northern Arizona University. She is internationally recognised for her research on inequality and justice, sex tourism, feminist criminology, and globalisation, migration and border performativity.

Acknowledgments

It has been a pleasure to work with the outstanding academics who have contributed to this collection. They have been patient and supportive and come together across a number of geographical and interdisciplinary borders.

We are indebted to Trish Luker for transforming our manuscript into a camera-ready document.

John Gaffey uncovered a wealth of material through his online voyages which contributed to the first two chapters.

This volume was improved by the comments of three anonymous reviewers as well as by valued colleagues at home and abroad including Dr. Jude McCulloch and Professor Ray Michaelowsi.

Welmoed Spahr has been an enthusiastic and committed publishing editor and we are grateful for her openness to our project and the publication of this work.

Sharon has been generously supported by Tom throughout the life of this collection, and its completion has been all the more exciting and wonderful with the arrival of Wesley.

Chapter 1

BORDERS, MOBILITY AND TECHNOLOGIES OF CONTROL

Sharon Pickering and Leanne Weber
Monash University and University of New South Wales

Borders, Mobility and Technologies of Control focuses on borders and the significance, from a criminological point of view, of the activities which take place on and around them. For many, the border is an everyday reality; a space in which to live; a land necessary to cross once, twice or many times; a space of sanctuary; a dangerous space. Often the border can be many or all of these things at once. For states, the border space increasingly requires protection and defence. It is also increasingly at the centre of state ideology and performance, the site for investing significant political and material resources, and is ultimately ungovernable.

In a rapidly globalising world, territorial borders are taking on a new significance, the implications of which are relatively unexplored within the discipline of criminology. Traditionally, criminology has aligned its own disciplinary boundaries with those of the nation-state, concerning itself with behaviours defined as criminal by state or national governments and with the institutions and enforcement practices of state actors confined within territorial boundaries and compared across territorially-bounded spaces. This approach is increasingly recognised as inadequate in the context of greatly increased levels of traditional cross-border crime, innovative technologies which create new opportunities both for criminal exploitation and new techniques of state control, and a widespread climate of fear and insecurity arising from global economic and political threats, transnational terrorism, and changing conceptions of the powers and responsibilities of the nation-state.

Borders, Mobility and Technologies of Control is specifically interested in how physical borders are impacting on the mobility of people. Concomitantly, it is concerned with how the state exercises its authority at and around the border and how it is experienced and understood by those

S. Pickering and L. Weber (eds.), Borders, Mobility and Technologies of Control, 1–19.
© 2006 Springer. Printed in the Netherlands.

involved in processes of exclusion. Criminalisation of 'unauthorised' border crossing has been a primary border control strategy in Europe, North America and Australia. Indeed, processes of criminalisation have largely come to reconstitute the circumstances and experiences of those who transgress borders. In turn, criminalisation has become central to the re-enforcement of territorial borders when, on many other levels, the role of national borders has been in decline. This collection will cover both how the border has been used in the construction of 'new' crimes, 'new' forms of law enforcement and processes of criminalisation, as well as how state practices at the border may themselves be considered criminally suspect.

1.   BORDERS

The border itself has been the focus of wide-ranging concern for social theorists and there is a growing body of literature that examines borders not simply as lines on maps, but rather as spaces of political, cultural and security significance. Heyman et al. (2002: 62), for example, conceives of borders as 'simultaneously structures and processes, things and relationships, histories and events'. Miller and Hashmi (2001) make a fundamental distinction between informal, social boundaries which are maintained by cultural and ethnic distinctions, and formal, territorial boundaries within which property and authority relations are exercised. They argue that modern states have attempted to dissolve this distinction by absorbing 'nationality'—the pre-eminent social boundary—within the concept of the nation-state, a process which they now observe is breaking down. They examine the justification for borders from a range of political and moral perspectives, including international human rights law, classical and egalitarian liberalism, Islam and Christianity.

One of the most comprehensive reviews of the treatment of borders within contemporary social thought comes from Donnan and Wilson (1999). They review how new conceptions of the border are emerging within the disciplines of geography (increasingly conceiving of borders in terms of function rather than form or place); history (where they argue causal links between territory, identity and sovereignty are being called into question); political science (where statist views of borders are being displaced by accounts of multidimensional frontiers where states exercise only limited control); cultural and comparative studies (where borders are viewed primarily as signifiers of culture and identity); and sociology (assessed by Donnan and Wilson in 1999 as still treating borders as a peripheral theme). Notably, criminology is not identified in this review as a discipline which has produced any significant literature on the subject of borders.

Operating from an anthropological perspective, Donnan and Wilson conceptualise borders as 'politicised boundaries' which are 'sites and symbols of power' that may be reinforced or neglected by states depending on the circumstances. Far from merely lines on a map, borders are understood as institutions, processes and markers of identity, and subject to competing definitions by the state and borderland populations. This is exemplified in the work of Ortiz (2001), who argues that the contested borderland between Mexico and the United States is best defined in terms of its ambiguity. He notes that local concerns compete with, but are generally subsumed by, imperatives arising from the region's status as a transit zone, leading to deeply asymmetrical experiences of borderland dwellers on either side.

Donnan and Wilson (1999: 15) propose that a border is constituted by three elements: a juridical borderline; the actions of state agents who operate in border areas but 'who also often penetrate deeply into the territory of the state'; and associated frontiers which are 'negotiated spaces which stretch across and away from state borders'. With borders no longer fixed and settled, the concept of frontierlands becomes more salient, denoting a space on and around the juridical border where power relations are uncertain and contested. These dimensions correspond to the different entities described by Nevins (cited in Pickering 2004) of the boundary (conceived as a strict line of separation); the border (a zone of gradual division and interaction); and the frontier (defined as a sparsely controlled zone of contact).

Writing in a slightly different context, geographer Howitt (2001: 234) proposes a transcendence of the limitations of both borders and frontiers, by drawing on the indeterminate and shifting concept of 'edges': 'I want to shift Australians' geographical imaginings away from the oppositional zoning of 'frontiers' and the categorical separateness of 'borders' to a liminal, multi-dimensional, real-world idea of edges as places with a more solid and changeable engagement with complexity'. Unlike the imagery of 'sharp edges' as used by Gready (2004) in his discussion of 'violently policed borders', Howitt's conception of edges recognises the possibility of peaceful coexistence, while frontiers imply lawlessness and conquest, a space beyond the rule of law where power prevails.

Donnan and Wilson (1999) argue that the concept of borders as sites for the expression of state power (which is prime analytical terrain for criminologists) has been relatively unexplored by anthropologists who favour analyses in terms of cultural meaning and identity. The theme of borders as sites for the expression of state power has been taken up in a study by Parsley (2003). Writing from a critical legal studies perspective, Parsley conceptualises the border as a 'narrative performance of nationalism', representing the organised power of the nation expressed through the decisions of border officials, and to be understood both as a site of great force and great weakness.

Primarily, criminologists have understood the border as increasingly the focus of securitisation and crime control. The nation-state has depended upon the border as a marker of territory and of inclusion and exclusion. The changing nature of borders, the occupation of the border space and border crossing increasingly brings the very nature of the state, and the state system, into question. Such border anxiety, and the increasing consideration of border crossing as a 'crime', has captured some criminological imagination and prompted critical forays into discussions of sovereignty and the terrain of traditional international relations.

Sovereignty has powerfully marked the boundaries between inside and outside and the debates covered in this collection engage with the ways the border has been an important marker of sovereign expression (see particularly chapters by Pickering and Carrington). As Devetak (1995) has argued, industrialisation, militarisation and colonialism have informed the powerful sovereign marking of inside from outside. Territorial sovereignty has been established and accepted as the normalising and cohering force from which life flows (Soguk 1999), a pre-existing state that is bordered and discernible. International relations traditionally conceived of the border in such ways that enabled criminology to continually domesticate its concerns within national borders, crossing borders only to study international crime and law enforcement where borders continued to be self-referential and unchallenged. However, new bodies of international relations thought unshackle the criminology of this volume to argue, in a similar fashion to Reus-Smit (2001), that borders are never self-referential but are always justified in relation to specific formations of legitimate statehood and state action. Such work problematises the notion of territorial sovereignty as absolute (Hoffman 1998) particularly in relation to understandings of human rights which no longer simply require the state to mediate their recognition and application. The work of Sassen (1996) clearly articulates how, for example, women have become important legal actors as they cross borders and challenge traditional versions of sovereignty. In this sense, sovereignty and territorial borders can be read as potentially emancipatory spaces. Moreover, statist expressions of territorially sovereign borders have also produced malleable borders where politically convenient, and unlock powerful new expressions of jurisdictionally-free political power. For criminologists, the increasing interdependencies of a globalised world are simultaneously challenging the bearers and enforcers of social order (Loader and Sparks 2002) to which criminology has traditionally adhered.

Borders, Mobility and Technologies of Control moves criminology into this challenging terrain to ascertain the intersections of legitimacy, force, sovereignty and resistance at the border. The contingency of sovereign territorial borders requires a rethinking of criminology's historical understanding of its core business being primarily inside the bordered nation-state. The contributions refute the marking of inside from outside that has historically occurred at the sovereign territorial border—both to document an alternate criminological account of the past and to consider possible futures—futures which will require states to come to terms with border crossing.

2. MOBILITY

According to the United Nations High Commission for Refugees (UNHCR), the mobility of people across borders in 'unauthorised' ways is increasing. The foreign-born population of the United States has been growing at an unprecedented rate since the 1990s, and up to one third of that growth has been attributed to unauthorised arrivals (Passel et al., cited in Cornelius 2005). In a statement released on 21 May 2004, the International Labour Organization (ILO) argued that 'the number of people crossing borders in search of work and financial security will increase rapidly in the next decades as globalization fails to provide them with jobs and economic opportunities' (United Nations 2004). Although the numbers of people arriving at the borders of affluent states via irregular means is still miniscule compared with the massive volume of commercial and recreational traffic, it is asylum applicants and other unauthorised arrivals who are defined as 'immigration problems', delaying the passage of 'legitimate' passengers at busy ports as they occupy the time of border officials, and threatening the economic and social fabric if allowed to remain within the community.

Unwanted border crossing is not, of course, a new phenomenon. In pre-industrial Britain (to draw on one of the best documented examples), the 'masterless men' and 'valiant beggars' who wandered from parish to parish in search of alms or work as agricultural labourers were greeted with similar suspicion to today's 'unauthorised arrivals' and 'bogus asylum seekers'. The perceived danger of their uncontrolled mobility was met with measures aimed to prevent free movement, justified 'by the belief that poverty, vagrancy, the spread of the plague, idleness, immorality, irreligion and crime were linked together' (Rawlings 2002: 45). Personal mobility of the newly 'emancipated' labouring classes did not fit with a system of government which rested on land, and so, according to Rawlings, was recast in terms of the 'sin of idleness and the crime of vagrancy'. In uncertain and changing times, mobility had come to connote disorder, especially in relation to the very sections of the population dislocated by the economic upheavals.

Then, just as today, efforts were made to separate the 'deserving' from the 'undeserving' in order to reconcile harsh treatment with the Christian (now humanitarian) duty to meet their needs. Relief for the deserving (immobile) poor was provided at parish level, while increasingly harsh punishments were scheduled for those who could not establish a link to any 'respectable' community, and were defined as vagrants. By Elizabethan times, Romany Gypsies, who were once reputedly welcomed at imperial courts as exotic and noble raconteurs, and whose nomadic way of life was valued for the services and entertainment it provided to rural villagers, faced execution or exile on the basis of both their ethnic identity and their itinerant habits (Acton 1974; Fraser 1992). This signified a racialisation of the measures to suppress mobility, and a shift towards defining the apparent enemy as originating from 'without' although residing 'within'.

At the same time, the British empire was redrawing borders and, by the forced deportation of many citizens to colonies around the globe, created and recreated states through the colonial project that similarly depended upon state-sponsored forced mobility based on social exclusion. In the modern British state, the cultural and administrative boundaries defined by parishes and counties which were once so vigorously defended hold diminished significance (although the early-modern attempts to control unwanted move-ments across local boundaries have resurfaced in contemporary public housing policies, which seek to eliminate applicants without a historic link to the local area). But what is different about the contemporary anxiety about border crossing is the global scope of mass population movements, the borders that are crossed, and the elimination of the state from the decision-making process. The borders being breached are now territorial boundaries, through which the modern state has come to define its identity and express its sovereign power. Viewed from a state-centred perspective, the 'problem' of uncontrolled border crossing signals the emergence of an army of 'global vagrants' who represent disorder on a global scale and embody the many insecurities arising from globalising trends in late modernity. In a world increasingly differentiated by access to mobility, Bauman describes two 'postmodern types': the tourists who 'pay for their freedom; the right to disregard native concerns and feelings, the right to spin their own meanings' (Bauman 1993: 241) and the vagabonds, for whom, more often than not, 'it will not be for him to decide when the stay will come to an end' (240).

Mobility is, therefore, once again both a serious and important topic for social analysis, and a basis for implementing exclusionary and criminalising policies. Urry is one commentator who has given mobility a central place in the development of his 'post-societal' sociology (Urry 2000a). His concern is to develop an analytical method which is applicable to an emergent 'global civil society', rather than provide an analysis or critique of the current plight of the globally mobile poor and insecure. Urry's forward-looking theorising imagines mobility as constitutive of a self-reproducing global order, and foresees the 'social as society' being transformed into the 'social as mobility' (186). On this view, contemporary social life is not merely fractured and transient, as described by many post-modern and late-modern theorists, it is fundamentally constituted by a range of mobilities of people, goods and information, including an unprecedented level of personal fluidity. On the most positive reading, this increasingly mobile world is tending towards some new equilibrium where mobility no longer signals instability, and where some form of mobile citizenship is possible. A special issue of the *Journal of Ethnic and Migration Studies* (Conradson and Latham 2005), has advanced this analysis through the concept of 'transnational urbanism' which is intended to convey both the inescapable emplacement of day to day life, and the possibility of achieving order through mobility.

On the journey to this possible new world, the opportunities of global mobility are not opening up equally to all the occupants of the planet. Urry refers to, but does not elaborate, what he calls the 'various kinds of disabling processes which limit or constrain the mobilities of many' (Urry 2000b: 50), and acknowledges that any 'full blown sociology of travel' would have to tackle these issues of inequality of access. Yeoh (2005: 412), commenting on the special issue of the *Journal of Ethnic and Migration Studies* referred to above, also challenges the tendency within the emerging field of transnational studies to assume that 'traversing of transnational space is smooth, painless and almost instantaneous'. In the same volume, Rogers (2005: 404), identifies an important question not addressed by the contributors, namely, how and why the 'transnational mobility of some is achieved at the cost of the relative immobility or entrapment of others'.

Empirical research into the motivations and constraints on border crossing by citizens from the 'suspect populations' of the world, such as a study by Carling (2002) on the gap between the desires and possibilities for foreign travel amongst Cape Verdeans, gives us concrete examples of the 'involuntary immobility' of those populations. Bauman provides a more general account in his theorising about the human consequences of globalisation, of the contrast between the 'extraterritoriality of the new global elites and the forced territoriality of the rest' (Bauman 2000: 221). In fact, Bauman (1998: 87) has argued that the capacity or incapacity to move has become the dominant new form of social stratification in a globalising world, and a powerful mediator of social inclusion and exclusion:

> The present-day combination of annulment of entry visas and the reinforcement of immigration controls has profound symbolic significance. It could be taken as the metaphor for the new, emergent, stratification. It lays bare the fact that it is now the 'access to global

mobility' which has been raised to the topmost rank among the stratifying factors.

Moreover, the same processes which are arguably producing an immobilised 'global underclass', continue to provide the imperative for them to cross borders in search of physical and economic security. In large part, of course, the immobilisation is a direct response to the unwanted mobility, in the face of security and employment needs which governments in host countries are unwilling or unable to address in relation to non-citizens. It is easier, of course, to focus on the mobility itself as the threat, than to come to terms with the underlying reasons for it. It is perhaps no coincidence that Romany asylum seekers, excluded from the contemporary exercise of nation-building in the ever-expanding 'European project' (Green and Grewcock 2002), and seemingly assigned a permanent status as itinerant and shiftless outsiders, continue to be singled out for particular vilification, as reflected, for example, in views expressed to one of the present authors by British immigration officers (Weber and Landman 2002). At the same time, Schuster's (2005) research with undocumented foreigners in Italy, and the analysis by Cornelius (2005) of unauthorised border crossing at the United States–Mexico border, reveal a variety of migration patterns, including what Schuster describes as 'shuttle migration', where stays in the host country are interspersed (border conditions permitting) with frequent returns to the country of origin. This flies in the face of official presumptions about the intentions of unauthorised entrants to stay permanently and 'milch' the host state.

In the face of inescapable changes associated with globalisation, affluent states and their inhabitants can either embrace a more mobile and inclusive world; seek to minimise and manage population movements through structural reform to create 'decent work' where people live, as argued by the ILO, or through conflict resolution and 'burden sharing', as proposed by the UNHCR; or attempt to pre-empt and expel unwanted arrivals. Juss (2004) has made the case that freedom of movement between territories is a fundamental human right, increasingly central to the realisation of other human aspirations, and could be incorporated into positive international law through an incremental process concentrating initially on employment-related mobility. Although engaged through international mechanisms in some of the migration management activities mentioned above, governments in the affluent world have overwhelmingly opted for restrictive measures, mobilising all the technologies of sovereignty at their disposal to defend their borders. As Bauman (2000: 214) argues: 'In the ever more insecure and uncertain world the withdrawal into the safe haven of territoriality is an intense temptation'.

3.   TECHNOLOGIES OF CONTROL

In fact, state responses to uncontrolled mobility continue to become more sophisticated and far reaching, employing highly technical, increasingly punitive and innovative methods of border control. The contributions in this volume seek to analyse these border technologies from a range of perspectives (see chapters by Carpenter, Carrington, Green, Hills and Pickering), and the chapter by Weber describes how the border *itself* has been manipulated as a technique of border control. Wonders points out the selectivity of these border technologies which are aimed at facilitating the travel of global elites while screening out unwanted arrivals and the chapters by Danner and Wilson stress their potential ubiquity when applied internally to citizen and non-citizen alike. Taken together, these measures produce an emerging class of the 'mobility poor' who seem destined, like the 'masterless men' and 'valiant beggars' of previous centuries, to shoulder the generalised anxieties of insecure and turbulent times. This network of selective controls designed to protect the secure and developed world from the incursions of the poor and insecure has been graphically described by Richmond (1994) as 'global apartheid'.

The techniques adopted to effect this separation align with other developments in the regulatory-yet-punitive state, where the means of social control are becoming increasingly automated and asocial (Braithwaite 2000), and operate through a variety of 'switch point(s) to be passed in order to access the benefits of liberty' (Rose 2000: 326). Wilson's chapter in this collection highlights the implications of the application of biometrics as the quintessentially asocial border technology. Furthermore, these information-based switch points increasingly apply not only at the physical border but reach both inwards and outwards from it. Health and welfare workers, teachers, employers and the general public are increasingly recruited in a web of surveillance aimed at identifying those who do not belong, and stand to be excluded not only from the provision of services but also from the physical territory (see chapters by Danner and Weber). And the actuarial logic of risk management, which pervades the governance of developed states under globalisation, has also pushed border controls outwards, both legally and physically, through visa regimes, carrier sanctions, overseas liaison officers, transnational disruption operations and information exchange networks, all aimed at preventing unwanted arrivals. These extra-territorial expressions of sovereign power (discussed most explicitly in the chapters by Carrington, Green and Weber) clearly rely on the doctrine of pre-emption which has made an emphatic appearance elsewhere on the global stage. The chapter by Hills highlights the complex, and often conflicting, demands being made in the name of border security.

As the concept of physical borders—the ultimate switch point governing movements between nation-states—is being reinterpreted, fragmented and manipulated, governments have also sought to reinforce the *symbolic* and *discursive* importance of borders as impenetrable barriers and have elevated border protection as the ultimate political objective (see chapter by Pickering). The political rhetoric about 'bogus asylum seekers' and 'illegal immigrants' which has accompanied coercive measures such as indefinite detention and forced deportations, has effectively redefined the act of border crossing as a 'crime of arrival' (Webber 1996). It has been widely observed that these policies have forced would-be border crossers into more irregular and dangerous modes of travel (see chapters by Carpenter and Green). This, in turn, has only heightened suspicions about their identity and intentions, thereby fuelling a cycle of 'deviancy amplification' (Weber and Bowling 2004) and a relentless procession of deaths at the literal and virtual border (Fekete 2003). It is notable that, while increasingly automated and infor-mation-based technologies are being employed at concentrated border points, such as busy commercial ports—where efficiency considerations often conflict with security demands in terms of passenger processing—less governable frontierlands, where the border dynamic is overwhelmingly one of the global south seeking access to the global north, have been subject to heavy militarisation and surveillance.

As a result of these attempts to make borders impenetrable, unauthorised border crossers have asphyxiated in lorries, been blown-up in minefields between Greece and Turkey, been crushed to death in the undercarriages of trains and frozen in the wheel compartments of planes. They have leapt to their death from balconies trying to elude immigration authorities, and their bodies are now washed ashore with casual regularity on Mediterranean beaches. They have perished in the Arizona desert, risking the most dangerous of crossings to avoid armed border patrols and vigilante groups, taken their own lives in detention centres, and have died at the hands of border guards, police, people smugglers, private security guards, immigration authorities and violent racists. Cornelius (2005) estimates that the fortified border between the United States and Mexico has been ten times deadlier over the last nine years for those attempting to enter the United States without permission, than was the Berlin wall to those attempting to leave East Germany during the entire 28 years of its existence. Not only this, but the United States border strategy has manifestly failed in its objective to curb unauthorised border crossing, and has, according to Cornelius (2005: 782), 'been more effective in bottling up unauthorised migrants inside the US than in deterring them from coming in the first place'.

The central normative question associated with border control is: 'What actions are states entitled to take—and where can they do this—in defence of their borders? For those who advocate a truly borderless world in the name of global justice, the answer is clear: no-one's mobility should be curtailed by state intervention, except, arguably, for the genuine and exceptional purpose of averting real and imminent harm (see, for example, Hayter 2000). Within the criminological literature, Grewcock (2003) has recently argued a radical open borders position. For those who strive to find a balance between freedom of movement and social stability within a transitional and inherently unstable global environment, the answer will be more elusive. Juss (2004) argues that legislation in favour of free movement rights is actually required in order to achieve global stability, but resiles from advocating a radical open borders agenda, in favour of an incremental achievement of positive rights within the existing system of international law. Sparrow (2003) provides a cogent discussion of the practical and philosophical difficulties from a position which is supportive of, but ultimately rejects, an open borders philosophy in favour of efforts to redress the gross inequalities in life opportunities that fuel mass population movements. Suffice to say that most contributors in this volume adopt a critical view of the coercive measures being adopted at present by states in the name of border protection, characterise them as backward-looking and based on a limited notion of the possibilities of state action, and seek to problematise the perception of 'harm' that informs governments' calculations of this balance. Indeed, the concept of balance seems ripe for serious criminological critique.

Clearly, there is also an economic dimension underpinning the legal, moral and political struggle over migration controls. The inability of states to maintain the huge costs of border protection (as detailed in the chapters by Danner and Wonders) could conceivably play a part in bringing about change. Juss (2004), for example, identifies the enormous costs of migration control as one argument for the abandonment of attempts to constrain mobility, advocating instead a 'creative accommodation' of new patterns of movement. Earlier in this discussion we drew attention to similarities between the criminalisation of the mobile poor of pre-industrial Britain and the present day reaction to unauthorised border crossing. According to Rawlings (2002), the plight of the mobile poor did not change much until they were recognised as a useful economic resource following Indus-trialisation. Perhaps the full resolution of the contemporary 'problem' of global mobility awaits the emergence of a truly global civil society, combining the 'fluid' society alluded to by Urry (2000b), which is constituted by individual mobility and transient membership, and the 'globalisation of labour' foreseen by Sassen (1996). In fact, it could be argued (for example, see Juss 2004), that the relaxation of migration restrictions is a necessary condition for the production of a more stable world order.

This is not to suggest that a society which has accommodated mobility is necessarily a just one, and opportunities for movement, and the degree of choice over individual mobility are likely to continue to be unevenly distributed. Moreover, opportunities for criminal activity and other security threats will no doubt continue to arise around residual borders, and challenge any utopian vision, although relaxation of border controls of itself would virtually eliminate one category of cross-border 'crime' by removing the market for 'people smuggling'. In the meantime, while nation-states persist in attempting to impose order on the emergent disorder using the traditional state-based methods that are available to them, there remains a considerable task of documenting and critiquing the changing meaning of territorial borders and contemporary state responses to border crossing.

4.   THE COLLECTION

This collection is concerned with the plurality and manipulation of borders in time and space, the constitution and communication of terri- torially sovereign borders, the gendered, racialised and classed dimensions of borders, the application of 'high-tech' sorting and surveillance techniques at and beyond borders, the defence of borders by a range of state actors, the violent actions and inactions of border officials as potent forms of state crime, and the historically cyclical nature of border exclusion.

Borders, Mobility and Technologies of Control brings together a range of accounts of the border from local expressions with international ramifications and international expressions with decidedly local consequences. The authors take a variety of approaches to conceptually locating and arguing the border, however the following characteristics, taken as a whole, reflect a commonality in approach which sets this collection apart from other attempts at understanding the border.

First, the contributors do not understand the border as a fixed entity, but rather as a space created and recreated by states and other actors in a way that is fundamentally gendered, raced and classed. Secondly, the border is seen to have both repressive and emancipatory potential, although it is clear that in the current global moment repression has the upper hand. Thirdly, the border is identified as a key focus for a critical criminology concerned with the theoretical and pragmatic expression of state power and alternative forms of power in late-modern societies under conditions of globalisation. Fourthly, the border is viewed as a window to examine key issues between the global north and global south indicative of changing world orders and criminological spaces no longer concerned solely with the preoccupations of the global elite.

This collection begins by tracing the changing locations of migration control. In Chapter 2, 'The Shifting Frontiers of Migration Control', Leanne Weber argues that, even in the post-September 11 world, the pass-key to many of the world's borders is still freely available to those possessing the requisite financial and social capital. For the remainder, an increasingly complex and interconnected system of transnational controls is aimed at ensuring immobility and exclusion, by repelling people at borders, preventing their initial departure or, when all else fails, punishing their arrival. Her chapter examines some recent innovations in border policing strategies which indicate a dynamic and shifting balance between pre-entry, border and in-country controls, drawing primarily on British and Australian examples. She argues that governments have introduced legal reforms and enforcement practices which effectively shift immigration controls in both time and space. This creates malleable and moveable borders which can be defined and redefined—functionally, geographically and legally—in line with differing policy objectives.

In Chapter 3, 'Border Narratives: From Talking Security to Performing Borderlands'*,* Sharon Pickering argues that borders are performed to multiple audiences and produce not only a range of words, languages and codes to communicate their location and function, but also generate the border itself. Increasingly, such border talk has involved the meshing of migration issues and the criminal justice apparatus as well as agents broadly denoted under the banner 'national security'. In this chapter, Pickering documents some of the many border languages used to convince multiple audiences as to the nature and function of borders (including the mechanisms used to erect and patrol borders) and the concomitant response of those audiences. She traces the discourses that the violent boundary inscription practices of statecraft depend upon to establish their legitimacy and the requisite reformulation of notions of territoriality and criminality.

In Chapter 4, 'Global Flows, Semi-Permeable Borders and New Channels of Inequality', Nancy Wonders notes that two of the most significant border flows in the contemporary period are migration and tourism. Importantly, these two global trends both involve the movement of people across borders, whether in search of jobs and security or leisure and luxury. Utilising the theoretical framework of 'border performativity', Wonders argues that nation-states today are engaging in border performances that ensure the semi-permeability of borders under globalisation. She analyses two technologies of control that help to ensure that borders facilitate the entry of some while limiting the entry of others: first, the social construction of 'illegals' and the criminalisation of vulnerable populations and, secondly, the 'securitisation of migration' and the creation of a border control industry that gives organisational architecture and durability to state performances of semi-permeable borders. By comparing the way that nations construct and enforce borders differently for different border crossers, much is revealed about the new channels of inequality that are being carved under globalisation. Given the many risks and benefits of both migrant workers and tourists to nation-states participating in the global economy, Wonders argues for more flexible and fairer borders for both kinds of travellers.

In Chapter 5, 'Biometrics, Borders and the Ideal Suspect', Dean Wilson examines the rise of biometrics in the drawing and enforcement of borders. Focusing on technology, social sorting and the surveillance of exclusion, Wilson traces the expansion of biometric technologies in the monitoring of populations following September 11 and the subsequent 'war on terror'. He finds that, since 2001, there has been a significantly expanded deployment of biometric identification technologies that seek to fix individual identities through the use of physical identifiers such as iris patterns and fingerprints. This is most evident at the borders between nation-states, where biometric passports and registration systems such as INSPASS in the United States are instrumental in processes of 'social sorting'. The concept of 'social sorting' refers to the coterminous construction of 'low risk' travellers, whose movements are characterised by unimpeded access and privileged citizenship, and 'high risk' travellers—those compelled to travel without documentation or with 'low-tech' documentation from the nation-states of the global south. Moreover, biometric technologies are pivotal to emerging cultures of securitisation that are enacted both internally and externally to the nation-state. Processes of exclusion and inclusion performed at ports of entry are thus analogous to state efforts to fix identities internally, most notably through the expanding number of states either establishing or considering national identification cards embedded with personal identifiers. Wilson concludes by arguing that the efficacy of such technologies is of less importance than their powerful signifying function in suggesting the continued capacity of the nation-state to monitor and demarcate populations in the global era.

In Chapter 6, 'Borders, Belonging and Homeland (In)Security', Mona Danner argues that the September 11 attacks in the United States emphasised some of the contradictory aspects of globalisation and borders. Following September 2001, the United States engaged in a war on terror that involved significantly tightening immigration procedures and border controls, and loosening legal standards related to surveillance and detention. Danner argues that the war on terror's emphasis on 'homeland security' actually camouflages the extensive growth in the last four decades of the state control orientation and apparatus found in the criminal justice system and the military. The consequences of control-oriented state expansion include staggering costs, decreased civil rights, and increased fear and sense of insecurity. On the ground in the United States, homeland security has translated into an attack on immigrants and suspicion of immigrant rights, especially against Arab and Muslim immigrants. It has also initiated a heightened attack on dissent and the criminalisation of some political expression. Both immigrants and dissenters sit on the border of legitimacy in the United States, suspected not to belong, lacking patriotism, and as terrorist-sympathisers, if not potential terrorists. Danner concludes that the increased scrutiny of these populations helps alleviate pressures on the state under globalisation and the intensification of the state security apparatus emphasises national security to the neglect of human security.

In Chapter 7, 'Control, Protection and Negligence: Border Security in the Western Balkans', Alice Hills examines the nuanced way in which borders express and symbolise national sovereignty, regional political imperatives and vested interests, the consistency of patterns of state action and the mobilisation of technologies across jurisdictions. Hills discusses these issues in the light of recent developments in functional border security in the western Balkans, illustrated by reference to the impact of the European Union's Schengen standards on border management in Bosnia Herzegovina (BiH), Macedonia and Albania. Two specific questions are considered. The first concerns the extent to which changes in the rationale underpinning border security are prioritised over the transformation of guarding structures. The second question relates to the nature of border guarding, which spans a range of military and police functions and roles. Hills concludes that trends in guarding are indicative of the ways in which states exercise authority at the border, and of the extent to which managing borders requires the integration of international, regional, and national interests.

In Chapter 8, 'State Crime Beyond Borders', Penny Green links changes in border security around the outer perimeter of the European Union with the commission of state crimes. European Union member states have, for a number of years, been developing partnership and regional agreements with non-European countries as part of a deliberate strategy to contain the arrival of irregular migrants and asylum seekers. Green examines the outsourcing of irregular migration control by the European Union by focusing on one partnership agreement, which has been negotiated between Italy and Libya. On average some 500 irregular migrants drown each year making the dangerous Mediterranean sea-crossing from Libya to Italy. Increased border controls, repatriation agreements, collective expulsions of irregular migrants, failure to process asylum claims and breaches of the *non-refoulement* principle of the 1951 Geneva Refugee Convention have led to a series of serious human rights abuses which are considered within a state crime framework. Despite these documented abuses, Green notes that Europe has indicated a clear desire to continue to devolve the responsibility for the management of irregular migration to countries of transit and origin. She concludes that this strategy of exporting European responsibility for refugee protection to nations of origin and transit will further increase the vulnerability of asylum seekers to criminal practices and omissions by states and their agents.

In Chapter 9, 'The Gender of Control', Jan Carpenter demonstrates how, as a result of the policy of militarisation of the United States border, women's bodies have become subject to militarized rape in a hypermasculinised climate of nationalism and fear. She argues that men are using rape on both sides of the border as a technology of control designed to terrorise and subordinate women in attempts to reproduce traditional hierarchical relationships during times of rapid social and economic change. Carpenter observes that US border policy has shifted the entry routes into the United States to dangerous and remote locations, producing a *de facto* return to the Bracero program that tends to encourage migration of young, fit male workers and exclude women and families. Politicians and employers reap the benefits of a policy biased against Mexican women and families without appearing to do so. Though many women negotiate increased social and economic power in the border region, these benefits can come with significant costs.

In Chapter 10, 'Law and Order on the Border in the Neo-Colonial Antipodes', Kerry Carrington brings the collection full circle, returning to a broad discussion of the border and examining the technologies and genealogies of border policing. Carrington argues that asylum seekers are caught between a borderless world, on the one hand, because persecution knows no borders, yet, on the other hand, destination countries in the European Union, North America and Australia have intensified efforts to tighten borders, assert sovereignty and exclude 'non-citizens' through technologies of expulsion and social control. Against this international backdrop, her chapter examines how a vast and growing network of policies and regimes of governance attempt to police Australian borders through regulatory techniques of socio-spatial ordering and control. Carrington argues that border protection measures deploy an array of jurisdictional and disciplinary technologies of population control that trace their genealogy to other forms of illiberal governance. First, the asylum seeker issue taps into deeply embedded anxieties about the fear of invasion in the largely unpopulated remote areas of northern Australia. Secondly, in many ways contemporary border control technologies mirror the historical efforts deployed to contain Aboriginal populations within white-made borders, such as reserves and missions, following Britain's proclamation of sovereignty over the island continent in 1788. And lastly, Carrington concludes that the practices of transportation mirror in vital respects the practices of deporting asylum seekers.

Both entail similar transport technologies (i.e. boats), as well as disciplinary technologies of population control, such as forced removal, containment, expulsion, and the mass movement of people across borders on an almost routine scale.

Collectively, these contributions from British, Australian and North American commentators take a step towards defining a new criminology which is informed and transformed by a critical, global perspective. They seek to redress the failure of criminology to question its own border blindness and transcend its conceptual boundedness, by making borders criminologically significant. It is important to clarify that *Borders, Mobility and Technologies of Control* is not a book which explores the legitimate threats posed by cross-border crime and transnational terror and seeks to describe effective means to counter them. No doubt many books have been, and will continue to be written with this practical objective. Nor is it our intention to provide an explicit critique of the 'securitisation agenda', although Danner's contribution in this volume tackles this issue directly in the context of borders and belonging, and Hills addresses the manifest security needs of the post-conflict Balkan region from a more pro-security position. Although securitisation provides the inescapable backdrop for any contemporary discussion about border crossing, the hijacking of so many social agendas by the securitisation discourse is in fact a path we wish to avoid. We therefore chose a different starting point. This book retains a primary focus throughout on borders and their meaning to those who seek to defend or to cross them.

REFERENCES

Acton, T., 1974, *Gypsy Politics and Social Change*, Routledge and Kegan Paul, London.
Bauman, Z., 1993, *Postmodern Ethics*, Blackwell Publishing, Oxford.
Bauman, Z., 1998, *Globalization: The Human Consequences*, Polity Press, Cambridge.
Bauman, Z., 2000, Social issues of law and order, *British Journal of Criminology*, Special Issue on Crime and Social Theory, **40(2): 205–221**.
Beck. U., 1999, *What is Globalization?*, Cambridge, Polity Press.
Braithwaite, J., 2000, The new regulatory state and the transformation of criminology, *British Journal of Criminology* Special Issue on Criminology and Social Theory, **40(2): 222–238**.
Carling, J., 2002, Migration in the age of involuntary immobility: theoretical reflections and Cape Verdean experiences, *Journal of Ethnic and Migration Studies*, **28: 5–42**.
Conradson, D. and Latham, A., 2005, Transnational urbanism: attending to everyday practices and mobilities, *Journal of Ethnic and Migration Studies*, Special Issue on Transnational Urbanism, **31(2): 227–233**.
Cornelius, W. A., 2005, Controlling 'unwanted' immigration: lessons from the United States, 1993–2004, *Journal of Ethnic and Migration Studies*, **31(4): 775–794**.

Devetak, R., 1995, Incomplete states: theories and practices of statecraft, in: *Boundaries in Question*, J. Macmillan and A. Linklater (eds), Pinter Publishers, London.

Donnan, H. and Wilson, T., 1999 *Borders: Frontiers of Identity, Nation and State*, Berg Publishers, Oxford.

Fekete, L., 2003, *Death at the Border—Who is to Blame?* Institute of Race Relations, London.

Fraser, A., 1992, *The Gypsies*, Blackwell Publishers, Oxford.

Gready, P., 2004, Conceptualising globalisation and human rights: boomerangs and borders, *International Journal of Human Rights*, **8**: 345–354.

Green, P. and Grewcock, M., 2002, The war against illegal immigration: state crime and the construction of a European identity, *Current Issues in Criminal Justice,* **14(1): 87–101**.

Grewcock, M., 2003, Irregular migration, identity and the state—the challenge for criminology, *Current Issues in Criminal Justice*, **15: 114–135**.

Hayter, T., 2000, *Open Borders: The Case Against Immigration Controls*, Pluto Press, London.

Heyman, J., Alvarez, R., Bariteau, C., Cole, J., et al., 2002, US immigration officers of Mexican ancestry as Mexican Americans, citizens and immigration police, *Current Anthropology*, **43(3): 479–509**.

Hoffman, J., 1998, *Sovereignty*, Open University Press, Buckingham.

Howitt, R., 2001, Frontiers, borders, edges: liminal challenges to the hegemony of exclusion, *Australian Geographical Studies,* **39: 233–245**.

Juss, S., 2004, Free movement and the world order, *International Journal of Refugee Law*, **16(3): 289–335**.

Loader, I. and Sparks, R., 2002, Contemporary landscapes of crime, in: *The Oxford Handbook of Criminology*, M. Maguire, R. Morgan, and R. Reiner, 3rd ed., Oxford University Press, Oxford.

McFarlane, J., 1998, Torres Strait: policing the open border, *Trends and Issues in Crime and Criminal Justice*, **92: 1-6**.

Miller, D. and Hashmi, S., 2001, *Boundaries and Justice: Diverse Ethical Perspectives*, Princeton University Press, Princeton.

Nevins, J., 2002, *Operation Gatekeeper: The Rise of the 'Illegal Alien' and the Making of the US–Mexico Boundary*, Routledge, New York.

Ortiz, V., 2001, The unbearable ambiguity of the border, *Social Justice*, **28(2): 96–112**.

Parsley, C., 2003, Performing the border: Australia's judgement of 'unauthorised arrivals' at the airport, *The Australian Feminist Law Journal*, **18: 55–75**.

Passel, J., Capps, R., and Fix, M., 2004, *Undocumented Immigrants: Facts and Figures*, Urban Institute Immigration Studies Program (12 January 2004).

Pickering, S., 2004, The production of sovereignty and the rise of transversal policing: people-smuggling and federal policing, *ANZ Journal of Criminology*, **37: 362–379**.

Rawlings, P., 2002, *Policing: A Short History*, Willan Publishing: Uffculme, Devon.

Reus-Smit, C., 2001, Human rights and the social construction of sovereignty, *Review of International Studies*, **27: 519–538**.

Richmond, A. H., 1994, *Global Apartheid: Refugees, Racism and the New World Order*, Oxford University Press, Oxford.

Rogers, A., 2005, Observations on transnational urbanism: broadening and narrowing the field, *Journal of Ethnic and Migration Studies*, Special Issue on Transnational Urbanism, **31(2): 403–407**.

Rose, N., 2000, Government and Control, *British Journal of Criminology*, Special Issue on Criminology and Social Theory, **40(2): 321–339**.

Sassen, S., 1996, *Sovereignty in an Age of Globalisation,* Columbia University Press, New York.

Sassen, S., 1998, *Globalization and Its Discontents: Essays on the New Mobility of People and Money,* The New Press, New York.

Sassen, S., 1999, *Guests and Aliens*, The New Press, New York.

Schuster, L., 2005, The continuing mobility of migrants in Italy: shifting between places and statuses, *Journal of Ethnic and Migration Studies*, **31(4): 757–774**.

Sheptycki, J., 2002, *In Search of Transnational Policing: Towards a Sociology of Global Policing*, Ashgate, Aldershot.

Soguk, N., 1999, *States and Strangers: Refugees and Displacements of Statecraft,* University of Minnesota Press: Minneapolis.

Sparrow, R. 2003, Border, states, freedom, and justice, *Arena Magazine* (August–September 2003).

United Nations, 2004, Migration could escalate as globalization fails to put jobs where needed, UN says, *UN News Service* (21 May 2004); http://www.un.org/apps/news/printnews.asp?nid=10834.

Urry, J., 2000a, Mobile sociology, *British Journal of Sociology*, **51(1): 185–203**.

Urry, J., 2000b, *Sociology Beyond Societies: Mobilities for the Twenty-first Century*, Routledge, London.

Webber, F., 1996, *Crimes of Arrival: Immigrants and Asylum Seekers in the New Europe*, Statewatch Publishing, London.

Weber, L., and Bowling, B., 2004, Policing migration: a framework for investigating the regulation of global mobility, *Policing and Society*, **14(3): 195–212**.

Weber, L., and Landman, T., 2002, *Deciding to Detain: The Organisational Context for Decisions to Detain Asylum Seekers at UK Ports*, Human Rights Centre, University of Essex, Colchester.

Yeoh, B., 2005, Observations on transnational urbanism: possibilities, politics and costs of simultaneity, *Journal of Ethnic and Migration Studies*, Special Issue on Transnational Urbanism, **31(2): 409–413**.

Chapter 2

THE SHIFTING FRONTIERS OF MIGRATION CONTROL

Leanne Weber
University of New South Wales

Halfway up the stairs isn't up and isn't down.
It isn't in the nursery. It isn't in the town.
And all sorts of funny thoughts run round my head.
It isn't really anywhere—it's somewhere else instead.

A.A. Milne, *Halfway Down the Stairs*

Every nationalist is haunted by the belief that the past can be altered.

George Orwell, cited by Stanley Cohen in *States of Denial*

1. FOOTPRINTS IN THE SAND

Just after midday on November 4th 2003, a 12-metre fishing boat, the *Minasa Bone*, carrying 14 Kurdish men, landed on Melville Island, 80 kilometres off the northern coastline of Australia. According to eye witnesses, two of the men waded ashore, scooped handfuls of sand from the beach and asked locals whether they had reached Australia (Morris 2004). When they were told that they had, the men are said to have danced for joy. Their elation was to be short-lived.

Local police and fishermen initially attended the scene. In the hours that followed, a navy warship was despatched to escort the *Minasa Bone* out to sea. An air navigation exclusion zone was declared over the island, preventing the arrival of the press or legal advisors. Customs, immigration and Australian Federal Police officers were flown to the scene. And the

S. Pickering and L. Weber (eds.), Borders, Mobility and Technologies of Control, 21–43.
© 2006 *Springer. Printed in the Netherlands.*

Governor-General was summoned from his official duties at Australia's most celebrated horserace, the Melbourne Cup, to give royal assent to statutory regulations that had been prepared for just such an occasion as this.[1] With the stroke of a pen, the official memory of the landing of those men on Australian soil had been erased. The 'finishing line', as some newspaper reports put it, had been shifted. The men had never really been in Australia, at least not in any way that could be of benefit to them.

These extraordinary events are the culmination of a spiralling cycle of border control measures directed almost exclusively at 'onshore' asylum seekers who arrive in Australia by sea. This reaction is rooted in Australia in an historical fear of invasion from the Asian north, but is also part of a larger story about the failure of governments around the developed world to deal constructively with the reality of contemporary migration. In their efforts to control unwanted arrivals, these governments have taken increasingly extreme measures to barricade their borders. But despite these efforts, people continue to do what they have always done, that is, to 'burst across borders, seeking new or better opportunities' (Horsman and Marshall 1994: 60). Faced with this prospect, some governments have moved their attention beyond the various control measures they have in place on and around their increasingly ungovernable borders, and have begun to manipulate the location and meaning of the borders themselves. The central thesis of my argument in this chapter is that, just as the contemporary citizen is increasingly 'on the move' (Valier 2003: 2), national borders are also becoming mobile in both time and space. Through rather mysterious official processes which will be outlined later, Melville Island can be 'Australia' one minute but 'not-really-Australia' the next.

Borders have traditionally marked the limits of sovereign territory and acted as the primary site of expression of the exclusionary powers of the state. In a globalising world, the ability for individuals to move and, more particularly, to cross borders, has emerged as a key social signifier, stratifying populations according to a 'global hierarchy of mobility' (Bauman 1998: 69). Bauman argues that, while global elites have always enjoyed transnational status, the prospect of the democratisation of mobility to allow the free movement of people in line with the lack of territorial constraints on commodities and capital, has been strongly resisted in developed states. Sassen (1996: xvi) interprets these trends as a 'denationa-lizing of economic space' alongside the 'renationalizing of politics', with border crossing emerging as a 'strategic site of inquiry about the limits of the new order'. She refers to a 'new geography of power', in which border control has become a ready vehicle through which the nationalist state retains its claim as an absolute sovereign in the realm of immigration control, while abdicating to denationalising forces in other areas of responsibility. The development of a transnational human rights regime which has forced a partial decentring of state sovereignty and begun to erode the distinction between 'citizen' and 'alien', is another factor on the denationalising side of the equation. Spontaneous and unauthorised border crossers clearly present a special challenge to sovereignty, while refugees, in particular, force a direct confrontation between nationalist politics and an ascendant—although still far from firmly established—international human rights regime.

The conflicting demands of globalisation have differential impacts on different borders and different categories of people who seek to cross them. Firstly, as Gready (2004: 350) has noted, 'globalisation erases certain borders while entrenching, establishing and redrawing others'. For example, the fortification of the external borders of the European Union alongside the relaxation of internal borders has been interpreted as part of the project to define a new European identity by delineating who is to be included and excluded (Green and Grewcock 2002). As Horsman and Marshall (1994: 59) observe, 'the erosion of the territorial state has not just made it easier to disregard frontiers within, for instance, Europe, it has also made it more difficult to ignore the frontier with the rest of the world.' And the heavily militarised United States border with Mexico (Cornelius 2005) is another clear example of the concentration of state resources to fortify the front line of a frontier struggle between the global north and global south. Gready (2004: 352) concludes: 'While it is true ... that globalisation erases borders, it is also true that those which remain are sharp edges, more closely policed, more violent'.

Borders also assert themselves differently in relation to different groups of border crossers. Against a backdrop of unprecedented mobility, the coming of the 21st century has been experienced by the majority of the world's population as an 'age of involuntary immobility' (Carling 2004: 37; see also Brown 2004). The internal borders of the European Union turn out to be not so relaxed after all in relation to the many thousands of 'third country nationals' who are legally resident in a European Union country, but unable to exercise the mobility rights associated with full European citizenship (McMaster 2001: 185). Bauman (1993: 241) argues that two 'postmodern types' have emerged with respect to global mobility, the welcome tourist and the unwelcome vagabond: 'Like the vagabond, the tourist is extraterritorial, but unlike the vagabond he (sic) lives his extraterritoriality as a privilege, as independence, as the right to be free, free to choose; as a licence to restructure the world'. Elsewhere, Bauman (1998: 89) has observed that, while borders are 'levelled down' for global business and cultural elites, the remainder face 'walls built of immigration controls'. Although government rhetoric is often aimed at reinforcing the idea of the border as solid and impenetrable, in line with these 'sharp' and 'solid' images, there is much to suggest that borders are becoming malleable and fluid. In order to meet the contradictory demands made on borders under globalisation, state borders could be said to operate as 'porous dams' (Joly 1994), expected to allow a steady and lucrative flow of welcome visitors, while holding back the floods of unwanted Others.

In this chapter, I try to capture some of the elusiveness and plurality of borders. It is a discussion about the extreme, often squalid, and sometimes bizarre attempts being made to selectively control global mobility through various techniques described by Perera (2002) as 'defensive geography'. I will build the discussion in four steps, using examples primarily from Australia and Britain. In the first section, I highlight the mobile nature of border controls which transcend the constraints of physical borders and operate both outside and within them. In the case of these *functionally mobile* borders, the border function is expressed at various sites of enforcement, but the location of the border and its symbolic value as a marker of territory remain unchallenged. Next I consider an Australian example of the *spatially mobile* border, where the physical location of the border is directly manipulated in the interests of border protection. This border manipulation is taken a step further in the case of *temporally mobile* borders which, remarkably, can be made to appear or disappear retrospectively as required. And finally I consider the possibility of fully *personalised borders* where the border is defined, not by a fixed geographical location, nor with reference to the location of border control activities, but is equated with the location of officially sanctioned border crossers, who legally *embody* the border.

2.   FUNCTIONALLY MOBILE BORDERS

For island nations such as Britain or Australia, checks at the border have long been the preferred method of immigration control, and Continental-style population surveillance measures involving identity cards and police checks have been strongly resisted. However, under pressure to control spontaneous migration, preventative and enforcement activity has shifted both inwards and outwards from the border. More recently, this expansion of internal checks and pre-emptive measures has also been justified in the name of combating both international and domestic terrorist threats. In relation to these initiatives, the border as a physical construct remains geographically fixed but it no longer retains a special significance as the exclusive, or even primary, site for migration control. Exclusionary processes operate at multiple sites and involve increasingly sophisticated and extensive networks of public and private agencies (Weber and Bowling 2004). The notion of the border retains enormous symbolic and political importance, but the reality is that in Britain, for example, resources have been moved away from border checks over the last decade, and the emphasis at ports of arrival has been on facilitating the efficient passage of desirable visitors, while streamlining efforts to screen out and deter the others (Crawley 1999).

Although front line immigration officers may perceive these changes to be an abandonment of political commitment to immigration control (Weber 2003), I will argue that they actually represent a strategic shift to a reconceived idea of borders and border protection. The state's arsenal of exclusionary devices increasingly involves pre-emptive measures to prevent and deter unauthorised arrival; efforts to increase the efficient sorting of desirable and undesirable passengers at the border, particularly through the application of new border technologies (such as biometric passports and advanced passenger processing systems); and punitive responses, such as administrative detention and forcible deportation, directed at those who enter or remain without authorisation. These shifts in the sites of migration control could be thought of as creating 'quasi-borders' where exclusionary powers are expressed far away from the designated border. The physical borders are not so much diminishing, but are changing towards 'smart borders',[2] while the border function is both trans-nationalised and internally dispersed. Motomura (1993) has pointed out that the legal precedent for the idea of 'functional borders' has been long established in American jurisprudence, although its application has been somewhat lopsided (I will discuss this below). For the purposes of this section, the border will be conceptualised according to Motomura's (1993: 712) analysis as: 'not a fixed location but rather wherever the government performs border functions'.

Many commentators have observed a gradual process of internalisation of immigration controls since the 1970s (reviewed in Weber and Bowling 2004). In Britain, this process accelerated in the 1990s with a raft of immigration legislation which led Anne Owers (now Her Majesty's Inspector of Prisons) to ask whether the country was entering a 'new age of internal controls' (Owers 1994). Developments during and since that time include *inter alia*: the formation of a specialist enforcement section in the United Kingdom Immigration Service and increased powers of search and arrest for immigration officers; the introduction of criminal sanctions against employers who fail to check the immigration status of employees; the establishment of highly publicised targets for the removal of 'failed asylum seekers' and 'immigration offenders'; the formation of specialist 'snatch squads' of police and immigration officers to effect forcible expulsions, and cooperation with other European Union countries to expel 'aliens' through jointly-administered charter flights; the increased use of administrative detention and expansion of the privately-run detention estate; the systematic withdrawal of welfare and legal support from asylum seekers; and dispersal into designated places of residence which has been linked to increased violence against asylum seekers and can be interpreted, at least in part, as a form of welfare-based surveillance. Further fuelled by post September 11 insecurity and the threat of home-grown terrorism following the London Underground bombings in July 2005, electronic tagging of asylum applicants has been trialled; a proposal for a national identity card, long resisted by the British public, has gone before Parliament; and members of the public are being encouraged to report suspected immigration offenders. Although there are many signs of resistance against being drawn into this web of immigration enforcement, for example, from health authorities, librarians and teachers, the official message seems to be that the functional border is everywhere, and internal controls can be operated by anyone at any time.

One powerful mechanism for the internal expression of sovereignty is administrative detention. The discretionary detention of asylum seekers in Britain has been highly controversial. But, amongst liberal democracies, it is the Australian Government which has made the most uncompromising claim of absolute sovereignty over its territorial borders, through its mandatory detention policies and its deliberate placement of detention centres in remote and hostile environments. The exclusionary power of these policies—both real and symbolic—has been graphically captured by Australian novelist Bernard Cohn: 'In those places, you see, they are not really in Australia. They are in the empty ungoverned space of their bodies, I guess, confined within not-Australia.' (cited in Perera 2002: 10). Internalised border controls shift the focus away from defending a physically-bounded territory towards a more dynamic delineation of those who do and do not belong. Dauvergne (2004: 601) argues that labelling certain people as 'illegal' shifts the boundaries of exclusion, allowing those whose presence is not wanted to be 'erased from within':

> Sovereignty in this picture is again seen to be about people not territory, as the label 'illegal' allows us to shift the US–THEM line from the border of the nation to within the nation, wherever it is required. In this way, cracking down on illegal migration functions as an assertion of both the internal and the external dimensions of sovereignty.

However, these mechanisms for maintaining the internal us–them border are fragile and are vulnerable to challenge through legal and political activism. States have therefore been reluctant to rely on them as the sole back-up for checks at the border. Morris (2003: 8) argues that: 'As the importance of being *legally* 'outside' (but physically within a state) has eroded in the context of domestic rights allocation, states have sought ways to reassert their sovereignty and, thus, their control over who remains *physically* 'outside' the demarcated territorial boundaries' (emphasis added). Similarly, Bauman (2002: 111) points to the political difficulties faced by governments when they are forced into violent and highly visible tactics against those who manage to breach border defences: 'Since deportations and expulsions make dramatic television and are likely to trigger a public outcry and tarnish the international credentials of the perpetrators, governments prefer to steer clear of trouble by locking the doors against all who knock asking for shelter'. The desire to lock the doors more effectively has resulted in a proliferation of externalised migration control measures intended to prevent unwanted arrivals. Former director of the European Council on Refugees and Exiles, Philip Rudge (1997: 72), has noted that there is a 'clear political will to move border controls back from the literal border' through mechanisms such as targeted visa regimes and carrier sanctions which 'appear to change the location of the world's borders'. Offshore, pre-emptive controls which stretch out from territorial borders to prevent unwanted arrivals are an obvious product of the actuarial calculus employed by governments of late-modernity, anxious to reduce their exposure to destabilising risks and to limit their own liability. The logic of these policies is simple: they transform 'an asylum seeker who would otherwise be "here" into an asylum seeker who is merely "there"' (Motomura 1993: 700).

Pre-emptive measures adopted in Britain include: the posting of overseas liaison officers to prevent the embarkation of targeted ethnic or national groups; explicit, publicly-announced targets for blanket reductions in asylum applications; and 'juxtaposed' border controls operated on behalf of the British Government in France, Belgium and the Netherlands, described by one British official as 'exporting our frontier controls to where they are most needed'.[3] With their universal visa system, well-developed overseas liaison network and computerised Advanced Passenger Processing (APP) system, Australia has, arguably, an even more comprehensive arsenal of offshore controls. Departmental reports describe their border strategy as follows: 'Australia manages the movement of non-citizens across its border by, in effect, pushing the border offshore. This means that checking and screening starts well before a person reaches our physical border.' (Department of Immigration, Multicultural and Indigenous Affairs 2004: 3)

Interdiction policies are perhaps the most coercive and controversial of these pre-emptive measures, as they provide the most direct challenge to the international legal order and human rights regimes: 'Located above and beyond the reach of the law, interdiction policies exist in a unique realm exploited by states to exert an unprecedented level of immigration control. ... These policies reflect a powerful reassertion of sovereignty on behalf of the state' (Morris 2003: 18). The best known example of this strategy in recent times was the interception by the United States coastguard of tens of thousands of Haitians who fled the Papa Doc regime by boat in the 1980s. The interdicted Haitians were either returned or redirected to detention centres at Guantanamo Bay (Magner 2004).

The parallels between this 'Caribbean solution' and Australia's more recent 'Pacific solution' are numerous and unmistakeable. On the 28 August 2001, following a spate of unauthorised arrivals of barely seaworthy fishing boats, the Norwegian merchant vessel *MV Tampa*, acting at the request of Australian authorities, rescued 430 asylum seekers whose boat had broken down 80 nautical miles from the remote Australian territory of Christmas Island. The events which followed gained widespread media coverage and have been well described elsewhere (see Magner 2004; Morris 2003; Mares 2001). As the humanitarian situation on board the overcrowded ship began to deteriorate, the response of the Australian Government was 'swift and decisive' (Howard 2003). Forty-five armed Special Air Services (SAS) troops boarded the *Tampa*. Most of the rescuees were taken aboard the warship *Manoora* to the impoverished Pacific nation of Nauru to be detained (under whose authority is a matter of debate) while their claims for refugee status were considered under international (not Australian) procedures. Academic lawyer Ernst Willheim claimed that asylum seekers diverted to the offshore detention centre at Nauru were being dealt with in a 'legal vacuum', paid for with Australian taxpayers' money, but recognised neither under Australian law nor the law of the host nation.[4] High Court judge Mary Gaudron likened the tactics employed by the Australian Government to the creation of a 'legal no man's land' by the United States Government at Guantanamo Bay (Banham 2004).

Legislation was rushed through both houses of parliament which retrospectively authorised the seizure of the *Tampa* and set in place additional authority for future action of a similar kind (Magner 2004). A naval blockade, *Operation Relex*, was established to 'deter and deny' suspected illegal entry vessels (SIEVs) and defence personnel were granted special authority to board vessels outside Australian territorial waters in the area of more diluted sovereignty known as the *contiguous zone* (Howard 2003). The British Government has responded with approval to these grossly disproportionate, yet seemingly effective, measures by making a series of proposals to the European Union for the establishment of 'regional protected zones' to operate in conjunction with naval interception programs (Sianni 2003). Zones near to countries of origin are reportedly now being favoured over the original idea of processing centres or transit zones on the periphery of the European Union, but other means have been used to enlist the support of a 'circle of friends' in North Africa, the Middle East and the former

Soviet Union, in order to create so-called 'frontiers of return' within which individuals can be intercepted and repelled, both within and beyond borders (Statewatch 2003).

Interdiction policies have demonstrated the 'lacuna between the physical spaces in which states exercise jurisdictional control and the spaces in which they will assume juridical responsibility' (Morris 2003: 2). They have done so by exploiting the grey areas at the boundaries of refugee law, international human rights law, and the law of the sea (Howard 2003: 21). While expanding the reach of the sovereign power to exclude, interdiction policies simultaneously challenge the wider jurisdiction of international law, for example, in relation to the law of the sea (with respect to the boarding of vessels), and *non-refoulement* of refugees. Australian interdiction policies have been described as efforts to 'draw a line in the sea', not merely against asylum seekers themselves, but also against the incursions of international law (Perera 2002: 3). In fact, a common feature of interdiction policies is the building in of immunity from judicial review, allowing unfettered expression of sovereign power over entry to territory (Motomura 1993). Douzinas (2002: 32) describes intercepted asylum seekers as being caught in a rights-free, unprotected zone from where 'they are chased away, kept from our borders lest they engage the law in responsibility'.

These developments have reportedly taken international human rights advocates by surprise, since the prospect that a contracting state would 'reach beyond its territory to seize and return refugees' would have been 'unimaginable' at the time the international legal regime for refugee protection was drafted (Magner 2004: 68). But even more unimaginable are the steps that have been taken by the Australian Government to strengthen its geographical defences still further by manipulating the physical location of the border itself. Even in the face of the relentless border protection measures described in this section, asylum seekers and other unauthorised border crossers have stubbornly refused to disappear. Instead, the Australian Government has resorted to making the borders themselves disappear.

3. SPATIALLY MOBILE BORDERS

A brief foray into maritime law reveals that Australia already operates many different borders. About 20 kilometres offshore is the boundary of Australia's 'territorial seas' which are subject to full Australian sovereignty. A 'contiguous zone' extends a further 20 kilometres within which Australia is entitled to take action to prevent and punish infringements of its domestic law, for example customs and immigration laws. And Australia has the right to exploit and manage natural resources for up to 200 nautical miles in the area known as the 'economic exclusion zone' (Coombs 2004). So the idea of a plurality of borders, each associated with different rights, responsibilities and functions, is already well established, although the meaning of each entity is by no means settled in practice.

In contrast to these entities which, however contested, are recognised under the United Nations *Convention on the Law of the Sea*, the idea of a *migration zone* is a construct defined solely within Australian law. In fact, High Court judge Mary Gaudron has described the very idea of a migration zone as a 'cute legal fiction' (Banham 2004). The *Migration Act 1958* defines the migration zone as 'the area of Australia where a non citizen must hold a visa in order to legally enter and remain in Australia' (DIMIA). For people travelling without visas, arrival in that zone subjects them to mandatory detention as 'unlawful non-citizens', but at least opens the possibility of applying for temporary protection as a refugee, and gives some limited access to Australian courts. It is the way in which this notional boundary has been manipulated to keep asylum seekers legally outside of Australia that has created so much controversy.

Australia has 37,000 kilometres of coastline and administers more than 8000 islands. The vast and sparsely populated northern shores of the continent, fringed by the crowded islands of Indonesia, have long been cast in the national imagination as a place of vulnerability to incursion from Asia. In the years leading up to the *Tampa* crisis, several outposts of Australian sovereignty, such as Christmas, Cocos and Ashmore Islands—which lie in the Indian Ocean much closer to Java than to the Australian mainland—were targeted by organised groups transporting asylum seekers and other irregular migrants via Indonesia. Melville Island, which was the setting for the events described at the beginning of this chapter, is comparatively close to the mainland and is inhabited by the Indigenous Tiwi people. In September 2001, in the continued flurry of law-making after the *Tampa* crisis, legislation was rushed through both houses of parliament which excised Christmas, Cocos and Ashmore Islands from the migration zone.[5] In future, any asylum seekers who slipped through the interdiction net and managed to land at any of these locations would be labelled 'offshore entry persons', and could be diverted into offshore processing centres along with passengers on boats intercepted on the open sea. In addition, the classification of Christmas Island as outside the migration zone cleared the way for a putative 'offshore' detention facility to be retained there, which, unlike Nauru, would be directly and openly under the control of the Australian Government.[6] The creation of a new legal category of 'offshore entry person' therefore provided a back-up strategy intended to deny asylum seekers any legal recourse should they penetrate the physical defences already associated with Australia's extended boundary (Morris 2003).

The excision of territory was seen by one leading commentator as a uniquely Australian innovation which added a new twist to the interdiction and offshore processing regimes pioneered by the United States: 'America's never gone so far as saying part of America's not America'.[7] Opposition politicians in Australia criticised the government's actions as either inhumane or foolish, the latter view based on indignation at the apparent ceding of Australian territory. In practice, any apparent loss of territorial sovereignty resulting from excisions was far outweighed by gains in functional sovereignty. The effect of excising territory from the migration zone is to deny people who land there (in not-really-Australia) access to Australian courts and refugee protection procedures, while still classifying their entry (into Australia) as unlawful.[8] This places 'offshore entry persons' in a perpetual state of non-arrival, true to Bauman's (2002: 112) description of refugees as people who 'do not *change* places; they lose a place on earth, they are catapulted into a nowhere'. In an insightful analysis of decisions to accept or reject asylum applicants at Australian airports, Parsley (2003: 75) has pointed out that even these routine performances of the border have the effect of denying arrival: 'The refugee, even as their body is acted upon and removed from Australian territory, awaits the recognition of themselves as ever having arrived'. In the remote, less-governable reaches of Australia's northern frontier, excision has been used to achieve the same effect. Australian sovereignty in these excised locations is deemed to exist for the purposes of exercising sovereign powers, but seems to vanish in relation to any associated domestic and international responsibilities:

> Thus the Australian state is simultaneously expanding, in terms of its extraterritorial immigration control operations, and shrinking in terms of the territory for which it is legally responsible. While interdiction exploits the gap between jurisdiction and juridical responsibility on the high seas, Australia's excision policy has created such a gap *on its own territory*. (Morris 2003: 14, emphasis added)

This win-win situation may have been a political coup for the conservative Coalition government, but was described by one legal commentator as making 'a mockery of basic principles of territoriality and legal certainty' (Crock, cited in Coombs 2004). United Nations High Commissioner for Refugees (UNHCR), Ruud Lubbers, referred to Australia's selective approach to the meaning of its borders as the 'law of the jungle' (cited by Magner 2004: 82) and another UNHCR spokesperson was quoted as saying: 'For us a country is a country, with all its territories, and any excising will have absolutely no bearing on the obligation of the country to abide by international obligations' (McCall 2003). Furthermore, the Australian Government's willingness to manipulate its borders to keep asylum seekers out stands in marked contrast to the stance they have adopted in their bid to draw a boundary around the Timor Gap oil and gas reserves which is favourable to Australian business interests. Faced with sustained criticism from international development and human rights non-government organisations (NGOs)[9] for its insistence that the boundary of the economic exclusion zone with Timor Leste be drawn at a location which would deny the emerging nation most of the proceeds, the Australian Foreign Minister is on the record as having stated: 'If there is an issue of economic disparity between Australia and East Timor, that should be addressed through aid programs … [it] should not be addressed through shifting boundaries and changing international law.'[10]

Debates over whether the Australian Government reneged on its international responsibilities in its interdiction and excision policies, particularly the duty of *non-refoulement* of refugees, have hinged on the crucial relationship between borders, border crossing and the rights and responsibilities associated with sovereign control of territorial space (see Magner 2004; Pallis 2002). Magner argues that the location of a 'frontier' for asylum seekers at sea is less obvious than a land border but, as a rule of thumb, is generally taken to be the edge of the territorial seas for most aspects of international law. The crossing of that frontier therefore evokes some obligations in international law, if not under domestic jurisdiction. Even so, the law of the sea confers rights on states which conflict with protection requirements, and states are prone to acting extra-legally in this disputed zone, as is evident in Australia's handling of the *Tampa* affair (Pallis 2002). Such exploitation of the watery borderlands which demarcate the various zones of power and responsibility around the country's coastline has particularly significant consequences for refugees. As noted by Perera (2002: 10): 'Lines in the water are such weighty and such ephemeral things: a mile this way or that is the line between life and death, safety and terror'.

Since the events surrounding the *MV Tampa*, Australia's excision legislation has had a mixed history. Regulations passed following the *Tampa* events allowed for excisions to be declared without reference to parliament, although they are subject to later review by the Senate. Attempts to excise a further 4000 islands in June 2002 were ultimately defeated in the upper house. A subsequent attempt was also rejected in December 2002, and a third in March 2003. The Coalition government finally succeeded in authorising further excisions in July 2005, after a federal election gave it control of the Senate. The historical record of the government's use of excision orders demonstrates the reactive and precipitate nature of these border-redefining procedures. According to an Australian Parliamentary Library report, Regulations that were gazetted in March 2003 to excise Bernier, Dorre, Dirk Hartog and Faure Islands when a boatload of suspected asylum seekers was seen approaching Australia's north-western coast, were later rescinded when the vessel was found to be a Sri Lankan fishing boat (Coombs 2004). A few months later, the arrival of a group of Kurdish asylum seekers on Melville Island took the excision strategy to a new level. Having been unable either to predict or pre-empt the arrival of the tiny *Mimosa Bone*, the Australian Government was forced to use its last trump card: the manipulation of borders not only in space, but also in time.

4.   TEMPORALLY MOBILE BORDERS

A fact sheet promulgated by the Australian immigration authorities includes in a list of changes associated with the *Border Protection Act 2001* 'measures to put beyond doubt the legality of the actions of the Government in relation to the *MV Tampa* and the *Aceng*, and additional statutory authority *for future action*' (emphasis added) (DIMIA). The Interpretation Notes for section 5 of the *Migration Act 1958*, as well as defining 'excised offshore places', include detailed definitions of 'excision time'.[11] These notes state specific times for already excised locations, and associate future excisions with the more open ended 'time when regulations commence'. When the Kurdish occupants of the tiny *Mimosa Bone* arrived at Melville Island around midday on 4 November 2003, they landed within Australia's migration zone and unwittingly set in train a series of pre-planned official actions. The ready-to-go regulation to excise the island received royal assent from the Governor-General that evening. (One can imagine the Queen's representative, still in the morning suit he had worn that day to the Melbourne Cup races, rushing to the urgent defence of his nation.) In contravention of long established principles of the non-retrospectivity of the law, the excision was deemed to have taken effect from the previous midnight. According to Australian immigration law, as it stood on the evening of 4 November, the Kurdish men who had waded ashore that day, had never set foot in Australia, and would have no access to Australian courts.

The Melville Island regulations were eventually overturned in the Senate in November 2003, and Attorney-General, Philip Ruddock, reported that the government was taking advice on other measures that could be used to achieve a similar effect.[12] But the brief window of opportunity afforded by the excision had given the government a legal veneer for its decision to return the *Mimosa Bone* to Indonesia, a country which has not signed the UN *Convention on the Status of Refugees*. In a bizarre twist in the border protection saga, the 14 Kurdish men had not been driven out of Australian waters by naval warships, but had instead been 'tricked out' (Perera 2002: 11).

A spokesperson from the NGO, *A Just Australia*, described the govern-ment's strategy of 'pretending that a boat hasn't really made it to Australia' as an 'Alice in Wonderland approach' (McCall 2003). Prominent refugee advocate and Jesuit priest, Frank Brennan, noted the irony of this official re-writing of history in a country colonised by British settlers who had them-selves arrived, uninvited, by sea: 'If only indigenous communities had been able to avail themselves of such legal artifices two centuries ago most of us could be deemed never to have arrived.'[13]

The public controversy surrounding the arrival of the Kurdish men glossed over these deeper questions and hinged primarily on whether or not they had asked the authorities for asylum. Immigration officials had reportedly instructed Melville Islanders not to speak to the media and the imposition of the exclusion zone hindered the construction of reliable, independent accounts.[14] Some press reports referred to the men as 'suspected' or 'apparent' asylum seekers (see, for example, Banham 2003). The Northern Territory fishing operator who was quoted earlier as saying the Kurds had 'danced for joy', said his first thoughts were that they were refugees.[15] Defence force and Australian Federal Police officers were also reported as saying that the men had described Turkey as 'no good', had said they did not want to go back, and had pointed to the word 'refugee' in a Turkish-English dictionary.[16] After repeated official denials, Immigration Minister Amanda Vanstone was finally forced to admit that the issue of asylum may have been raised. The multi-agency People Smuggling Task Force accepted responsibility for the error, but played its trump card to get out of trouble, claiming it was irrelevant anyway because of the excision. The *Minasa Bone* was towed out to sea by a naval vessel on Tuesday night, and by Saturday was back in Indonesia. It is in doubt whether Indonesia ever formally agreed to the arrangement.

In an interview conducted after the Kurdish men had returned to Indonesia, Immigration Minister Vanstone is quoted as saying: 'We're not going to let our borders get eaten away bit by bit'.[17] According to the 'Alice in Wonderland view', it was the arrival of the asylum seekers, rather than the excision of sovereign territories from the migration zone, which threatened to diminish Australia's borders. The Leader of the Opposition, interviewed on ABC radio on 23 January 2004, criticised the government's actions, not for the violation of fundamental legal principles or the shirking of responsibilities under the *Convention on the Status of Refugees*, but because, he said, Labor would have taken a tougher approach and apprehended the crew as people smugglers.[18] He argued that borders should not be protected by wiping them out, and criticised the government for cutbacks to *Operation Relex* which had allowed the boat to slip through the nation's defences.

The cessation of unauthorised boat arrivals has obviated the need for any further twists in the Australian Government's spatial and temporal manipulation of its borders (although further excisions are being enacted, as discussed earlier). One is left to speculate about how much further this strategy could be taken. One clue might be found in the Migration Act Interpretation Notes which specify that the migration zone includes, *inter alia*, 'land that is part of a State or territory at mean low water'.[19] This raises the spectre of asylum seekers being peremptorily turned away after stepping ashore at an exceptionally low tide. This possibility may perhaps stretch the boundaries of the official imagination too far, but my final example, namely the creation of personalised borders in Britain, takes border manipulation in an equally surprising direction.

5.   PERSONALISED BORDERS

Compared with these dramatic and highly publicised events off Australian shores, the quiet revolution in the location and meaning of borders that has taken place in Britain has gone virtually unnoticed. I owe my knowledge of this interesting development to an article by legal commentator, Elspeth Guild (2000: 228), where she makes the astonishing claim that: 'The UK border for persons has become entirely personal to the individual and unrelated to the physical territory over which the UK is sovereign'. New immigration Rules came into force in April 2000 which, according to Guild, shifted the moment at which entry to Britain is officially granted away from the stamping of a passport at the border, and attached it instead to the time a visa is issued by a consular official overseas. The intention was to expedite passport checks at busy airports, where immigration officials are expected to rapidly sort 'undesirable' from 'desirable' visitors with minimal inconvenience to the latter. For the purposes of United Kingdom immigration law, the holder of a valid entry visa was henceforth to be considered, not just entry cleared, but actually legally present in the United Kingdom. On the other hand, Guild points out (and this was nothing new), persons could be physically present within the United Kingdom having entered clandestinely or fraudulently, without having ever been granted leave to enter. Not only can some individuals be legally nowhere (either in the weaker sense of being denied legal recognition of entry to sovereign territory, or in the stronger sense of existing in the legal 'no man's land' of Nauru or Guantanamo Bay), it seems that the holder of a British visa can now be simultaneously in two places on the globe. On this interpretation, British borders can be conceptualised as fragmented and fully portable, their location defined, not by sites of enforcement action by state officials (as discussed earlier), but in terms of the current whereabouts of certain intending visitors. In an ironic reversal of the patriotic poem by Rupert Brooke,[20] it seems that British sovereign territory is no longer manifest abroad through the bodies of fallen British soldiers whose burial sites remain 'forever England', but through the living bodies of non-British visa holders. The holders of valid British entry visas could be said to embody the externalised border. This seemingly modest development, inspired more by financial incentives to facilitate commercially valuable travel than by political imperatives to suppress unauthorised arrivals, takes the re-imagining of borders by the state a step further. The border is not fixed to a particular location for a particular purpose, or even explicitly redefined with reference to a particular group at a particular point of time, but effectively tracks the movements of each holder of a British visa as they go about their daily affairs. If this sounds rather reckless in relation to border control, it may simply reflect the chasm that has opened up between globally mobile elites and those who are marked for enforced immobility. Since Britain operates a selective rather than universal visa system, these living embodiments of the British border are likely to be 'desirable' individuals from countries which otherwise have been targeted for strict controls.

Ortiz (2001: 6), writing about the United States–Mexico border, has also described the social exclusion of Mexican Americans living legally on the United States side of the border in terms of embodiment, albeit an embodiment where ethnic categories surmount legal ones: 'Even when they constitute over 70% of the city's population, Mexican Americans embody the border in their skins or in their last names'. Perhaps the personalisation of borders was foreshadowed in these comments by Sassen (1996: 69) in a 1996 address: 'The framework for immigration singles out the border *and the individuals* as the sites for regulatory enforcement' (emphasis added). The guaranteed, personalised border for the favoured guest, and the physically elusive border—often violently policed and sometimes virtually unknowable—for the unwanted guest, can be seen as complementary aspects of the same process.

6.   RECONSTITUTING SOVEREIGNTY AND DECRIMINALISING BORDER CROSSING

These changes in the way borders are interpreted by states reflect altered expressions of sovereignty that need to be considered by a globally aware criminology. The voluminous literatures on sovereignty, citizenship and globalisation are unfamiliar and perhaps forbidding territory for most crimi-nologists. However, a rudimentary appreciation of these developments (and this is all I attempt here), is crucial in understanding present strategies of border control, and speculating about future prospects for the democratisation of mobility.

According to Dauvergne (2004: 593), some theorists detect the demise of sovereignty and the nation-state in the face of globalisation; others assign a continuing relevance to transformed or partial manifestations of sovereignty; while others remain 'globalisation sceptics'. The border practices which have been analysed here support the second of these positions, and illustrate one aspect of what Sassen (1996) describes as the 'unbundling' of sovereignty. While seeking to divest itself of international responsibilities and abdicating many of the obligations associated with economic regulation, the late-modern state increasingly expresses its sovereign power through asserting, relocating and redefining its borders. Territorial borders remain as 'sites and symbols of power' which stand as a 'testament to the adaptability of the state' and can be reinforced or neglected depending on circumstances (Donnan and Wilson 1999).

This matters to critical criminologists because there are important parallels between the rise of border protection as an external expression of an unbundled sovereignty in the face of globalising processes, and domestic developments associated with the emergence of a late-modern state which is regulatory (in the economic sphere) yet selectively punitive (in the social sphere) (Braithwaite 2000; Garland 1996). Similar exclusionary and criminalising strategies have been employed by states against perceived sources of instability from without (i.e. illegal immigrants), and from within (i.e. criminals). Coutin (2005: 22) has argued that 'the convergence of policies that target illegal immigrants and those directed at criminals more generally makes it useful to bring illegal immigration into the purview of criminology'. She cites in evidence of this convergence the use of immigration law, which offers few constitutional protections, to hold detainees associated with the September 11 attacks, and observes that recent immigration reforms are following a crime control model based on increased penalties, detention and enforcement. As Garland (1996) acknowledges in his influential article about the limits of the sovereign state, the development of selectively punitive crime policies in many affluent states raises important questions about the contemporary expression of sovereign power. A critical criminology which looks beyond borders raises even more, and arguably more complex, questions about the responsibilities and powers of sovereign states with respect, not just to their existing populations, but to the citizens of other countries.

Looking beyond borders opens up a highly adversarial space where new challenges to territorial sovereignty are being played out. Bauman (2002: 90) has observed that 'global space has assumed the character of a frontier-land', a place of contested sovereignty in which adversaries are constantly on the move. The struggle between individual rights to global freedom of movement and sovereign rights to control access to territory and citizenship is the central dynamic of this unfolding process. The contest, as we have seen, is rather lopsided at present, and recognition of mobility rights is highly selective and contingent. Not surprisingly, international lawyers propose solutions that involve expanding the jurisdiction of international human rights law into these disputed frontier zones, to counter-balance the reach of externalised expressions of sovereign power: 'The violence of population mobility and immobility; conflicts, intervention and non-intervention; the global economy and contemporary politics, is nothing if not a call for genuinely *human* rights, accessible on the borders, carried across borders' (Gready 2004: 352).

Possible strategies to prevent 'untouchable states' exploiting what Morris (2003) calls the 'extraterritoriality gap' include applying the notion of the 'functional equivalent of the border' (evoked earlier in relation to sites of enforcement for migration controls), to force states to accept their international responsibilities (Motomura, cited in Morris 2003: 16). The rationale for such a requirement, which Motomura borrows from the United States domestic criminal jurisdiction, is based on the proposition that 'the government's affirmative acts may expand the territorial scope of its obligations' (1993: 710). A more recent review of the jurisprudence of the European Court of Human Rights, the Inter-American Commission on Human Rights and the United Nations Human Rights Committee, has concluded that findings of extra-territorial responsibility have become the norm, rather than the exception, and that interpreters of human rights law have deemed 'the manner and the character of the state act more crucial than the territory where the act took place' (Mantouvalou 2005: 153).

The vision of these commentators is not of a world without borders, but one in which the meaning and significance of territorial borders is dramatically altered. McCorquodale (2001: 155) has argued that '[t]here are new ways to imagine the international legal role of territorial boundaries' which depend on new 'liberating' forms of governance not based on territory. Pangalangan (2001: 165) advocates a reconception of sovereignty based on the governance of people not place, the result of which is to 'recast territorial sovereignty from a source of power to a basis of responsibility' (see also Deng, cited in Juss 2004). And Horsman and Marshall (1994: 44) propose that borders can be re-imagined by the 'force of humanity on the move', that is, through a bottom-up globalisation process, leading ultimately, perhaps, to Urry's (2000) vision of a self-reinforcing 'global civil society' in which mobility is not a threat but an accepted and defining feature. A new global citizenship able to cope with mobility and transience might be based on notions of 'cultural citizenship' (McMaster 2001, citing Turner) or the 'citizen pilgrim' (McMaster 2001, citing Falk). This mobile citizen could be thought of as a merging of Bauman's (1993) two 'postmodern types'—a combination of an empowered and freely choosing global 'vagabond' and a culturally engaged and socially responsible 'tourist'.

Nevins (2001), for one, proposes freedom of movement to be a basic human right, derived from the universal right to work and live in dignity, and the necessity of migration, in many cases, in order to achieve these (see also Juss 2004). He imagines a universal community capable of guaranteeing these rights, constructed from a vision that puts humanity above national citizenry; a community where 'membership becomes a function of participation within a social, cultural and political-economic entity not limited to national boundaries' (Nevins 2001: 7). But a new type of fluid citizenship can also be imagined as arising, not from transnational structures or a truly global society, but from a reconceived nation-state 'founded upon a post-national sense of common purpose, which is a creative and productive life of boundary crossing, multiple identities, difficult dialogues, and the continuous hybrid reconstruction of our selves' (McMaster 2001: 188, citing an unpublished speech by Kalantzis). Importantly, from a criminological perspective, these images of a renegotiated citizenship offer the possibility to 'redefine the space occupied by unauthorized immigrants by contesting their state-defined status of criminality, and transforming the concepts of illegal presence, illicit labour and temporary legal status' (Coutin 2005: 22).

A regime of individual rights and protections which transcends physical location and applies equally to all in practice is a still-distant, arguably unattainable, cosmopolitan dream. Even Mantouvalou's promising account of directions in the juridical recognition of the extra-territorial responsibility of states recognises that this does not yet extend to an expectation of shared governmental responsibility for the protection of the full range of positive and negative human rights, regardless of the nationality of their holder (Mantouvalou 2005). Many other complex questions arise which go beyond the scope of this discussion. (See Brock 2005 for an accomplished discussion from a global contractarian position.) How can citizenship rights as we know them be guaranteed without a definable boundary? What circumstances could bring these transformations about, and to whom are these universal rights claims to be made? Ironically, the dismantling of state welfare systems and the promotion of radical individualism under neo-liberal policies, which have been the target of ongoing and justified criticism from critical criminologists and other commentators, might ultimately contribute to the conditions of possibility for the renegotiation of a new global contract, a reconnection of newly constituted communities, and the universalisation of mobility rights, as individual claims for security and wellbeing cease to be linked to citizenship of a territorially-defined state. The unbundling of sovereignty, which so far has empowered states to increase their freedom of action while reneging on their responsibilities, might conceivably create possibilities for some components of citizenship to be offered more freely within a transformed, but still state-based system (McMaster 2001). And changes in the economic calculus of individual mobility would need also to occur in order to bring about a real, if not necessarily just, 'globalisation of labour' (Sassen 1996).

Until such time as this new world arrives, there is much new territory to explore for a critical criminology which is aware of the changing significance of borders under globalisation. Its task will be to analyse the dynamics of frontier battles over access to territory; to challenge official discourses which seek to criminalise unauthorised, but otherwise benign, border crossers; to document and critique the often violent technologies of border policing; to promote due process approaches, or other liberating models, in place of purely control orientated policies; and to articulate the underlying social and structural changes which are fuelling the moral panic over population movements. Only when the establishment of a new and stable global order creates an acceptance of universal mobility (or perhaps the reverse, as Juss (2004) argues) and prompts a decriminalisation of border crossing, will the control of global mobility be once again beyond the boundaries of criminology.

---

1   There are two sources for this account: Mr Killesteyn, Chair of People Smuggling Task Force, questioned by the Senate Legal and Constitutional Legislation Committee (25 November 2003); http://parlinfoweb.aph.gov.au/piweb/view_document.aspx?id=82201& table=ESTIMATE, and *Weekend Australian*, Vanstone approved boat plan day before (8 November 2003).

2   A term used, for example, by Greek Foreign Minister, George Papandreou, quoted in *Statewatch*; http://www.statewatch/org/news/2003/jun/07eubuffer.htm.

3   Immigration Service Director of Border Control, quoted in BBC news story, 'Immigration checks move to Belgium' (April 2004); http://news.bbc.co.uk/go/pr/fr/-/hi/uk_politics/ 3626355.stm.

4   'A lack of respect for rule of law', *Canberra Times* (18 November 2003), http://www.abc.net.au.

5   *Migration Amendment (Excision from Migration Zone) Act 2001.*

6   See Barry York, Social Policy Group, Department of Parliamentary Library, *Australia and Refugees, 1901-220: Annotated Chronology based on Official Sources, Summary* (16 June 2003); http://www.aph.gov.au/library/pubs/chron/2002-03/03chr02.pdf.

7   Mary Crock, quoted in 'Kurds and ways to a no zone', *Canberra Times* (8 November 2003).

8   Rather confusingly, another DIMIA briefing note states that excised offshore places remain not only part of Australia's territory, but also part of the migration zone so that all normal migration provisions apply. The only effect, it seems, is to prevent engagement of

Australia's refugee determination system and bar any recourse to Australian courts;
9   http://www.immi.gov.au/legislation/refugee/02.htm.

Oxfam Australia, 'Australia Pushing East Timor to Brink of Becoming Failed State', Press Release (20 May 2004); http://www.oxfam.org.uk/press/releases/etimor 2000504.htm.
10

Alexander Downer interviewed on ABC TV Four Corners program 'Rich Man, Poor Man' (10 May 2004); http://www.abc.net.au/4corners/content/2004/s1105310.htm.
11   Available at http://www.austlii.edu.au/legis/cth/consol_act/ma1958118/s5.html.
12

ABC Online, 'Govt considers options on migration zone', (25 November 2003); http://www.abc.net.au. The necessity for the government to pursue these other channels has since been diminished by the government's ability to pass its legislation through both houses of parliament.
13

Father Frank Brennan's address to the National Press Club, 'Time to stop tampering with asylum', (5 November 2003) Canberra; http://www.uniya.org/talks/brennan_5nov03.html.
14

15 'New bid to repel asylum seekers', *The Australian*, 5 November 2003.

'Kurds "danced for joy" on island', ABC News Online (12 November 2003); http://www.abc.net.au.

16 Reported by Mr Killesteyn, Chair of the People Smuggling Task Force to the Legal and Constitutional Legislation Committee (25 November 2003); http://www.parlinfoweb. aph.gov.au.

17 ABC Online 'Turkish asylum seekers now in Indonesia' (9 November 2003); http://www.abc.net.au.

18 ABC Online, 'PM—Labor gets tough on people smuggling'; http://www.abc.net.au.

19 http://www.austlii.edu.au/legis/cth/consol_act/ma1958118/s5.html.

20 The first lines of *The Soldier* by Rupert Brooke (1887-1915) read: 'If I should die, think only this of me: That there's some corner of a foreign field that is forever England.'

REFERENCES

Baldaccini, A., 2004, *Providing Protection in the 21st Century: Refugee Rights at the Heart of UK Asylum Policy,* Asylum Rights Campaign, London.

Banham, C., 2004, New boat arrival tests migration zone, *Sydney Morning Herald* (5 March 2004); http://www.smh.com.

Bauman, Z., 1993, *Postmodern Ethics*, Blackwell, Oxford.

Bauman, Z., 1998, *Globalization*, Polity Press, Cambridge.

Bauman, Z., 2002, *Society under Siege*, Polity Press, Cambridge.

Braithwaite, J., 2000, The new regulatory state and the transformation of criminology, *British Journal of Criminology*, Special Issue on Criminology and Social Theory, **40(2): 222–238**.

Brock, G., 2005, Does obligation diminish with distance?, *Ethics Place and Environment*, **8(1): 3–20**.

Brown, A., 2004, The immobile mass: movement restrictions in the West Bank, *Social and Legal Studies*, **13: 501–521**.

Carling, J., 2004, Migration in the age of involuntary immobility: theoretical reflections and Cape Verdean experiences, *Journal of Ethnic and Migration Studies*, **28: 5–42**.

Cohen, S., 2001, *States of Denial: Knowing About Atrocities and Suffering*, Polity Press, Cambridge.

Coombs, M., 2004, *Excisions from the Migration Zone—Policy and Practice*, Research Note No. 42, 2003–04, Parliamentary Library of Australia; http://www.aph.gov.au/library/pubs/RN/2003-04/04rn42.htm.

Cornelius, W. A., 2005, Controlling 'unwanted' immigration: lessons from the United States 1993–2004, *Journal of Ethnic and Migration Studies*, **31**: 775–794.

Coutin, S., 2005, Contesting criminality: illegal immigration and the spatialization of legality, *Theoretical Criminology*, **9(1)**: 5–33.

Crawley, H., 1999, *Breaking Down the Barriers: A Report on the Conduct of Asylum Interviews at Ports*. ILPA, London.

Dauvergne, C., 2004, Sovereignty, migration and the rule of law in global times, *The Modern Law Review*, **67**: 588–615.

Department of Immigration, Multiculturalism and Indigenous Affairs (DIMIA), 2004, *Managing the Border: Immigration Compliance*, Canberra.

Department of Immigration, Multicultural and Indigenous Affairs (DIMIA), *Fact Sheet 71*; http://www.immi.gov.au.

Donnan, H., and Wilson, T., 1999, *Borders: Frontiers of Identity, Nation and State*, Berg Publishers, Oxford.

Douzinis, C., 2002, Postmodern just wars: Kosovo, Afghanistan and the new world order, in: *Law After Ground Zero*, J. Strawson, ed., Cavendish, London.

Garland, D., 1996, The limits of the sovereign state: strategies of crime control in contemporary society, *British Journal of Criminology*, **36**: 445–471.

Gready, P., 2004, Conceptualising globalisation and human rights: boomerangs and borders, *International Journal of Human Rights*, **8**: 345–354.

Green, P., and Grewcock, M., 2002, The war against illegal immigration: state crime and the construction of a European identity, *Current Issues in Criminal Justice*, **14**: 87–101.

Guild, E., 2000, Entry into the UK: the changing nature of national borders, *Immigration and Nationality Law and Practice*, **14(4)**: 227–238.

Horsman, M., and Marshall, A., 1994, *After the Nation-State: Citizens, Tribalism and the New World Order*, Harper-Collins, New York.

Howard, J. 2003, To deter and deny: Australia and the interdiction of asylum seekers, *Refuge*, **21(4)**: 35–50.

Juss, S., 2004, Free movement and the world order, *International Journal of Refugee Law*, **16(3)**: 289–335.

Joly, D., 1994, The porous dam: European harmonization on asylum in the nineties, *International Journal of Refugee Law*, **6(2)**: 159–193.

Magner, T., 2004, A less than 'Pacific' solution for asylum seekers in Australia, *International Journal of Refugee Law*, **16(1)**: 53–90.

Mantouvalou, V., 2005, Extending judicial control in international law: human rights treaties and extraterritoriality, *International Journal of Human Rights*, **9(2)**: 147–163.

Mares, P., 2001, *Borderline*, University of NSW Press, Sydney.

McCall, C., 2003, UN blasts Australia for 'off the map' stance on 14 Kurdish asylum seekers, Agence France-Press, via Clari-Net (5 November 2003); http://quickstart.clari.net.

McCorquodale, R., 2001, International law, boundaries and imagination, in: *Boundaries and Justice: Diverse Ethical Perspectives*, D. Miller and S. Hashmi, eds., Princeton University Press, Princeton and Oxford.

McMaster, D., 2001, *Asylum Seekers: Australia's Response to Refugees*, Melbourne University Press, Melbourne.

Morris, J., 2003, The spaces in between: American and Australian interdiction policies and their implications for the refugee protection regime, *Refuge*, **21(4)**: 51–62.

Morris, S., 2004, Government under fire over Kurdish asylum seekers, *The Human Rights Defender*, Amnesty International, **22(6)**.

Motomura, H., 1993, Haitian asylum seekers: 'interdiction and immigrants' rights, *Cornell International Law Journal*, **26: 698–717**.

Nevins, J., 2001, Searching for security: boundary and immigration enforcement in an age of intensifying globalization, *Social Justice*, **28(2): 132–148**.

Ortiz, V., 2001, The unbearable ambiguity of the border, *Social Justice*, **28(2): 96–112**.

Owers, A., 1994, The age of internal controls? in: *Strangers and Citizens: A Positive Approach to Migrants and Refugees*, S. Spencer, ed., Institute of Public Policy Research/Rivers Oram, London.

Pallis, M., 2002, Obligations of states towards asylum seekers at sea: interactions and conflicts between legal regimes, *International Journal of Refugee Law*, **14: 329–364**.

Pangalangan, R., 2001, Territorial sovereignty: command, title, and the expanding claims of the commons, in: *Boundaries and Justice: Diverse Ethical Perspectives*, D. Miller and S. Hashmi, eds., Princeton University Press, Oxford.

Parsley, C., 2003, Performing the border: Australia's judgement of 'unauthorised arrivals' at the airport, *The Australian Feminist Law Journal*, **18: 55–75**.

Perera, S. 2002, A line in the sea, *Race & Class*, **44(2): 23–39**.

Rudge, P., 1997, Free circulation: a socio-political point of view, in: *Europe and Refugees: A Challenge?*, J. Y. Carlier and D. Vanheule, eds., Kluwer, The Hague.

Sassen, S. 1996, *Sovereignty in an Age of Globalisation*, Columbia University Press, New York.

Sianni, A. 2003, Interception practices in Europe and their implications, *Refuge*, **21(4): 25–34**.

Statewatch. 2003, EU uffer states and UNHCR 'processing centres' and 'safe havens', *Statewatch*, June; http://www.statewatch.org/news/2003/jun/07eubuffer.htm.

Urry, J. 2000, Mobile sociology, *British Journal of Sociology*, **51: 185–203**.

Valier, C., 2003, Foreigners, crime and changing mobilities, *British Journal of Criminology*, **43: 1–21**.

Weber, L., 2003, Down that wrong road: discretion in decisions to detain asylum seekers arriving at UK ports, *The Howard Journal of Criminal Justice*, **42: 248-262**.

Weber, L., and Bowling, B., 2004, Policing migration: a framework for investigating the regulation of global mobility, *Policing and Society*, **14(3): 195–212**.

Chapter 3

BORDER NARRATIVES
From talking security to performing borderlands

Sharon Pickering
Monash University

1.   INTRODUCTION

National borders more than physically bound a territory; they also conceptually bound ideologies of the state and migration. In turn, the regulatory capacity of the state at the border produces and reproduces the individuals and places that exist within (and indeed constitute) what can be increasingly referred to as the borderland. How that border is narrated in public discourse points to how we can understand everyday deployments of ideologies of state and migration. Importantly, it also tells us how we routinely inscribe borders with meaning that serve to reinforce particular border imaginations, especially the practices of border policing.

Borders are performed to multiple audiences and produce not only a range of words, languages and codes to communicate their location and function, but also the border itself. Increasingly, such border talk has involved the meshing of migration issues and the criminal justice apparatus, as well as agents broadly denoted under the banner 'national security'. Elsewhere I have talked about this in terms of statecraft (Pickering 2005) and the many border narratives used to convince multiple audiences as to the nature and function of borders (including the mechanisms used to erect and patrol borders) (Pickering 2006).

In this chapter, I analyse the contradictory development of border narratives that aid understandings of migration, state and regulation. I do so by focussing on the production of the United States–Mexico border in the media. However, such an analysis could equally begin on the Thai–Burma border, the Australasian rim, the borders of the European Union or in a

45

S. Pickering and L. Weber (eds.), Borders, Mobility and Technologies of Control, 45–62.

number of other locales. All these sites yield their own narratives of the border that states depend upon to produce their border performances. While these narratives are not identical, they do suggest similar border languages at work in the development of border narratives that bolster border policing efforts. Such border narratives are often repressive but also yield important moments of potential resistance to the repressive border moment.

The first narrative I focus on in this chapter is that of *security* and the relationship between security and attempts to regulate unauthorised migration from Mexico to the United States. The second narrative is the construction of a United States–Mexico *borderland*. These two predominant narratives evident in press reporting help shed light on broader discussions of the nature of migration (circular, linear, stoppable); interstate relations, trans-nationalisation of regions and the reconfiguration of the territorial sovereign state; and the capacity of the state to regulate borders through law enforcement. Ultimately, I argue that the United States–Mexico border is constructed by these often mutually exclusive narratives almost as much as it depends upon their occasional conflation. I will argue that both narratives are underpinned by flawed understandings of irregular migration, law enforcement and sovereignty that perform unpredictable, yet critical, functions in shoring up state legitimacy.

A focus on border talk is only interesting because it is intimately linked to very real physical and material consequences. The violent boundary-inscription practices of statecraft depend on performances of the border to establish their legitimacy. In this chapter, I use the example of press representations of the United States–Mexico border to outline the predominant narratives explaining border policing and the movement of people across the border. I question how these predominant narratives co-exist and in turn inform (and are informed by) discourses of deviancy. I will contrast this United States–Mexico research to some of the research I have conducted on the border policing that has emerged simultaneously with border narratives in Australia, the Thai–Burma border, Spain and South Africa. While this approach seeks to briefly chart how the predominant narratives can obscure or reveal the symbiotic relationship between unauthorised border crossings and law enforcement discernable in the borderlands, it then takes the next step to ask what happens when we attempt to go beyond the borderland into what I consider to be the violent counter-geographies of state survival at the border.

For criminology, border narratives have contributed to the traffic or trade in repelling people away from the global north, but those discourses have also opened up an understanding of the border as a space, a borderland, as yet inadequately considered within criminology. While some of the discourses of the borderland have offered cogent critiques of the focus on securitisation and control, the borderland has also become a discourse—and indeed a space—for unchecked violence not only as a site of expulsion but also as a space of exception. Therefore, in this chapter I conclude by examining what such a space potentially holds for critical criminological inquiry.

In short, the normalisation of border talk has provided criminology with some traditional purchase in tracing criminalisation strategies and the concomitant expansionist and opportunistic logic of criminal justice agencies at the border. I have been examining border discourses through media, government and other public documents (see, for example, Pickering 2001). In this chapter, I will predominantly draw on my work on the United States–Mexico border, which I believe presents some of the greatest contradictions, in terms of border talk, of any border currently attracting significant state attention. This work is based on critical discourse analysis of *The Arizona Republic* (a state broadsheet newspaper) from mid-October 2003 to mid-November 2003. This period coincided with the visit of Mexican President Vicenze Fox to Arizona, a state which shares a 2000 kilometre border with Mexico.

This research found that two border narratives exist simultaneously, partly in contradiction and partly in concert. The first narrative is that of security. This is not surprising and is evident in other works focusing on representations of the border in other parts of the world (Pickering 2002, 2006). The second narrative is that of the borderland.

2.   SECURITY NARRATIVES

Turning first to security narratives: a basic lexical analysis reveals that those who cross the border are referred to as 'aliens', 'illegals', 'criminal aliens' and 'bad guys'; they are an 'exportable commodity' that undertake 'illegal border crossings' and 'should get in line for legal opportunities', they are 'people who broke our laws', can become 'stolen human cargo' and are brought across the border by 'coyotes' who partake in 'bloody violence' and remain ultimately 'Mexico's burden'. Immigration is a matter of protecting 'our borders', 'our economic security' and 'our jobs'; it is also about 'deadlocking passions', and is currently at a 'stalemate' for 'our nation' is 'more vulnerable to terrorism' through this 'notorious smuggling corridor'. Those that patrol the border 'detain', 'repatriate,' 'rescue' and 'discover people in the desert'. Law enforcement 'sorts out' these 'illegal aliens'; they are 'hunters' that have 'sicced' the smugglers that they 'blame for violence'. Security, as a border narrative, and not surprisingly, is almost completely organised through exclusionary dichotomies.

Drawing on discourses of deviancy, the security lexicon has three main parts: economic security, border security and national security. These three discourses are often interdependent. For example, Republican Congressman Hayworth wrote an open 'letter' to United States President Bush regarding the upcoming visit of the Mexican President published in *The Arizona Republic* during the sample period (*The Arizona Republic*, 31 October 2003, p. B11). The article attracted published responses in the days following its release, including direct comment from the Mexican President. In many ways it represents the codification of the key security discourses identified throughout the sample period. For these reasons it warrants detailed comment as an influential piece deploying the security narrative in this study.

The article implored the President to 'make clear this nation's determination to establish and enforce an immigration policy that celebrates our immigrant heritage, secures our borders, draws a bright line between legal and illegal aliens, and rejects any and all forms of amnesty.' This opening statement gives primacy to enforcement, and utilises an 'immigrant heritage' that, through the use of the term 'heritage', is disconnected from the immigration present. It links immigration to 'our' heritage and not the heritage of current immigrants. It requires a 'bright line' to be drawn, which is a reference to the need to shore-up borders and to reinscribe them as powerful exclusionary cartographic barriers. The body of *The Arizona Republic* article then contains an ideologically powerful list of how this needs to be done in the name of security:

> ... what we consider to be bedrock principles of a sane, effective and productive immigration policy:
>
> – Our national security against terrorism must be built on secure borders, and we intend to invest whatever manpower and technological resources are required to close our borders to terrorists, drug smugglers and illegal aliens;
>
> – Our national allegiance is to one indivisible nation, and we will not allow or condone the balkanisation of the United States of America;
>
> – ... we can no longer blur the line between legal and illegal immigration and we must vigorously enforce our immigration laws;
>
> – The nation's economic security and that of our workers, particularly low-income and underemployed Americans, must not be undercut by exploited, unskilled illegal alien workers.

– Our national treasure is of, by and for Americans ... and should not be further depleted to aid, abet, or encourage persons who are here illegally;

– Our previous experiments with direct or indirect amnesty have failed ... because amnesty rewards lawbreakers and discriminates against those who seek legal entry into this country; therefore every vestige of amnesty must be rooted out of federal laws, regulations and policies. (*The Arizona Republic*, 31 October 2003, p. B11)

As the threat slips from a criminal to a national security matter, it is in the techno-military (more so than the techno-legal) that the solution can be found: if only there could be greater border enforcement (militarised law enforcement) then immigration/drugs/terror could be stopped. Traditionally, criminality was seen to threaten individual safety, and national security threatened the nation. However, in the reporting period I examined in the research, individual security is increasingly considered to be shaped by the effects of a globalised world (that is, by the unauthorised movement of people) and the implicit threat to the sovereign territorial nation-state they represent. In conflating border crossing with the terrorist threat, it is catapulted to a matter of national security that is experienced primarily as a threat to personal dominion *because* it is a threat to national sovereignty under conditions of globalisation. The nation and the citizen become one. The requisite security response to such threats requires unending material and political resources and the assumption that law enforcement is always a *response* to a problem rather than contributing to that problem or having particular investments in the construction of a 'criminal problem'. In the requisite policing response of re-securing the border, immigration fades as the issue and the security star continues to rise. In this narrative, security can only ever be read as a matter of security that is primarily external to the state.

In locating the security threat as external to the United States, the article states:

... we expect Mexico to be an integral part of this effort. For far too long Mexico has acted more as an accomplice in illegal immigration than a partner preventing it ... [it] has a responsibility to help control this runaway problem that is largely of its own making (*The Arizona Republic*, 31 October 2003, p. B11).

The national security problem—that is, the United States–Mexico border—is seen to have been produced by Mexico, not the United States. Security discourses rest on assessing the threat as external and unrelated to actions of those internal to the state being protected. To acknowledge a connection would make the border combat and enforcement approach impossible because the target could not be expurgated from the body of the nation, for it would be the nation itself. Throughout the reporting period, the United States was often represented as the vulnerable nation that needs to be 'rescued' from its own poor policy. The consequences of failing to enforce the border are measured in economic rationalist terms of costs. The very future of the nation (a future primarily measures in fiscal terms) is at stake if the border is not secured.

Economic security has often been a key theme in discourses of security. However, the threat of unregulated migrant labour has not consistently been a concern in relation to the United States–Mexican border. This is because the United States economy has heavily relied on 'illegal' labour in a number of key sectors, and many have documented how the United States economy has become dependent upon it (Sassen 1998, 1999). However, the contribution of unregulated or 'illegal' labour to the overall security discourse is currently reaching a peak as the economy shifts and the impact of Mexican migration is positioned not only as 'stealing jobs' but also as placing a significant burden on state health and education services. Immigration is primarily linked to economic demand, and when the demand wanes, so should the supply of immigrants. However, there is also a powerful national *social* discourse at work in this article that destabilises the purity of the economics. Mexican labour is desirable only if it is not part of a family. Unregulated labour can be desirable if it remains circular, never actually integrating via the familial unit and getting a foothold in the body of the nation. As 'legal' and 'illegal' labour are discursively run together, the ultimate threat becomes located in the ability of immigrants to breed themselves into the legitimate economy. The implicit meshing of family, reproduction and race is significant in the formation of this security narrative. A number of articles in the sample focused on how Mexicans were breeding themselves into an economy which they should be considered outside of because they are precluded from taxable working conditions. This discourse erases histories of economic exploitation in favour of assumed and implicit understandings of racially defined biological threats.

The security narrative evident in representations of the United States–Mexican border is not dissimilar to those identified in Australia and other places. In what I have identified elsewhere as the mundane process of criminalisation (Pickering 2005), security-type narratives have been central in media reporting of refugee movements from the global south to the global north. Such narratives have depended upon locating security in relation to the integrity of the nation-state, race, disease and the 'loopholes' of the legal system. They have relied as much on implicit messages in the 'quality' press as they have explicit discourses in more tabloid-style journalism. The deviancy of those who cross borders in an unauthorised way has become a matter of 'common sense', in terms of Gramscian notions of ideological work that is carried out by the media. The deviancy of those crossing is represented through the transgression of many boundaries—physical and geographic as well as linguistic, legal, national social and political. Importantly, the power of language in the representation of deviance and security at the border is only matched by the power of enforcement that such representations routinely call for. However, such narratives, in establishing themselves in the everyday representation of those who move irregularly across borders, have also become the foundation for moments of what I have called spectacle, where national and international media become focused on a particular border moment. It is often in these moments of spectacle, where those who cross borders in an irregular fashion become the subject of often frenzied media attention, where the language of reporting amplifies the deviancy of those who cross borders and obfuscates the legality of state actions—where the discourse of security disallows any discourse of human rights.

Security, as deployed in this narrative, is narrow, fixed and coercive. It has its roots in fear of the Other and is in and of itself a constant state of anxiety. It is a singular kind of security being deployed, one in which 'our' (United States) security cannot be their (Mexican) security. It is a security which absorbs the fears of individuals as to their everyday safety into concerns for national security whereby the nation-state remains the principle referent. Security comes to define the modern territorial state, as the territorial state defines the nature and parameters of security. Concomitantly, the border features in the security narrative as a fixed cartographic and physical characteristic, inscribed with clear social, cultural, political and legal legitimacy. The border is the focus to deter both the individual immigrant as well as the Mexican state. It is the line, the place where massive border enforcement can be rolled out, where violent boundary inscription practices define and redefine national, social, political and cultural points of inclusion and exclusion. This security narrative exists alongside a growing and more contradictory narrative that I identify as that of 'borderland'. I will come to argue that these two narratives inform what Nevins (2002) has called the 'schizophrenia' of United States thought on immigration.

3.   BORDERLANDS NARRATIVE

What I am calling the borderlands narrative routinely refers to those who cross the border with a larger range of lexical items than is evident in the above security narrative. They are 'undocumented immigrants', 'migrants', 'undocumented workers', 'workers'; they are 'Latinos', 'Mexicans' and 'Hispanics'; they are 'American Mexicans' and 'Mexican Americans'; they are 'non-citizens' and increasingly 'employees', 'guest workers', 'young workers', 'human energy'; they are 'good', 'decent', 'diligent' people, even 'people' who 'die in the desert' seeking a 'better life'. However, 'they' remain 'the problem'. The United States is routinely referred to as having an 'unworkable', 'unfair' and 'cruel' immigration policy; the United States also has an 'ageing workforce' with 'unscrupulous employers'. The 'constant drumbeat' of immigration is a 'Fight with the devil for fairness', it is a 'problem that plagues Arizona' and is 'emotional'. Mostly immigration is a 'unilateral decision' by Washington rather than a policy determined by local authorities. There is 'death along the border' with Mexico, a country that is a 'natural geographical asset' for the United States. The border is a 'region' where greater 'regional cooperation' is called for and 'closer trade and immigration' links desired. The borderlands lexicon differs significantly from security narratives. It does not routinely draw on deviancy discourses to depict those crossing the border. Those that cross the border are usually referred to in relation to work, nationality or ethnicity. The United States immigration policy is the focus for the most vitriolic condemnation in this narrative, followed closely by those who exploit unregulated labour. The border is a land, a space (rather than a line); it is both part of and apart from the United States and Mexican states.

Borderlands narratives have four major foci: the failure of law enforcement and the rise in immigrant deaths; the immigration/trade nexus; state-based relations with Mexico; and discourses of responsibility. Taken collectively, these foci contribute to the development of a borderland narrative. Articles contributing to the borderlands narrative usually contain some or all of the following elements: current immigration policy is undesirable and unworkable; concern over the rising number of deaths along the border; the role of law enforcement in those deaths and the futility of law enforcement more generally in policing the border; the tightening nexus between immigration and trade and the development of a border economy (which is estimated to have a worth comparable to the GDP of Poland); and, finally, the need to attribute responsibility across the United States Government, United States employers and the Mexican state for current border practices. In contrast with the security narrative, the borderlands narrative usually relies, at least in part, on stories of migrants or statements by migrant advocates.

'Death along the border' was *the* predominant issue for articles read as contributing to a borderlands narrative. The deaths of Mexicans attempting to cross into the United States came to fix a notion of the borderland, as a shared space in which both countries experience the humanitarian crisis. Repeatedly, the deaths were seen as primarily a consequence of United States border enforcement, a strategy that has not only reconfigured the nature of migration to the United States but also made the risks too great:

> The hypocrisy is tragically clear. Laws against hiring the undocumented are rarely enforced, creating an irresistible lure to desperately poor people south of the border. A zone of heavy enforcement in selected areas along the border pushes would-be workers into dangerous desert crossings, creating yet another record year for deaths along Arizona's southern border. That human tragedy remains the best and most compelling reasons for reforming this nations immigration laws. (*The Arizona Republic*, 2 November 2003, Section 5).

However, articles contributing to a borderlands narrative did not consistently advocate wide ranging federal law reform but routinely called for greater localised organisation of the borderland. One such example was debate over the *matricular*. The *matricular* is a form of identification that those who have crossed the border irregularly can use. When articles contributing to a borderlands narrative raised the issue of the *matricular* there was rarely mention of national security concerns, but rather concern for the welfare of Mexicans:

> Fox and Napolitano likely will discuss illegal immigration, vigilante groups and the matricula consular, the ID that Mexican consulates issue to Mexican nationals and that a growing number of local governments and banks accept for identification in transactions. Because the matricula can be issued to Mexicans who are not legal residents of the United States, it has faced opposition from anti-immigrant groups who see it as a 'back door amnesty'. Fox is expected to push for statewide recognition of the matricular and to lobby for legislation to allow Mexican immigrants to obtain drivers licenses. He is also expected to reiterate concerns to Napolitano about bands of border ranchers who detain migrants but he likely will save his push on an immigration deal for his next meeting with President Bush (*The Arizona Republic*, 2 November 2003, p. A1).

The *matricular* can be read as a feature of the borderlands narrative in which alternative understandings of mobility were becoming established in representations of the United States–Mexico border. For example, the following article, in discussing the *matricular* stated:

> It does not dissuade me from urging the federal government to re-examine its immigration policies. We bear the brunt of a policy that does

not recognize the need for a flow of people back and forth.' Gov Janet Napolitano (*The Arizona Republic*, 5 November 2003, p. A1).

However, the borderlands narrative does reflect some of the aspects of security narratives, in particular depicting immigration as an emotive site. Repeatedly, articles contributing to a borderlands narrative linked immigration with emotion, and were often seen as a matter for welfare-type organisations, whereas the key issue to solving the border crisis was trade, which needed to remain a matter of reason. For example,

> Much good and strengthened relations, economic and otherwise, can come from today's face-to-face meetings and conversations … However, the many opportunities before us can easily become eclipsed because of the raw emotions surrounding illegal immigration. Please, let's not let this happen (*The Arizona Republic*, 4 November 2003, p. B8).

Notably, the development of the borderlands narrative only partly relied upon the introduction of rights-based discourses. For example:

> … immigration will be the centrepiece of many of today's discussions, as it should be. Mexicans are dying in record numbers as they try to get to United States business owners who need and want them. Human rights and common decency demand changes to the United States immigration policy that led to this situation… *(The Arizona Republic*, 4 November 2003, p. B8).

This is perhaps not surprising considering that the strength of rights-based discourses has historically been linked to the established and regularised relationship between the individual and the state and that increasingly, sovereign rights have been considered as 'trumping' the rights of the individual. This has been particularly evident in security discourses where governments have espoused the 'right to security' as the greatest of human rights and have sought to negate any rights talk that promoted common understanding between those internal and external to the state. In response to the difficulty of gaining traction in relation to human rights discourses, borderlands narratives have repeatedly depended upon familial narratives to promote common identification with those who move across borders. For example: 'The migration of its people northward corrodes Mexico's soul. Children grow up fatherless because men find no hope in Mexico. Children grow up in communities of old people because their mothers also seek opportunity across the border.' And:

> The ceaseless march of generations of migrants etches a devastatingly negative image of Mexico in the hearts and minds of its people. That's the unintended consequence of seeing people as an exportable commodity

instead of a national resource worth cultivating and developing (*The Arizona Republic*, 2 November 2003, p. V1).

The clearest differentiation between those articles that consider the border as a cartographic line and those that represent it as a shared space is the location of 'the problem' within issues of global trade. In short, the borderlands narrative depends upon a more global understanding of mobility and economics and a critical appreciation of the role of border policing and the legal apparatus required to realise the securitisation of the border. For example:

> A prosperous Mexican economy is the long term key to easing the crisis of illegal immigration that claims the lives of hundreds of migrants a year along Arizona's southern border. ... The boom in foreign investment from the North America Free Trade Agreement is waning. In recent years Mexico has lost hundreds of manufacturing jobs to China, and economists don't expect those jobs to return. ... Reforms that recognise the need to help Mexico's poor learn, earn and prosper in their own country will not only benefit Mexico. It will provide a more dynamic trading opportunities for the United States and reduce illegal immigration (*The Arizona Republic*, 8 November 2003, p. B8).

Indeed the language and representation of the borderlands narrative has not been about demarcation or even simple exclusion, but rather the construction of a shared space that is somewhat beyond the state. It is a space that simultaneously requires securitisation and the possibility of movement, trade, exchange, and protection. It partly draws on rights discourses, but is more likely to appeal to common understanding and humanity. Whether the borderland narrative has emancipatory potential is still too difficult to determine but it is clear that the borderland offers alternative discourses in the performance of the border to that of the predominant security narrative.

4. FROM NARRATIVES OF SECURITY TO NEW/RENEWED POLICING PRACTICES IN THE BORDERLANDS

The United States–Mexico border case study indicates that alternative discourses to that of border security are possible. While such discourses are of course locally grounded, they indicate that the border talk of a fixed line in need of unending security can be challenged. Yet this alternative discourse needs to be cognizant of the increasing development of violent counter-geographies of state survival that also rely on the development of the borderland narrative. In short, while the borderland may be seen as countering powerful securitisation discourses of the border, it can also be drawn upon by states seeking to unshackle themselves from legal regulation historically linked to clear border markings and language. The new crafting of the border policing effort indicates the importance of borderland narratives in the reshaping of new, or at least reinvigorated, policing of frontierlands evident in border policing practices.

The narratives of the border, particularly those of security and state practices in the borderland, are primarily about the justification of border policing measures. In the name of security, border policing has sought to ensure the protection of the nation through defensive policing at the border and internal to the receiving state, and offensive intervention in the sending nations. While this has primarily been performed through security narratives, it may be argued that state actions may be read as a flip side to more progressive readings of the borderlands narrative. In short, a borderland narrative can equally support repressive security practices on the border in ways that evidence a borderland both internal and external to the state, and upon and away from the traditionally defined border.

As the state propagates security narratives, their performances of the borderland can also be traced. These are most evident in the border policing practices on the United States–Mexico border, as well as on the borders of Australia and South Africa, on the Thai–Burma border and in Spain. It is well documented that these borders have also been the subject of security narratives and yielded some potential for the development of alternative borderland narratives. It is through the increased material and political power of the border policing effort that consequences of security narratives coupled with the development of a state-sponsored borderlands performance can be seen. The following examples suggest that security narratives may be realised through the development of a re-imagined internal, external and extended policing borderland.

Irregular border crossings have been located as a policing matter in South Africa where nearly 200,000 'illegal aliens' are removed annually (Department of Home Affairs 1994–1999). Arrest records indicate that locating undocumented migrants is a key priority for South African police (Human Rights Watch 1998). It has been suggested that migrants are often arrested in order to boost overall police arrest rates. The South African National Defence Force (SANDF) plays an important role in the detection and arrest of 'illegal aliens' as they police the Mozambican border (Klaaren and Ramji 2001), including the operation of the 3300 volt electrified fence that is set up along parts of the border. Since the fence became operational in 1987, over 100 people have been killed by the lethal operation of the fence (Human

Rights Watch 1998). The police have encouraged participation of the public by advertising toll-free 'crime stop' numbers which people call to report undocumented migrants and by offering reward money for reporting undocumented migrants (Human Rights Watch 1998).

The border policing effort in South Africa has increasingly depended upon particularly problematic internal policing practices that extend the border into the South African state. An investigation into the treatment of undocumented migrants, asylum seekers and refugees in South Africa in 1996 and 1997 found that abuse was occurring in all border control agencies. It was found that authorities identified undocumented migrants through unreliable and stereotypical characteristics such as complexion, accent or inoculation marks. The report concluded that 20 percent of people detained by the police on suspicion of being undocumented migrants are later released after proving their identity as South African citizens or lawful residents.

It has been estimated that there are 200,000 undocumented immigrants in Spain (Eurostat 2001). Human Rights Watch (2002) has documented that the experiences of 'illegal immigrants' in Spain depends upon their point of entry or place of detention. These differences exist because the law allows for extensive policing discretion and provides few guidelines for policing officials. Spanish police officers implement the law in their local areas and the national police frequently exercise their powers arbitrarily or erroneously.

Similar to South Africa, internal policing frontierlands has developed in Spain through the unchecked powers of state policing and administrative agencies. For example, Human Rights Watch (2002) concluded that the lack of checks on the power to make immigration control decisions combined with unchecked police discretion, have resulted in arbitrary differences in the treatment of similarly situated migrants. Such arbitrary treatment has resulted in two major forms of state violence: expulsion and ill-treatment. Indeed Amnesty International has concluded that torture and ill-treatment of Spanish and foreign nationals by state agents (namely police officers) is increasing.

The Thai–Burma border has long seen the movement of people across unmarked and marked borders. The expansive border camps and the elaborate relations between the Thai state, police, intelligence, Burmese military and refugees has constituted a transversal space (See Pickering and O'Kane 2002) that may be seen as a borderland *par excellence*. Since the mid-1980s hundreds of thousands of Burmese have fled to Thailand to escape gross human rights abuses committed by the Burmese military government (Human Rights Watch 1997).

One of the increasingly worrying forms of violence in the patrol of this borderland has been the indiscriminate use of deportation. The Thai Government depends heavily upon the deportation of Burmese back across the border (running at approximately 10,000 per month, Human Rights Watch 2004) a practice which has been routinely considered as breaching the principle of *non-refoulement* with many facing persecution or ill treatment by Burmese government soldiers.

Australian border policing efforts have relied on refugee policy which has become explicitly deterrent focused, despite the fact that Australia still receives relatively few unauthorised arrivals by international comparison. In late August 2001, the *MV Tampa* rescued a boat in distress carrying asylum seekers to Australia. As the *Tampa* incident unfolded, the government legislated to excise remote Australian islands from Australia's migration zone, meaning that asylum seekers who landed there could not invoke Australia's protection obligations under international law. Instead, asylum seekers would be taken by the Royal Australian Navy to 'declared countries' for processing. Significantly, those who arrive in an excised zone are prohibited from bringing legal action challenging their treatment by Australia. This sought to locate Australia's borders beyond territorial Australia and into the territory of other nations. The border policing became external and reached deeply into other, often poorer sending and transit nations. Border policing is a matter of interdiction, disruption, deterrence and detention for all those who sought to enter Australia unlawfully and apply for asylum. State responses to unauthorised border crossing have become a matter of border protection and a matter of transnational crime.

Border protection dependent upon external policing has required Australia to develop de-territorialised spaces in which to enact its regime. Asylum seekers attempting to reach Australia between 2001 and 2005 were taken to either Nauru or Papua New Guinea. Australia secured arrangements for the introduction of the 'Pacific solution' bound up with increased aid that was now to be focused on law and order. Australian police are now present in most Pacific islands with significant contingents in the Solomon Islands, East Timor and Papua New Guinea. The federal policing agency responsible has shifted from having a relatively low status to a high political and material profile.

Transnational policing arrangements have now been separated from the traditionally domestic base of policing to work with various Indonesian authorities. While being premised on stopping the inhumane treatment of asylum seekers by people smugglers, the policing effort against people smuggling places it on the frontline of ensuring Australia's refugee protection obligations are never invoked. Moreover, a number of questions have been raised regarding the Australian police involvement in the sabotage of boats leaving Indonesia for Australia. The Indonesian Government has raised concerns about these activities, as has the Australian Senate. However, the nature of the police presence and their working relationship with Indonesian police and military remains unknown.

The above border policing practices indicates the development of elaborate intra- and extraterritorial policing in relation to unauthorised border crossing that is embedded within security discourses but increasingly and collectively demonstrates the development of a borderland from which policing out refugees/unauthorised migrants has depended upon systematic criminalisation, through the discourse of criminality and security. In addition, policing out refugees/unauthorised migrants has seen the development of de-territorialised policing borderlands (sometimes internal, sometimes external to the territorial nation-state), all of which depend upon the extension of the policing function to a rights-free zone not subject to the rule of law. On the back of the unauthorised mobile, we can discern the development of transversal policing which has fundamentally depended upon consistently violent state action that, if exercised against ordinary citizens or those with regularised migration status, would be unacceptable. (Pickering forthcoming).

In short, a condition of unchecked violence against those who cross borders in an unauthorised fashion has developed. Under conditions of globalisation, borderlands, or what I have previously called frontierlands, are increasingly evident. These are spaces which have been crafted through security narratives but through the development of actual borderlands. In response to increased unauthorised mobility, state sponsored meshing of security narratives and borderland realities has unleashed some violent counter geographies of state survival.

5.   TALKING SECURITY AND PERFORMING THE BORDERLAND

The speaking of security, coupled with the policing practices of the borderland, has opened up spaces both internal and external to the nation-state where the censuring gaze has been removed or rebuffed. While Bauman (2002) has suggested that refugees and their haphazard border crossings are the waste of the global frontierland, based on my research on border narratives, I suggest that it is on the backs of those that irregularly cross borders, at least in part, that the state has been able to finally and violently craft the borderlands—those who cross are not its *waste*, but rather its *rationale*.

Whether internal to the territorial nation-state or part of the de-territorialised repulsion of those not authorised to cross, using a security narrative and a borderland reality, the state has successfully shaken off the various regulatory apparatuses that have restricted absolute expressions of sovereignty between the state and the individual that international norms, mechanisms and processes had historically sought to prevent.

It has been argued first, that we are witnessing the development of a highly complex and elaborate body of law securing exclusive territoriality of the nation-state that has not been seen before, and, secondly, that we are simultaneously witnessing the internationalising of the rights of non-citizens (Sassen 1996). The combat between these is neutralised in the global borderlands, where the language of security and the material and political benefit of state agencies creating and recreating the borderland, make the second all but impossible. Moreover, in the borderlands, violence against the unauthorised mobile represents the coming together of a new repertoire of violence (compare this with Tilly 1986), a repertoire adopted from the policing of marginalised and dispossessed groups. While the violence is not continuous but has 'inflexions and ruptures', it globally paralyses, in small and large ways, the condition of survival mobility. It seeks to end the counter geographies of survival that unregulated movements have repre-sented and at the same time has liberated the executive and the policing function in their own counter geographies under conditions of globalisation. As Andreas (2000) and Nevins (2002) have both so cogently argued, the border enforcement apparatus is intimately linked to the increased crimi-nality required to cross borders and that symbiotic relationship is emblematic of the complexity and contradictions of the border. Moreover, it is the policing apparatus that stands to benefit most from the deployment of the security narrative *and* the reality of a borderland space in which it may develop its non-checked practices.

6.   CRIMINOLOGY OF THE BORDERLANDS

Agamben (1995, 2005) has argued that increasingly we are faced with states of exception: states of emergency extended indefinitely, detention extended indefinitely. According to Agamben, in the state of exception questions concerning the legality or illegality of what happens simply make no sense. He makes this point in relation to the camp, in which subjective rights and juridical protections no longer make sense and where we move into a zone of indistinction between outside and inside, exception and rule, legal and illegal. This is the space of the borderland; the borderland is the state of exception. The '"juridically empty" space of the state of exception has transgressed its spatiotemporal boundaries' (Agamben 1995: 38).

I have attempted to demonstrate that contradictory discourses of the border simultaneously exist that raise the spectre of a fixed geographic border and the development of a borderland. Both rely on varying rationales of citizen, non-citizen and state, and varying understandings of the necessity of state military and policing responses. While there is some emancipatory potential in the borderlands discourse, it can only be real if it can tackle what may be called the extra- and intra-territorial policing frontierlands which indeed have become zones of indistinction in which not just laws, but principles of law, have been disappeared.

There is more to be done in our theorisations of the border and the sovereign to enable criminological engagement with the state of exception in the borderland. States of exception can be seen as depriving us of criminological purchase—a difficulty of assigning legality and illegality in what is often a legal void. The real question becomes how can criminology intercede in such states of exception that borderlands produce?

REFERENCES

Agamben, G., 1995, *Homo Sacer: Sovereign Power and Bare Life*, Daniel Heller-Roazen, trans., Stanford University Press, Stanford.

Agamben, G., 2005, *State of Exception*, Kevin Attell, trans., Chicago University Press, Chicago.

Andreas, P., 2000, *Border Games: Policing the US Mexico Divide*, University of Cornell Press, Ithaca.

Bauman, Z., 2002, Reconnaissance wars of the planetary frontierland, *Theory, Culture and Society*, **19: 81–90**.

Department of Home Affairs [South Africa], 1994–1999, *Annual Reports*, Government Printer, Pretoria, South Africa.

Eurostat, 2001, *Statistics in Focus: Populations and Social Conditions: Theme 3-19/2001, Population and Living Conditions*, European Communities, Luxembourg.

Human Rights Watch, 1997, *Burma/Thailand: No Safety in Burma, No Sanctuary in Thailand*, New York.

Human Rights Watch, 1998, *Prohibited Persons: Abuse of Undocumented Migrants, Asylum-Seekers, and Refugees in South Africa*, New York.

Human Rights Watch, 2002, *Discretion Without Bounds: The Arbitrary Application of Spanish Immigration Law*, New York.

Human Rights Watch, 2004, *Out of Sight, Out of Mind: Thai Policy Toward Burmese Refugees*, New York.

Klaaren, J. and Ramji, J. 2001, Inside illegality: migration policing in South Africa after apartheid, *Africa Today*, Fall, **48: 34–46**.

Nevins, J., 2002, *Operation Gatekeeper: The Rise of the 'Illegal Alien' and the Making of the US–Mexico Boundary*, Routledge, New York.

Pickering, S., 2001, Common sense and original deviancy: news discourses and asylum seekers in Australia, *Journal of Refugee Studies*, **14(2): 169–186**.

Pickering, S., and O'Kane, M., 2002, Policing, exile and gender in states' borderlands, *Current Issues in Criminal Justice,* Special Edition on Refugee Issues and Criminology, **14(1): 106–110**.

Pickering, S., 2005, *Refugees and State Crime*, The Federation Press, Sydney.

Pickering, S., 2006, The globalisation of violence against refugees, in: *The Globalisation of Violence*, R. Devetak and C. Hughes, eds., Routledge, London.

Sassen, S., 1996, *Losing Control? Sovereignty in an Age of Globalisation*, Columbia University Press, New York.

Sassen, S., 1998, *Globalization and its Discontents*, The New Press, New York.

Sassen, S., 1999, *Guests and Aliens*, The New Press, New York.

Tilly, C., 1986, War making and state making as organised crime, in: *Bringing the State Back In*, P. Evans, D. Rueschemeyer, and T. Skocpol, eds., Cambridge University Press, Cambridge.

Chapter 4

GLOBAL FLOWS, SEMI-PERMEABLE BORDERS AND NEW CHANNELS OF INEQUALITY
Border crossers and border performativity

Nancy A. Wonders
Northern Arizona University

> In the imagery [of globalisation] ... the flow is valorized, but not the carving of the channel (Tsing 2000: 334)

> Everyone has the right to freedom of movement and residence within the borders of each state' and 'Everyone has the right to leave any country, including his own, and to return to his country (*Universal Declaration of Human Rights*, Article 13)

There is little doubt that one of the most important features of globalisation is mobility. An enormous and still growing body of literature addresses the importance of capital mobility for facilitating the rise of transnational corporations, supranational institutions, and global commerce (Sassen 1998, 2002; Schaeffer 2003). This literature heralds the construction of 'porous borders' under globalisation; as Dauvergne (2004: 595) writes, 'The stock story of globalization is one of fluidity. More and more things are moving at faster and faster rates.' Globalisation theorists argue that corporations and nation-states facilitate the free flow of capital by developing channels and networks—an 'organisational architecture'— which links disparate locales and lubricates and regulates international exchange. Importantly, '[a] central feature of this organizational architecture is that it contains not only the capacities for enormous geographic dispersal and mobility but also pronounced territorial concentrations of resources necessary for the management and servicing of that dispersal and mobility' (Sassen 2002: 2).

S. Pickering and L. Weber (eds.), Borders, Mobility and Technologies of Control, 63–86.

In this chapter, I argue that broad claims about porous borders obscure the complexities of changing contemporary border constructions, particularly the 'pronounced territorial concentrations of resources' which have been deployed to manage and service the mobility of people. While is it evident that globalisation has facilitated the free flow of capital, in contrast, borders are increasingly constructed in ways that rigidly channel the waves of humanity who seek freedom of movement. As I will elaborate, there is no question that people are on the move, whether in search of jobs and security or in search of leisure and luxury. But for many ordinary people, borders are far from porous. Rather, borders and the technologies of control that enforce them have become ever more important as vehicles for restricting rights and constructing new channels of inequality.

In this chapter, I explore the semi-permeability of borders under globalisation. I do so by examining the different ways that borders are constructed to facilitate the entry of some but to deter the entry of others. As noted by Guiraudon and Joppke (2003: 2), '[i]n the multidisciplinary field of migration studies there is a peculiar divide between the study of migration flows and the study of state policies that seek to solicit, channel or contain those flows.' In this chapter, I highlight the technologies of control used to fashion the semi-permeability of today's borders by examining state responses to two of the most significant flows of people in the contemporary period: migration and tourism. By juxtaposing the way that nations construct and enforce borders differently for tourists and migrants, much is revealed about the racialised, gendered, and classist divides that borders today actually seek to enforce. Although a more global world has enormous potential for reducing inequality, in many wealthy countries, national borders are rapidly being reconstituted to function as a hard metal sieve, sifting and sorting people in ways that (re)produce global stratification.

Like many other scholars, in this analysis, I will use the term 'the border' to refer primarily to 'the wall around the west' and the efforts of developed nations to protect their wealth and privilege from others (see, for example, Andreas and Snyder 2000; Cunningham 2004). Because it provides such stark illustration of the arguments put forward here, many examples will be drawn from the United States–Mexico border. As Alvarez (1995: 451) puts it: 'No other border in the world exhibits the inequality of power, economics, and the human condition as does this one.'

I first provide a brief overview of the broad theoretical framing provided by the concept of border performativity. Border performativity takes as its theoretical starting point the idea that borders are not only geographically constituted, but are socially constructed via the performance of various state actors in an elaborate dance with ordinary people who seek freedom of movement and identification. The choreography for this dance is shaped by state policies and laws, but it is increasingly shaped by larger global forces as well. I then briefly sketch contemporary analyses of the extent and sources of international migration and tourism. While distinct literatures have developed that segregate these human flows, in this section, I conclude with a brief analysis of the symbiotic relationship between these two global trends.

Subsequently, I explore the changing role of the state relative to the global movement of people across borders. I argue that global challenges to both sovereignty and citizenship have led developed nations to restrict access and rights for some border crossers, particularly those viewed as socially needy, marginalised, or powerless; in contrast, those with resources are further privileged by their differential access to citizenship, rights, and mobility.

Next, I explore two specific technologies of control nation-states in the west are using to channel and (re)produce global social stratification. First, the social construction of the 'illegal' and the criminalisation of vulnerable populations and secondly, the 'securitisation of migration' and the creation of a border control industry that gives organisational architecture and durability to state performances of semi-permeable borders. By analysing these technologies of control, it becomes more transparent that borders are intentionally performed in ways that encourage some to cross them and to restrain others from doing so. Though regulation of migrants is often framed in terms of traditional crime control concerns, particularly the risk of criminal activity and the dangers of victimisation, in this chapter I argue that both migrants and tourists offer quite similar risks and benefits for nation-states. Yet, despite these similarities, the rhetoric of threat is only used to describe border crossings by migrant workers; in contrast, nation-states often go to great lengths to welcome the border crossings of tourists, thus carving still deeper the channels of inequality that divide these social groups.

Finally, I argue for greater consistency in contemporary border performances. Rather than relying on abstract, rhetorical conceptions of criminal threat, border constructions and enforcement should be more closely linked to the actual dangers posted by various kinds of border crossers. Given the many risks and benefits of both migrant workers and tourists to nation-states participating in the global economy, I argue for more flexible and fairer borders for both kinds of travellers.

1.   BORDER PERFORMATIVITY

The concept of border performativity serves as an analytic tool for exploring borders and border constructions. In my previous work (Wonders

2004a, 2004b), I combined relational theories of the state (for example, Jessop 1990) with feminist social constructionist theory (for example, Foster 1998) to develop a new theoretical approach to borders, called 'border performativity'. This theoretical approach argues that, although states attempt to choreograph national borders, often in response to global pressures, these state policies have little meaning until they are 'performed' by state agents or by border crossers. Although some border performances occur in the vicinity of the physical border of the nation-state, many other border performances occur in locations that may be far from the actual geographic border, such as in airport terminals, in the offices of social service workers who refuse assistance to non-citizens, or in workplaces raided by border agents in pursuit of illegal border crossers (Sole and Parella 2003). Border agents and state bureaucrats play a critical role in determining where, how, and on whose body a border will be performed. Border performances are shaped by many factors, but concerns related to processes of globalisation are increasingly salient.

Importantly, border performances are embodied. For example, in most developed countries today, some (mostly male) bodies enforce borders, while other (mostly female) bodies are subject to border enforcement. Thus, border performances are not gender-neutral, but are instead highly gendered (Wonders 2004b). Similarly, border performances are also classed and racialised (Driessen 1996). Indeed, those belonging to some racial groups and social classes may be welcomed by a country that strictly enforces borders crossings by 'Others'. This is particularly true in the post 9/11 world.

Importantly, the character of border enforcement practices is not only related to the identities of border agents and border crossers; it is also shaped by the cultural and economic location of various groups within the destination country. The body of law, rights, and opportunities available to those with citizenship has bearing on the extent to which borders are used to limit the rights and opportunities of others. Again, state performativity of borders is literally an embodied activity that is shaped by gender, race, and class relations. The utility of the concept of border performativity is illuminated by examining state responses to two different categories of border crossers: migrants and tourists.

2.   EMBODIED GLOBAL FLOWS

In this section, I begin by briefly outlining traditional framings of migration and tourism, with particular emphasis on how they shape our understanding of the differences between 'migrants' and 'tourists'.

2.1   Migrants

As many scholars have documented, one of the most important consequences of globalisation has been mass migration (Tirman 2004). Most migration statistics define an immigrant as 'a person who settles for some time in a given country from outside that country' (Council of Europe 1984: 8, as cited in Lahav 2004: 33).

According to the United Nations (2002: 2):

> Around 175 million persons currently reside in a country other than where they were born, which is about 3 percent of world population. The number of migrants has more than doubled since 1970. Sixty percent of the world's migrants currently reside in the more developed regions and 40 percent in the less developed regions. Most of the world's migrants live in Europe (56 million), Asia (50 million) and Northern America (41 million). Almost one of every 10 persons living in the more developed regions is a migrant.

These numbers, while striking, actually underestimate the disparate impact of migration on specific locales. For example, although to the European Union immigration constitutes 'only 4 percent of a population of 330 million, in countries such as France 11 percent of the population are foreign-born' (Lahav 2004: 32). Twelve percent of the United States population, or 288 million people, in 2004 were foreign-born, and it is estimated that about ten million were 'living in the United States without authorization' (Congressional Budget Office 2005: 4). However, in some states, like California and Texas, the percentage of foreign-born is much higher. In fact, for immigrants who work, 'two-thirds of them reside in just six states'; remarkably, 'the foreign-born constitute 32 percent of the labor force in California and 21 percent of the labor force' in the five other states, and 'over half of the foreign-born workers live in [just] seven consolidated metropolitan areas'(Congressional Budget Office 2005: 3). Thus, in Europe and in the United States, research indicates that the spatial concentration of immigrants is significant.

Researchers and scholars have played an important role in creating a separate conceptual category for people who cross borders as 'migrants'. A brief glance at the justifications for these migratory trends provides an important backdrop for understanding the segregation of 'migrants' from tourists and other border crossers. Generally, migrants are characterised as border crossers who move because of poverty, danger, or economic necessity.

First, the literature suggests that a substantial portion of today's migrants are ordinary people who have been displaced from traditional, largely agrarian, ways of life due to the widespread impact of structural adjustment programs and land privatisation (Kingfisher 2002; Wonders and Danner 2002). Migration as a result of structural adjustment programs has especially affected women, who constitute the majority of the world's farmers (Eschle 2002). Research has demonstrated that the migration of poor, uneducated and under-skilled women and men in search of a means of survival has inspired much of the new border choreography taking place in industrialised countries today (Peterson and Runyan 1999).

In addition to the poor, research has evidenced that people from diverse social backgrounds are also represented in recent waves of migration. For example, women and children from all social classes are disproportionately displaced by environmental damage, as well as by war and internal conflicts within nations (Peterson and Runyon 1999).

An additional catalyst for migration is the increase in mobility made possible by relatively accessible international transportation and the rise of new communication technologies. The ease of travel and the growing accessibility of information about other locales have been especially important for opening the floodgates for cross-border flows of middle-class professionals and educated students from countries with struggling economies, fostering a brain drain in many parts of the world (Dauvergne 2004).

Another key source of much migration is revealed by social network analysis. Numerous studies have evidenced the importance of existing social relationships on the behaviour of recent migrants; informal information sharing about employment opportunities, strategies for border crossing, and supportive resettlement locales have heightened family reunification and friendship networking in the recent wave of global migration (Mendelson 2004).

Despite the many sources of international migration, it is important to recognise that 'crossing the border remains a very difficult proposition for much of the world's population' (Cunningham 2004: 333). Although the number of migrants increased by 14 percent between 1990 and 2000, as noted earlier, only three percent of the world's population currently reside in a country other than where they were born (United Nations 2002). Thus, it is important to appreciate that the moral panic about migration is not a 'global' phenomenon; instead, it is a 'western' phenomenon related to the fact that today's migrants disproportionately seek entrance into wealthy developed countries (United Nations 2002).

Again, while technically migration simply involves the movement of people from one place to another—a right protected under the *Universal Declaration of Human Rights*—the discourse and research on migration has framed this current of human mobility in terms of economic necessity and poverty. As a result, in the popular mind, migrants are individuals who are disproportionately poor, economically needy, dark-skinned, from the global south, and increasingly female. Or, perhaps, because some border crossers manifest particular identities, their mobility becomes suspect and worthy of heightened attention as 'illegals'—a point to which I will return.

2.2 Tourism

A second global flow that has been primed by globalisation is international tourism. Over the last two decades, the development and impact of global tourism has been immense. 'Between 1981 and 1997, the number of tourist arrivals rose from 292 to 613 million per year at the international level. Tourism receipts increased even more dramatically, from U.S. \$106 billion to U.S. \$447 billion' (Brenner 2002: 504). International tourism brought in receipts of €455 billion in 2003 (World Tourism Organization 2004). It is estimated that approximately ten percent of all consumer spending is devoted to tourism, making it one the largest industries in the world (Theobald 1998).

Again, scholars, policy makers and others have played an important role in creating a separate conceptual category for people who cross borders as 'tourists'. Generally, tourists are characterised as border crossers with resources who move in search of leisure or pleasure.

Globalisation has facilitated the global flow of tourists in several ways. First, the advent of mass communication and transportation, particularly the aeroplane, literally made the world a smaller place spatially (Urry 1990). Additionally, as has been pointed out by numerous authors, rising incomes and leisure time in developed countries created the material and social conditions for the growth of mass tourism (Brenner 2002; Urry 1990).

More recently, tourism development in many nations has become a strategy to promote economic growth, new jobs, construction, and to finance urban centres (Brenner 2002). Tourism development has also played an important role in the phenomenal growth of the service sector, as I will elaborate below.

It is important to note that tourism dollars disproportionately benefit the already wealthy west. 'The majority of tourist activities are located in the developed countries, mainly in Western Europe and in the U.S. These two areas concentrated almost 70 percent of tourist arrivals and 70 percent of income generated by tourist services during the 1990s' (Brenner 2002: 504).

Significantly, the characterisation of tourists in the literature and in popular discourse is almost the polar opposite of the migrant. According to experts, today's tourists are disproportionately wealthy, white and male

(Urry 1990). It is, therefore, not surprising that few constraints are placed on the mobility of tourists in the globalised world.

3.   EMBODIED FLOWS AND EDDIES

Although justifications for mobility may differ, it is important to realise that migratory and tourist flows merge together and eddy in complex ways. This is true despite the way that ordinary discourse and state border performances seek to divide these two categories of border crossers.

Ironically, but significantly, the desire of the tourist to move freely across borders is an important source of the demand for cheap labour that fuels economic migration. In general, tourism is associated with the rise of the service sector, 'involving as it does financial, insurance, transportation, accommodation, restaurant, and recreational services' (Meethan 2004: 112). As Brenner (2002: 500) notes, '[o]ne of the most significant developments of the last few decades in the global economy has been the rapid growth of the service sector. It is increasingly the major source of employment and a dominant contributor to the gross domestic product (GDP) in most developing countries.'

There is no question that tourist development in the industrialised world plays a critical role in shaping the demand for labour in the service industry, particularly for construction workers, and for employees in domestic service, and food services (Cunningham 2004). The service sector is characterised by jobs that are typically low wage, require little education or advance training, are part-time and/or temporary, and which have few benefits; jobs that are disproportionately occupied by the foreign-born.

The relationship between migration and tourism can be illustrated by using the United States as an example, as documented in a recent a report, *The Role of Immigrants in the U.S. Labor Market* (Congressional Budget Office 2005). This report concludes that '[i]n 2004, more than 21 million workers—one in seven workers in the United States—were foreign born, and half had arrived since 1990. Almost 40 percent of foreign-born workers were from Mexico and Central America' (2005: 1). The report goes on to note the distribution of foreign-born workers in a variety of sectors of the economy. These statistics tell a powerful story about the relationship between tourists and migrants in the new United States service economy, including that:

- 'During the past decade, foreign-born workers accounted for more than half of the growth of the U.S. labor force. The number of foreign-born workers increased from 13 million in 1994 to 21 million in 2004. About 40 percent of foreign-born workers are U.S. citizens. Possibly half (6 million to 7 million) of the remaining foreign born workers are unauthorized' (2005: 2).

- 'In 2004, three-quarters of all workers born in Mexico and Central America were employed in occupations that have minimal educational requirements, such as construction laborer and dishwasher; only one-quarter of all native workers held such jobs' (2005: 1).
- 'On average, the weekly earnings of men from Mexico and Central American who worked full-time were about half those of native born men; women from Mexico and Central America earned about three fifths of the average weekly earnings of native-born women' (2005: 1).
- 'Workers from Mexico and Central America fill large proportions of low-education jobs on construction sites and at restaurants' (2005: 13).
- 'Over one-third of all dishwashers, janitors, maids, and cooks are foreign born' (2005: 20).

Because the tourism and leisure industries depend upon consumers with resources, these industries are primarily located in wealthy countries of the west. Workers who supply this industry with labour cannot just work anywhere; as the Congressional Budget Office (2005: 20) aptly points out, 'many immigrants, especially those with very low levels of education, were doing work—for example, washing dishes or cleaning hotel rooms—that cannot be done in another country. If the work they did was to be performed at all, it had to be performed in the United States'. The dependence of the tourism industry on immigrant labour is significant in virtually all industrialised nations. This dependence is also fuelled by racist, classist and sexist stereotypes about who 'ought' perform unskilled and low wage labour (Sole and Parella 2003).

The stratified character of work within the tourism industry is, in part, shaped by the demands created by wealthy, white, mostly male leisure travellers and the businesses that seek to attract them. For many male leisure travellers, access to the emotional and sexual services traditionally provided by women is an especially important feature of desirable tourist destinations. Much recent research reveals that sex tourism is a major source of economic development for developing countries, with Thailand being the clearest example (Kempadoo and Doezman 1998). However, it is also the case that gendered and racialised labour expectations shape the competition for the tourist dollars associated with the male leisure travellers in the west (Wonders and Michalowski 2001).

In many cities, a focus on 'service with a smile' has created demand for large numbers of workers across a variety of service jobs, including front desk operators, massage therapists and maids. This focus on emotional labour has led to an increase in the demand for women's labour in particular (Adkins 1995). In other cities, sexual services flourish, such as in the

Amsterdam's red light district (Wonders 2004a), Spain's coastal tourist cities, as well as in other major cities in the industrialised world. In many of these locales, male consumer desire for the exotic 'Other' helps to fuel the disproportionate demand for women of colour. The fact that tourists demand sexual services creates a huge incentive for women (and some men) to migrate to these areas to meet the demand (Wonders and Michalowski 2001).

What should be evident from this analysis is the relational character of these two types of mobility. Both tourist and migrant flows emerge from powerful currents of change in the global economy, but each flow depends upon the other in important ways, despite their very different treatment by policy-makers and border officials.

4.   NARROWED CHANNELS FOR BORDER FLOWS: THE CHANGING ROLE OF THE STATE

While globalisation has created the conditions for unprecedented global mobility, restrictions on some kinds of movement are growing at a similarly remarkable rate. In this section, I describe several reasons that nation-states are constructing more rigid borders for some.

While some scholars have argued that state power has declined under globalisation (Cohen 1996), many others note the way that state power has simply been restructured in the contemporary period (Kingfisher 2002). In fact, most theorists today argue that the nation-state is essential to the broader project of globalisation (Sassen 1998). One important site of state power is the border.

Borders have long served to define and divide nations but, historically, border performances did not revolve around restricting the right of movement for border crossers. As Dauvergne (2004: 589) puts it:

> Worldwide regulation of migration was a twentieth century invention. Although it was certainly the case that passports and border controls emerged at an earlier point in time, it was not until the beginning of the twentieth century that the world was fully and firmly divided by borders, and the requirement of passports and visas to cross them.

Though a detailed analysis of the impact of globalisation on the nation-state is beyond the scope of this chapter, it is important to note a few of the reasons that nation-states in the west were compelled to perform borders differently by the late 1980s, once globalisation's effects began to reverberate more broadly.

Globalisation created a powerful threat to the traditional power of nation-states and to national sovereignty (Dauvergne 2004). Once capital was freed from its traditional time, geographic and spatial moorings, the boundaries of the nation were thrown into question, as were the parameters of state power. In part, border performances today reflect an attempt by the state to preserve some aspects of sovereignty.

Embedded in larger forms of global capital and transnational labor, borders are clearly important sites for the study of how mobilities are being organised and contested in the context of enclosures across a global landscape. They also distinctly illustrate the manifold ways in which the state (as a complex of different agencies and actors) continues to powerfully monitor movement across nations and to mount different models for doing so (Cunningham 2004: 345).

Today, nation-states seek to restrict mobility in order to narrow the channels by which people can make claims upon the state via citizenship.

Citizenship is a mechanism for allocating rights and claims through political membership. In the past two centuries or so, citizenship has been nested in nation-states. Globalization is a package of transnational flows—of people, production, investment, information, ideas and authority. As exchange intensifies across borders, such globalization changes the nature of citizenship (Brysk and Shafir 2004: 3).

The changing character of citizenship is complex and a source of widespread debate, but it is evident throughout the literature that citizenship claims today are highly contested in part because of the crisis of the welfare state that has been precipitated by globalisation (Kingfisher 2002).

In the rhetoric of global capitalists, nations with expensive costs of doing business, including those with high taxes in support of social services, state pensions and health care, have simply priced themselves out of the global marketplace. In response to this rhetoric, and at times in active support of it, many developed nations have laid siege to the broad social welfare benefits that had been developed over the last half century. As benefits to citizens in the west have declined, the general public has become more agitated about others who wish to make citizenship claims, frequently supporting constricted borders in large numbers. Politicians further prey on public fears by framing the economy as a zero-sum game, suggesting that if more people cross the border, those already within the country should expect to get 'less'. The effectiveness of this political rhetoric depends on the fact that such claims are typically directed at border crossers from already marginalised groups.

The development of international human rights law has also fed the anxiety of nation-states concerned about their declining ability to satisfy citizens. In particular, the development of refugee law placed a new burden on signatory nations who became obligated to accept those who met the legal definition of a 'refugee'. As Dauvergne (2004: 596) argues: '[r]efugees are people fleeing persecution on the basis of one of five grounds (race, religion, nationality, particular social group, or political opinion)' but in order to claim refugee status, one must make that claim from 'somewhere'. Once a person claiming refugee status sets foot in a country and puts forward a request for protection, the nation-state is generally obligated to provide support for the refugee, including during the time it takes for the claim to be fully processed. For this reason, wealthy nation-states have focused on strategies to tighten borders, place limits on refugee admissions and restrict entry. The goal is to prevent potential refugees from entering in the first place, an objective which extends to many other border crossers as well, particularly to those who seek the ever elusive rights associated with citizenship.

This brief overview of the changing role of the state highlights the importance of changing border performances for (re)establishing the boundaries of sovereignty and restricting access to citizenship rights. In the next section, I explore some of the specific control strategies nation-states have utilised to segregate and channel diverse border crossers.

5.   SEMI-PERMEABLE BORDERS
AND TECHNOLOGIES OF CONTROL

Although many view the border as a fixed geographic line, the concept of border performativity draws attention to the way that borders shift and change as a result of new state policies, everyday practice and the utilisation of new technologies of control. In this section, I explore two technologies of control that are currently being used in the west to construct semi-permeable borders, arguing that these control strategies are creating new channels of inequality in an already deeply divided world. The technologies of control addressed here include discourses, practices and polices associated with, first, the social construction of 'illegals' and the criminalisation of vulnerable populations, and secondly, the 'securitisation of the border' and the development of an entrenched border control industry.

5.1 The Making of 'Illegals': Criminalisation of Vulnerable Populations

Perhaps the most powerful tool in any nation's arsenal is the ability to frame discourse and how citizens imagine the world around them. 'Discourse is not a thing or a conversation between individuals. Rather, the term refers to particular ways of collectively talking about, writing about, practicing or performing aspects of the social world around us. Discursive practices, and the languages they rely on, provide the themes that shape how reality is understood' (Neysmith and Chen 2002: 247).

Border performances today are dominated by the development and use of linguistic codes that create stark separations between border crossers and serve to justify differential treatment. In particular, the construction of the category of 'the illegal' serves as a rhetorical and real device for denying access to citizenship rights for certain kinds of people. The category 'illegal' masks classed, raced, and gendered judgments about who can cross borders and who cannot. This is best illustrated by examining the differential labeling that is attached to various border crossers. Here, I explore the sharp divide between tourists and migrants, as well as the numerous categories that have been constructed to bridge the contradictions created by radically different treatment of these two groups.

The contradictory and rather arbitrary categorisation of border crossers has begun to receive attention within both the tourism and the migration literature. For example, Rodriguez (2001: 52) argues that '[t]he concepts of tourism and residency are intrinsically confusing in that they confront the notion of mobility, associated with the rhythms of individuals' working or leisure hours and the degree of permanency of time spent in leisure spaces.' He goes on to note that conceptual divides are difficult given that '[t]ourists and residents usually share the same space, time and way of life' (2001: 54). A recent anthology on tourism tries to clarify by stating that 'there is increasing international agreement that "tourism" refers to all visitor activities', but the authors also note that experts still need to 'address the arbitrary boundaries between tourism and leisure, and tourism and migration' (Hall et al., 2004: 5). Further, they highlight the dialectic between tourism and other forms of mobility when they write that 'tourism constitutes just one form of leisure-oriented temporary mobility; and in being part of that mobility, it is also both *shaped by* and *shaping it*' (2004: 5, emphasis mine).

It is especially difficult to draw a bright line between tourists and migrants given that tourism, like migration, can lead to semi-permanent or permanent relocation. As Truly (2002: 264) notes, '[r]ecreational travel and tourism are common forms of temporary migration that are typically planned two-way trips; however, these trips can lead to the purchase of a vacation or second home' which then makes the tourist rather indistinguishable from the migrant or from the permanent resident (who may also leave on vacation from time to time). Research has established that tourism is a significant source of retirement migration; indeed, 'there is considerable evidence of the importance of previous tourism experiences to resident retirees' (Rodriguez 2001: 56). Although a deluge of foreign senior citizens may not seem threatening in the abstract, such waves of new residents have utterly transformed coastal regions in Spain and Mexico, as well as in other regions of the world. While this transformation has fuelled the economy in some ways, it has also had numerous deleterious consequences including increased demands on natural resources such as water, devastation of coastal ecosystems and pollution.

In reality, the fairly regular transition from temporary 'visitor' to permanent 'resident' found among tourists is not so different in many ways from patterns found among so-called 'migrants'. For example, migrants to the United States historically crossed the border seasonally or temporarily, but generally returned home. Today's migrants are less likely to return regularly to their home country, but research has evidenced that this is a response to harsher border enforcement, rather than a cause of it. 'One of the unintended consequences of making border crossings more difficult was to persuade many illegal Mexican immigrants to end their long-established circular patterns of annual rotation between Mexico and the United States, hoping for another amnesty and an opportunity to get their families north of the border' (Daniels 2004: 244).

The very narrow construction of who is 'illegal' has often led to contradictory, adverse and unintended consequences. For example, the criminalisation of adult migrants has profound implications for others in their social network, but most profoundly for children. '[N]early one out of ten families with children in the United States is a mixed-immigration status family; that is, at least one of the parents is a non-citizen and at least one of the children is a citizen' (Romero 2005: 63). Parents may be 'migrants' but their children are often 'citizens'; restrictive border policies that define 'illegals' narrowly divide such families into those with rights and those without.

In order to resolve some of the contradictory consequences of the narrow framing of the 'illegal', the United States and other western countries are constantly creating new categories to bridge the canyon between the tourist and the migrant. For example, the category of 'legal resident' was created to extend certain rights to migrant crossers from some countries with whom the government had sympathies (Daniels 2004: 247). The myriad of special visas and permitted seasonal workers in the United States reveals an immigration system that is explicitly set up to engage in classed, raced and gendered social segregation of border crossers. In general, people who already have resources and educational advantage are given even greater advantage in this complex visa system. These permutations illustrate the performative quality of borders in the contemporary period. Nevins (2002: 11) articulates this well when he writes that:

> Opportunistic politicians and nativist organisations presented the 'illegal' immigrant not only as a lawbreaker, but more importantly as a threat to national sovereignty and the American social and economic fabric … the state did not simply respond to public concern with the supposed crisis of 'illegal' immigration. Rather, it has helped to create the 'illegal' through the construction of the boundary and the expansion of the INSs enforcement capacity.

All of this is to say that the problem is not necessarily migration, but the way that the mobility of some is framed. A powerful example is provided by Guiraduon and Joppke (2003: 4) in their prescient analysis of migration to France, a country that solicited permanent immigration for several decades, but saw declining immigration throughout the 1990s; so much so that:

> … it would be far-fetched to deem France in a 'migration crisis.' However, ever since a right-wing party, Le Pen's National Front, had been luring big chunks of the electorate with its demagogic demand to expel most (Muslim) immigrants from France, immigration had become more politicised than anywhere else in Europe …

I would argue that media representations that blame the November 2005 unrest in France on immigration have missed this central analytic point; it was this politicised climate which marginalised immigrant communities and led to their extensive rioting in France.

Similarly, in Spain, research has evidenced the way that border performances today create the 'illegal'; as Merino (2004: 247) emphasises, in Spain the 'vision of the immigrant's presence as a problem and the creation of the category "illegal immigrant"' have been used to justify changing border practices. In her work on both Spain and Italy, Calavita (2005: 164) concurs that the construction of the 'illegal' is itself the problem; 'immigrants who are marked both by their economic marginality and, relatedly, by perceived racial difference are not just excluded but are stigmatized as not "suitable" for inclusion.' And Mountz (2003: 624) has documented this process in Canada, arguing that the Department of Citizenship and Immigration 'constructs the identities of transnational migrants through its immigration programs by categorizing them along a spectrum of desirability. Through such bureaucratic practices, nation-states can legalize forms of belonging.'

Thus, illegality is a forced identity category imposed upon some individuals and groups by nation-states reluctant to provide access and/or citizenship rights to those considered undesirable. This identity category is used to demarcate the boundary between citizen and outsider, but it does so by excluding the most vulnerable portions of the world's population, despite the fact that border crossers come in all shapes and sizes. Dauvergne (2004: 599) captures this contradiction:

> Technically, anyone who is present in a nation state without either nationality or authorisation under law is an illegal migrant. Many people around the world who have no legal migration status have overstayed tourist, student or work visas. ... The term 'illegal' has escaped its legal, and even grammatical, moorings and now stands alone as a noun. It does not conjure British backpackers overstaying on Australia's Gold Coast, or Kiwi's working in London's pubs. It conjures sweatshops and sex shops, poverty and race. The face of the imaginary illegal is poor and brown and destitute.

Thus, the construction of 'the illegal' reflects, not mobility or border crossing *per se*, but rather the identity of particular border crossers. The concept of 'the illegal' also represents an important technology of control in the construction of semi-permeable borders, particularly since it not only shapes border flows and citizenship, but also our imagination.

5.2   'Securitisation' of the Border: Terrorism, Tourists and the Border Control Industry

A second technology of border control is the creation of a security-focused organisational architecture for enforcing borders in a way that ensures their semi-permeability. The framing of some border crossers as 'illegal' has legitimated the creation, financing and deployment of special police forces charged with border patrol at the physical frontier and in airports, governmental offices, and other public spaces. Particularly after 9/11, borders have been reframed as zones of threatened security, leading to what has been called the 'securitisation' of the border (Tirman 2004).

By 2000, in Europe '"[n]ew security" issues (i.e. ethnic conflict, terrorism, Islamic fundamentalism, and drug and human smuggling), which supplanted Cold War ideology, became the dark side of globalisation that linked migration to crime, smuggling, terrorism and other policy issues of law and order' (Lahav 2004: 31). Similarly, in the United States, by the mid-1990s a sense of the migrant as a threat emerged; though the reasons for this shift in public attitudes were complex, 'the association of immigrants with crime, heightened by the Mariel boatlift from Cuba, and Hollywood's often glamorised and overemphasised treatment of not only the Italian "mafia", but also of alleged Russian and Chinese "mafias", surely had its effects' (Daniels 2004: 239).

In both the United States and Europe, the framing of immigration as a threat led to a significant and relatively new deployment of border police, a reconfiguration and proliferation of border-related agencies, and an infusion of expensive new technologies, leading some to suggest the development of a 'border control industry' (Davis 2002: x). In the United States, 'The INS [Immigration and Naturalization Service] budget for enforcement efforts along the southwest boundary, for example, grew from $400 million in fiscal year (FY) 1993 to $800 million in FY 1997' (Nevins 2002: 4). Additionally, '[i]n the seven years following NAFTA, the number of border agents more than doubled to 9,335' (Cunningham 2004: 337). With this increase, the United States Border Patrol during the 1990s became 'the largest and least professional federal law enforcement agency' (Daniels 2004: 241).

This militarisation of the border is also occurring in border regions in Europe, including in Spain, Italy and Germany (Nevins 2002). Lahav (2004: 44) documents that '[a]s a consequence of EU and Schengen commitments to strengthen external frontiers, all the Southern European member-states increased coastguard patrols, police checks on third-country nationals, and deportations'. Importantly, he also notes that '[t]he upshot of immigration cooperation was protectionism'. The goal of keeping people out was actually to keep citizenship, resources and privilege 'in'.

Significantly, the criminalisation of some forms of border crossing has been accompanied by concern that border policy *not* restrict socially desirable border crossers; of special concern is the free movement of business travellers, students, and tourists. This social sorting requires that special staff and equipment be provided at key border points to ensure the ease of entry for some. Throughout the west, but particularly in the United States, new technologies of control have been recently installed in airports that seek to screen potential 'terrorists'. Visitors from some countries are subject to this increased surveillance, while visitors from other (more white and affluent) countries are treated as 'tourists' rather than as terrorist threats. The costs of this effort are staggering. Estimates of the monthly costs of private airport security in the United States in 2001 ran as much as $211 million a month for passenger-screening services from private firms (De Lollis 2002). Another report in the same year put the world cost of airport security at $7 billion, a figure that has surely increased each year (World Airport Week 2002). More recently, the cost of one mismanaged United

States government contract to hire and train over 60,000 airport screeners costs over $300 million (Higham and O'Harrow 2005).

Whether trying to keep people out or helping them come in, border officials must rely heavily on strategies like race and class profiling and individualised conceptions of risk and harm when doing their jobs. Where these policies are not officially sanctioned, the impetus for such profiling remains strong. As one border official complained:

> We're not allowed to do our job because they don't want us to hurt anyone's feelings; for example, they tell us to catch Middle East terrorists, but in no way should we racially profile anyone. What does that mean? Catch Middle East terrorists but don't racially profile. That's two of the greatest contradictions there are (Krauss and Pacheco 2004: 178).

Despite this complaint, there is ample evidence that border officials frequently utilise profiles to do their jobs. Attitudes like the one expressed above are particularly unfortunate for those ordinary citizens who are not security threats, but who otherwise fit racial or ethnic profiles. This is true, for example, of the 'estimated 3 million people in the US [who] trace their origins to the Arabic-speaking world' (Nagel and Staeheli 2004: 8). As Romero (2005: 25) cautions 'because of the high correlation between national origin and racial, ethnic and religious profiling, the federal government should be wary about using such accidents of birth and culture as proximities for disloyalty, especially when such profiling promotes essentialist stereotyping and subordination without the promise of enhanced security.'

While there are some social and security risks associated with migrants, there is little evidence thus far to suggest that they are a greater risk than other, more affluent border crossers. In general, the evidence thus far suggests that migrants—whether legal or illegal—are net contributors in most destination countries, particularly in terms of their overall economic contributions (Congressional Budget Office 2005). In fact, most developed countries desperately need low-wage workers and will continue to do so given sharply declining birth rates throughout the industrialised world (Congressional Budget Office 2005; Raghuram 2004).

When migrants do engage in harmful activity, it is all too frequently an accommodation to the adverse consequences of social policies that lead to their marginalisation within their host country. Although many people associate immigrants with increased crime, Guiraudon and Joppke (2003: 16) point out that:

until the early 1970s, there was actually little reason for such fears: the evidence was overwhelming, in the United States, Australia, and Europe alike, that immigrants committed fewer crime than the native population. However, from the mid-70s on—that is, immediately after the recruitment stop in Europe—there has been a reverse trend of increased crime rated among immigrants, especially in the second generation.

They go on to comment that 'the turn to zero-immigration policies transformed demand-into-supply-side driven immigration, with a higher proportion of irregular immigration and a greater propensity for risk-taking among those who still dare to migrate despite and against states' control policies'. Thus, '[a]ccordingly, the proportion of irregular immigrants—asylum-seekers, tourists, illegals, and transitory migrants—among criminal immigrants is exceedingly high everywhere' (17). Thus, increased crime among migrants is associated with border tightening as the cost and risk associated with border crossing is heightened and the avenues for legal participation in social, political and economic life are blocked.

In contrast, despite the efforts to throw open the borders for tourism, the damaging consequences of global tourism are well documented. The adverse impacts of tourism on the natural environment include: pressure on natural resources, including energy depletion, water supply, land use and soil erosion; harm to wildlife/habitat and biodiversity loss as a result of trampling and clearance of vegetation, loss of forest cover, disturbance to wildlife, damage to coral reefs, damage to species; pollution, including air and water pollution, as well as solid waste and litter and noise pollution (Wong 2004).

In the state of Arizona, which has the largest stretch of shared border with Mexico and had the largest influx of 'illegal' migrant crossings in 2004, politicians and citizens are outraged over the environmental damage done to fragile desert ecosystems by border crossers. However, little public outcry has accompanied the construction of thousands of water-intensive golf courses for tourists in an arid and water-short desert landscape. If risk, threat, and harm justify targeted enforcement policies, surely some of contemporary border performativity ought be directed toward tourists.

Migrants are even more likely to be viewed as threats since 9/11. The threat of terrorism has also fuelled the growth of the border control industry. As a result of the terrorist attacks in New York, some illegal aliens became 'enemy aliens' who constituted national security threats (Cole 2003). 'After the September 11 attacks, the culprits of American vulnerability were widely identified as porous borders, generous entry policies, violations of the terms of entry, and the entry of immigrants from the Middle East more generally' (Tirman 2004: 2). All migrants came to be defined as 'security risks'.

What has been interesting about border enforcement since 9/11 is how much the United States response, which is largely aimed at migrants, fails to address the actual facts of the terrorists' border crossing. 'Though the 9/11 terrorists evidently entered in the United States legally as visa students and not as immigrants or even refugee claimants, and a few had resided there for some years, according to a nationwide poll in the United States, two-thirds of those polled (68 percent) believed that enforcement of immigration laws and the border had been too lax' (Adelman 2004: 124). In addition, '[p]olls reported that nearly 60 percent of the American public favored ethnic profiling, at least as long as it was directed at Arabs and Muslims' (Cole 2003: 48). Though the Bush administration has denied the use of racial profiling, it's actions, which have included random interviewing, widespread detention, and selective deportation, suggest a clear policy of targeting Arabs and Muslims (Cole 2003). The close link between immigration and concern about terrorism is also 'strong in the European Union, where inter-governmental cooperation on immigration affairs has from the start occurred in the context of fighting international crime and terrorism and protecting external borders' (Guiraudon and Joppke 2003: 15).

But the truth is that targeting tourists might be more successful than targeting migrants since '[t]errorists (especially those conducting recon-naissance) behave remarkable like tourists—by happenstance and design. Both travel to the United States from foreign countries in small (sometimes familial) groups, visit the nation's most identifiable landmarks, and take endless photographs' (Bulletin of the Atomic Scientists, 2005: 8).

The point is that restricting the rights of border crossers is an ineffective strategy for identifying terrorists. Additionally, assuming that terrorists look more like migrants than like tourists mistakes the performed border for the very real politics behind border stratification in a globalised world. What has been revealed in this analysis is the development of an organisational architecture—the border patrol industry—that is designed to ensure the semi-permeability of borders, granting free access to flows of socially-desirable border crossers while restricting the rights of those deemed threatening to those who already have privilege.

6.   ON SEMI-PERMEABLE BORDERS: FROM CONTRADICTION TO CONSISTENCY

Migration and tourism constitute global flows that spring from the same fundamental source: the growing global belief that all people have a fundamental right to mobility, as guaranteed in the *Universal Declaration of Human Rights*. However, people caught up in these border flows today are not encountering the porous borders that have been so closely associated with capital flows. Nation-states in the developed world face many challenges as a result of globalisation, including threats to sovereignty and pressure to reduce the entitlements historically associated with citizenship in wealthy welfare states. These challenges have resulted in a strategic recons-truction of the border as 'semi-permeable', easing the mobility of tourists and those with resources while restricting access for vulnerable and marginalised populations who might make claims upon nation-states' diminishing capacity to serve citizens. The analysis here highlights the fundamental unfairness of such an approach.

The concept of border performativity has offered a valuable framing for analysis of this border reconstruction project since it draws attention to the relational and performative character of border control strategies. Border control strategies are not fixed, but rather shift and change in response to particular kinds of border flows and in response to particular kinds of border crossers. This chapter has focused on two control strategies that play an important role in creating new channels of global inequality: first, the social construction of 'the illegal' and its carefully crafted linkage to already disadvantaged populations and, second, the securitisation of the border which has been accomplished by the development of a large, costly, and growing border control industry.

The strong currents of change may yet wash away the rigid channels nation-states seek to construct for some border crossers. Low birth rates and the critical need for migrant labour in the west are likely to continue to siphon people toward wealthy countries. An ironic feature of the demand for labor in the west is that tourism, a valorised border flow, has facilitated the creation of a large and growing service sector that is fundamentally dependent upon the labour of another stream of border crossers, migrants. The dialectical relationship between the demand for mobility as a luxury good for wealthy and middle-class consumers in the west and the mobility associated with economic need and migrant labour is an understudied, but critical aspect of border performativity in today's global context. As I have illustrated, despite the relational quality of migration and tourism flows, there is much evidence that wealthy countries have tremendous motivation to simply build more effective strategies to control and channel who gets in to the developed world and, more importantly, what rights they will be able to claim once they arrive. It is essential that criminologists provide research that details the real (in contrast to the 'imagined') risks and harms associated with cross-border flows, and that reveals the deep channels of inequality that are being carved by contemporary border performances. There is every reason to believe that the current border flows of humanity may yet become tidal waves, and criminologists must be prepared to engage this sea of change.

REFERENCES

Adelman, H., 2004, Governance, immigration policy, and security: Canada and the United States post-9/11, in: *The Maze of Fear: Security and Migration After 9/11*, J. Tirman, ed., The New Press, New York, **pp. 109–130**.

Adkins, L., 1995, *Gendered Work: Sexuality, Family, and the Labor Market*, Open University Press, Philadelphia.

Alvarez, R. M., Jr., 1995, The Mexican-U.S. border: the making of an anthropology of borderlands, *Annual Review of Anthropology*, **24: 447–470**.

Andreas, P., and Synder, T., 2000, *The Wall Around the West: State Borders and Immigration Controls in North America and Europe*, Rowman and Littlefield, Landham.

Brenner, L., 2002, Luxury tourism and regional economic development in Mexico, *The Professional Geographer*, **54(4): 500–520**.

Brysk, A., and Shafir, G., 2004, *People Out of Place: Globalization, Human Rights and the Citizenship Gap*, Routledge, New York.

Bulletin of the Atomic Scientists, 2005, Homeland security: terrorism takes a holiday, **(July/August) pp. 8–9**.

Calavita, K., 2005, *Immigrants at the Margins: Law, Race, and Exclusion in Southern Europe*, Cambridge University Press, Cambridge.

Cohen, M. G., 1996, Women, democracy and the future of nations, in: *States Against Markets: The Limits of Globalization*, R. Boyer and D. Drache eds., Routledge, London, **pp. 383–414**.

Cole, D., 2003, *Enemy Aliens: Double Standards and Constitutional Freedoms in the War on Terrorism*, The New Press, New York.

Congressional Budget Office, 2005, *The Role of Immigrants in the U.S. Labor Market*, Congress of the United States, Congressional Budget Office, Washington, DC.

Cunningham, H., 2004, Nations rebound?: crossing borders in a gated globe, *Identities: Global Studies in Culture and Power*, **11: 329–350**.

Daniels, R., 2004, *Guarding the Door: American Immigration Policy and Immigrants Since 1882*, Hill and Wang, New York.

Dauvergne, C., 2004, Sovereignty, migration, and the rule of law in global times, *The Modern Law Review*, **67(4): 588–615**.

Davis, M., 2002, Foreword, in: *Operation Gatekeeper: the Rise of the 'Illegal Alien' and the Making of the U.S.-Mexico Boundary*, J. Nevins, Routledge, New York, **pp. ix–xi**.

De Lollis, B., 2002, Cost of airport security soaring' *USA Today*, April 11.

Driessen, H., 1996, At the edge of Europe: crossing the Mediterranean divide, in: *Borders, Nations and State*, L. O'Dowd and T. M. Wilson, eds., Ashgate Publishing, Brookfield, Vermont, **pp. 179–198**.

Eschle, C., 2002, Engendering global democracy, I*nternational Feminist Journal of Politics*, **4(3): 315–341**.

Foster, S.L., 1998, Choreographies of gender, *Signs*, **24(1): 1–22**.

Guiraudon, V., and Joppke, C., 2003, *Controlling a New Migration World*, Routledge, London.

Hall, C. M., Williams, A. M., and Lew. A. A., 2004, Tourism: conceptualizations, institutions, and issues, in: *A Companion to Tourism*, A. A. Lew, C. M. Hall, and A. M. Williams, eds., Blackwell Publishing, Malden, MA, **pp. 3–21**.

Higham, S., and O'Harrow, R., Jr., 2005, The high cost of a rush to security, *Washington Post* (30 June 2005).

Jessop, B., 1990, *State Theory: Putting the Capitalist State in its Place*, Pennsylvania State University Press, University Park, PA.

Kempadoo, K., and Doezema, J., 1998, G*lobal Sex Workers: Rights, Resistance and Redefinition*, Routledge, London.

Kingfisher, C., 2002, *Western Welfare in Decline: Globalization and Women's Poverty*, University of Pennsylvania Press, Philadelphia.

Krauss, E., and Pacheco, A., 2004, *On the Line: Inside the U.S. Border Patrol*, Citadel Press, New York.

Lahav, G., 2004, *Immigration and Politics in the New Europe*, Cambridge University Press, Cambridge.

Meethan, K., 2004, Transnational corporations, globalization, and tourism, in: *A Companion to Tourism*, A. A. Lew, C. M. Hall, and A M. Williams, eds., Blackwell Publishing, Malden, MA, **pp. 110–121**.

Mendelson, M., 2004, The legal production of identities: a narrative analysis of conversations with undocumented women, *Berkeley Womens Law Journal*, **19: 138–216**.

Merino, A., 2004, Politics of identity and identity policies in Europe: the case of Peruvian immigrants in Spain, *Identities:Global Studies in Culture and Power*, **11: 241–264**.

Mountz, A., 2003, Human smuggling, the transnational imaginary, and everyday geographies of the nation-state, *Antipode*, **35(3): 622–645**.

Nagel, C. R., and Staeheli, L. A., 2004, Citizenship, identity and transnational migration: Arab immigrants to the United States, *Space and Polity*, **8(1): 3–23**.

Nevins, J., 2002, *Operation Gatekeeper: The Rise of the 'Illegal Alien' and the Making of the US–Mexico Boundary*, Routledge, New York.

Neysmith, S., and Chen., X., 2002, Understanding how globalization and restructuring affect women's lives: implications for comparative policy analysis, *International Journal of Social Welfare*, **11: 243–253**.

Peterson V. S., and Runyan, S. A., 1999, *Global Gender Issues*, Westview Press, Boulder, Colorado.

Raghuram, P., 2004, Crossing borders: gender and migration, in: *Mapping Women, Making Politics: Feminist Perspectives on Political Geography*, L. A. Staeheli, E. Kofman, and L. J. Peake, eds., Routledge, New York, **pp. 185–198**.

Rodriguez, V., 2001, Tourism as recruiting post for retirement migration, *Tourism Geographies*, **3(1): 52–63**.

Romero, V., 2005, *Alienated: Immigrant Rights, the Constitution and Equality in America*, New York University Press, New York.

Sassen, S., 1998, *Globalization and its Discontents: Essays on the New Mobility of People and Money*, The New Press, New York.

Sassen, S., 2002, *Global Networks, Linked Cities*, Routledge, New York.

Schaeffer, R. K. 2003, *Understanding Globalization: The Social Consequences of Political, Economic, and Environmental Change*, Rowman and Littlefield, New York.

Sole, C., and Parella, S., 2003, The labor market and racial discrimination in Spain, *Journal of Ethnic and Migration Studies*, **29(1): 121–141**.

Tirman, J., 2004, *The Maze of Fear: Security and Migration After 9/11*, The New Press, New York.

Truly, D., 2002, International retirement migration and tourism along Lake Chapala Riviera: developing a matrix of retirement migration behaviour, *Tourism Geographies*, **4(3): 261–281**.

Tsing, A., 2000, The global situation, *Cultural Anthropology*, **15(3): 327–361**.

United Nations, 1948, *Universal Declaration of Human Rights*, United Nations, New York.

United Nations, 2002, *International Migration Report*, Department of Economic and Social Affairs, Population Division, United Nations, New York.

Urry, J., 1990, *The Tourist Gaze*, Sage, London.

Wonders, N., 2004a, Seks en de aandacht van de toerist in Amsterdam, transl: Sex and the tourist gaze in Amsterdam, *Rooilijn*, **7 (September): 325–331**.

Wonders, N., 2004b, Bodies, borders and state performativity in a globalized world, Unpublished paper presented at the Gendered Borders: International Conference on Women and Immigration Law in Europe, Amsterdam, The Netherlands.

Wonders, N. A., and Danner, M., 2002, Globalization, state-corporate crime, and women: the strategic role of women's NGOs in the new world order, in: *Controversies in White Collar Crime,* G. W. Potter, ed., Anderson, **pp. 165–184**.

Wonders, N.A., and Michalowski, R., 2001, Bodies, borders and sex tourism in a globalized world: a tale of two cities—Amsterdam and Havana, *Social Problems,* **48(4): 546–572**.

Wong, P. P., 2004, Environmental impacts of tourism, in: *A Companion to Tourism,* A.A. Lew, C. M. Hall, and A. M. Williams, eds., Blackwell Publishing, Malden, MA, **pp. 450–461**.

World Airport Week, 2002, Airport security costs could skyrocket to $7 billion this year, (24 April 2002); http://static.highbeam.com/w/worldairportweek/april242002.

World Tourism Organization, 2004, Tourism is on the rise again, says world tourism organization; http://www.world-tourism.org.

Chapter 5

BIOMETRICS, BORDERS AND THE IDEAL SUSPECT

Dean Wilson
Monash University

1.   INTRODUCTION

In March 2004, Italian philosopher Giorgio Agamben was scheduled to teach at New York University. Cancelling the course, Agamben cited his reason as his objection to the requirement that all foreign visitors to the United States submit to biometric fingerprinting. For Agamben, the collection and filing of this data bears ominous implications. Indeed, he suggested these biometric databases portend the criminalisation of entire populations. Writing in the French newspaper *Le Monde* (2004), he argued that 'by applying these techniques and these devices invented for the dangerous classes to a citizen, or rather to a human being as such, states, which should constitute the precise space of political life, have made the person the ideal suspect, to the point that it's humanity itself that has become the dangerous class'. While initially limited to those in transit, Agamben sounds a warning that such measures are 'a precursor to what we will be asked to accept later as the normal identity registration of a good citizen in the state's gears and mechanisms'. In this chapter, I chart how biometric surveillance technologies are seeping from the physical borders of the nation-state to become systems of automated surveillance, classifying and coding general populations. They are therefore intertwined with, and constitutive of, new manifestations of state power.

In the wake of 9/11 and the subsequent 'war on terror', there has been an exponential increase in the deployment of biometric technologies—automated systems that use biological or behavioural characteristics to identify individuals. In the context of a 'globalisation of fear' (Davis 2001),

S. Pickering and L. Weber (eds.), Borders, Mobility and Technologies of Control, 87–109.
© 2006 *Springer. Printed in the Netherlands.*

hi-tech solutions to problems of security—such as facial recognition technology, iris and retina scans, and smart identity cards—have proven incredibly persuasive and ascendant (Van der Ploeg 2003; Zuriek and Hindle 2004). The proliferation of biometric technologies has been most evident at the borders between nation-states, where the use of biometric passports matched with surveillance tools such as face and iris recognition technologies are being rapidly deployed at airports and other land and sea border posts. However, while biometric technologies have initially been introduced in relation to specific categories of people—such as travellers, welfare recipients, and asylum seekers—the reach of biometric identification systems is expanding to encompass whole national populations. Citizens are being reconfigured as ideal suspects.

While avoiding technological determinism, it is nevertheless important to see biometric technologies as both symbolic and constitutive of new expressions of state sovereignty. Biometric technology is being deployed in the broader context of a neo-liberal refashioning that has witnessed a 'hollowing out' of the state. During the 1980s, states moved away from the provision of services to promoting and promising safety—a promise intertwined with the rise of 'law and order' politics, particularly in the United States, United Kingdom and Australia (Brake and Hale 1992; Beckett 1997; Downes and Morgan 2002; McCulloch 2004a). The retreat of governments from the provision of services and the rush to privatisation has been accompanied by increasing levels of domestic militarisation. The militarisation of policing (McCulloch 2004b) is one manifestation of the progressive securitisation and militarisation of societies in the affluent global north. Prior to 9/11, Simon (1997) noted the increased tendency to 'govern through crime', whereby states increasingly criminalise, and advance criminal justice solutions for, social problems (Giroux 2002). Post 9/11, there has been an amplification of this trend as social and economic problems are progressively reconfigured and interpreted through the prism of security (McCulloch 2004b).

The 'law and order' agenda that facilitates nation-states 'governing through crime' internally is intertwined with external expressions of sovereignty that configure the control of immigration and mobility between states as a problem of security. Monopolising the legitimate means of movement within and across its boundaries is one of the core characteristics of the modern state (Torpey 2000: 7), and traditionally one of the most absolute expressions of sovereignty has been the right to include and exclude non-citizens. These practices of inclusion and exclusion are not only expressions of the power of the nation-state, they are performances of 'statecraft' by which state sovereignty is simultaneously enacted and constituted (Doty 1996). Such 'performances' of the nation-state have a heightened pull for the 'hollowed out' states of late-modernity, whose sovereign powers have been pierced and curtailed by the forces of deregulation and globalisation. Biometric technology thus provides a fecund reservoir of imagery for new performances of sovereign control that refashion the nation-state as the ultimate arbiter of security. Advanced technological screening and database compilation embody compelling symbolism that projects the continued sovereignty of the nation-state and an invigorated capacity to ensure internal and external security.

In this chapter, I begin by considering the theoretical significance of biometric technologies. While technological discourse fashions biometric technologies as neutral tools of authentication and verification, I suggest that the technology is deeply embedded and constitutive of emerging processes of social classification and discrimination. Following this, I consider the role of the 'fear economy' in the diffusion of biometric technologies. Post 9/11, the marketplace for high-technology security products has increased exponentially, with the governments of nation-states emerging as major consumers. The consumption of biometric technologies, I argue, has little to do with the capacity of the technology. Rather, it is based upon the symbolism of biometrics, which is engaged by nation-states as a signifier of the renewal of sovereign power in the context of a global 'fear economy'. I then consider how biometric technology is being deployed. High technology, in the form of biometrics, has been touted as the antidote to the problem of securing porous borders. While biometric technology has been used for some time in border control, post 9/11 its use has expanded, becoming integrated into the international passport system. Increasingly this involves the collection, filing and coding of biometric identifiers on a hitherto unknown scale in order to trace 'non-citizens'. The proliferation of border controls and the securitisation of migration is also evident in the engagement of biometric technologies to control and monitor asylum seekers within nation-states. The issuing of smart entitlement cards and the coding of 'illegal' migrants with biometric technologies serves to merge discourses of mobility with those of terrorism and transnational organised crime.

Post 9/11, heightened concerns surrounding borders and mobility have been coterminous with an increased securitisation of societies *within* the boundaries of the nation-state (Bigo 2002b; Lyon 2004), and this is evidenced by the spread of biometric identification systems to encompass entire national populations. The desire of nation-states to maintain greater surveillance over internal populations is evident in the expanding number of states either establishing or considering national identity cards embedded with personal identifiers (Stalder and Lyon 2003). The impact of this is that the experience of being included or excluded can be reproduced anywhere and is no longer restricted to the geographical boundary of the nation-state.

As Lyon suggests, 'the border is everywhere' (2004: 2). Moreover, in the present 'state of exception' (Agamben 2005), where nation-states increase-ingly act outside the limits of normative law, the categories of inclusion and exclusion are continually reinvented. Through codes of biometric identification, the spaces of citizenship are reconfigured as spaces of suspicion occupied by the increasingly ubiquitous identity of the ideal suspect.

2.   DIGITAL RULE

To posit a significant symbolic and constitutive role to biometric technologies in reconfigurations of state power may at first glance appear technologically deterministic. After all, what is biometric technology? In general, it involves the collection of digital representations of physiological features unique to an individual, like fingerprints, patterns of the iris and the retina, voice patterns; it may also include typical behavioural patterns such as typing or writing a signature. Digital representations are then normally transformed by means of an algorithm to construct a template. These templates are accumulated in a centralised database that is accessed when, on subsequent occasions, the finger, hand, face, eye or voice is presented to the system. If a matching template is found, the person is acknowledged and counts as known to the system. In some instances, the representation may be stored on a chipcard rather than a template. Users then have to present the chipcards and requested body parts to prove they are the legitimate users of the cards (van der Ploeg 1999: 37).

Biometric technology uses two main methods for identity checks: verification and identification. Verification is essentially confirming people are who they say they are, and is achieved through one-to-one matching. One-to-one matching is used, for example, in the identification of people travelling on false passports, but might also be used to facilitate more rapid immigration procedures for those possessing the designated biometric documents (Clarke 2003). Biometric technologies are also increasingly utilised in identification (that is, determining who the person is, or, in some instances, is not) through one-to-many matching. The clearest example of one-to-many matching is evident in the use of facial recognition technology matched to CCTV cameras. Air passengers may have their faces scanned and checked against a database of 'terrorists' or other 'wanted' people (Lyon 2003: 77).

Such procedures superficially indicate that biometric technology does little more than enact automated functions of verification and authentication. Some commentators have posited that these remote modes of digital classification may herald the end of discriminatory enforcement. Lianos and Douglas suggest that 'it is the first time in history that we have the opportunity to experience forms of control that do not take into account any category of social division' (2000: 266). Automated systems, it might be suggested, reduce questions of discretion and discrimination to the abstracted issue of whether one is granted or denied access. It is this superficial neutrality that problematises the analysis of the constitutive role of biometric technology in developing practices of exclusion. Technological discourse frequently constructs biometrics as a neutral security tool enacting abstracted processes of authentication and verification. As Muller (2004: 286) notes, 'why biometrics is so successful in concealing its exclusionary and discriminatory character is the way in which it tries to hide the question of identity behind the preoccupation with authenticity'.

These technological systems are not neutral as they are actively constituted in relation to social practices and decisions. As Graham and Wood (2003: 229) note of digital surveillance systems, while they may be characterised by flexibility and ambivalence, and contingent upon judgements of social and economic worth built into their design, they are 'likely to be strongly biased by the political, economic and social conditions that shape the principles embedded in their design and implementation'. It would be simplistic to imply inevitable socio-political consequences as somehow inherent in biometric technology. Nevertheless, biometric identification systems are being deployed within a specific global political context, where their meanings are fashioned by the 'extension of the U.S. "law and order" state to the transnational arena' (Jayasuriya 2002). Bauman (2000: 205) has suggested that a political process focused upon crime and control gives rise to a 'logic of exclusion and fortification'. This logic of exclusion is frequently linked to discourses of 'risk management', whereby populations who conform to certain criteria are pre-emptively immobilised. The capacity of surveillance hardware in the form of CCTV to enact this exclusionary logic is already well documented (Coleman and Sim 2000; Norris and Armstrong 1999). However, the development of biometric technologies linked to databases elevates this exclusionary potential to new heights.

Biometric technologies are thus not neutral but both constitutive and symbolic of transformations in the exercise of state power and in the spaces of politics. By their very nature, biometrics form components of technological systems that imply the assembling of digitised databases on an unprecedented scale. The cause of concern is that such databases are being assembled amidst a 'state of exception', whereby nation-states increasingly enact decisions based upon political will rather than the constraints of normative law (Agamben 2005). Biometrics is thus deployed within a social context and organising logic that inevitably heads towards exclusionary rather than inclusionary functioning. The potential for 'actuarial justice', where the objective is risk management rather than rehabilitation, and where predictors of dangerousness are engaged to pre-emptively target 'problem' populations (Feeley and Simon 1994), becomes amplified.

Far from being neutral technological tools of access and authentication, biometric technologies are deeply embedded within new modalities of power. Digital biometric identifiers become vital tokens of contemporary citizenship, and an integral aspect of what Jones (2001) terms 'digital rule'. 'Digital rule' refers to the capacity of control agents to assign access and authorisation. Punishment increasingly takes the form of 'withdrawal of access privileges'. This is a form of remote rule based upon databases and codes. The capability of remotely granting or denying access through biometric technologies linked to databases thus contains the capacity to deepen and widen social discrimination. Biometric technologies are hastening processes of social sorting where populations are digitally catagorised as 'worthy' and 'unworthy', 'included' and 'excluded' (Lyon 2003: 81). Moreover, as the net of suspicion appears to ever-widen, so the category of ideal suspect is more broadly applied and normalised as the routine identity of the nation-state.

3.   BIOMETRICS AND THE FEAR ECONOMY

Prior to 9/11, late-modern societies had witnessed an expansion of the commercial security sector that frequently fuelled public anxieties in relation to crime control while claiming to allay them (Garland 2001: 161). The already expansionist trajectory of the security sector received a massive boost from the climate of heightened anxiety following 9/11. As Davis (2001: 45) predicted, 'the "Fear Economy", as the business press has labelled the complex of military and security firms rushing to exploit the national nervous breakdown, will grow fat amidst the general famine'. And grow fat they have. Estimates suggest the global homeland security market in 2005 to be worth $42 billion (Lynn 2005). The impact of 9/11 on the private industries developing biometric technologies has been nothing short of staggering. Prior to 9/11, biometrics was a fringe element of the security industry widely regarded as being of limited application and subject to significant errors. Subsequently, growth trends have been inexorably skyward. A recent report estimates the size of the biometric market as likely to exceed US$4 billion by 2007, which would represent an 80 percent increase since 2001 (Zuriek and Hindle 2004: 121).

Moreover, particularly in the United States, the size of the government pie being expended on security technologies continues to grow ever larger.

In 2003, the Bush administration earmarked $38 billion in new spending for homeland security, while security budgets in Europe and Australia also continue to rise (Zuriek and Hindle 2004: 121). In 2005, the Australian federal government budget allocated $182 million to biometrics, including $67 million over four years for the implementation of biometric passports and $74.6 million towards facial recognition technology to 'automate border processing using ePassports' (Bajkowski 2005).

In this climate, the biometrics industry has been well organised to claim market share and gain 'brand recognition' for biometrics as a security technology. Security technology companies were aggressively marketing their wares to airport officials within days of the 9/11 attacks (American Civil Liberties Union (ACLU) 2004a: 27). Within a fortnight of 9/11, the International Biometrics Industry Association (IBIA), an advocacy organisation representing major biometric companies in the United States, issued a press release highlighting the role of biometrics in the fight against terrorism. Visionics—a manufacturer of facial recognition technology— suggested in a white paper entitled *Protecting Civilization from the Faces of Terror*, that airport security—in the United States the responsibility of the federal government—'demands substantial financial resources' to develop 'technology that can be implemented to immediately spot terrorists and prevent their actions'. Boarding a plane, the white paper suggested, should no longer be considered 'a right granted to all, but as a privilege accorded to those who can be cleared of as having no terrorist or dangerous affiliations' (cited in Zuriek and Hindle 2004: 122).

The sums of government money being expended on security technologies are significant, and many private companies are therefore aggressively lobbying and cultivating political connections. In the United States, one 2003 study found that 569 companies had registered a homeland security lobbyist (ACLU 2004a: 28). In Australia, direct links between the biometrics industry and government are evident with the establishment of the Biometrics Institute in 2001. Nominally set up to encourage public debate and discussion, the Biometrics Institute is a 'not-for-profit' trade association funded through a federal government grant whose mission is 'to be a forum for biometric users and other interested parties and to facilitate the responsible use of biometrics'. Close links between technology companies and government are evident in the composition of the board, which includes government appointees as well as significant industry representatives (Biometrics Institute 2005).

Biometric technologies have been heavily promoted as infallible despite their actual efficacy remaining highly questionable. At Palm Beach International Airport in the United States, a trial of facial recognition technology failed to recognise participating airport employees 53 percent of the time

(Scheers 2002). Results of independent evaluations of facial recognition technology in other locations suggest similarly dismal results (Clarke 2003). Accuracy rates for facial recognition and fingerprint scanning remain problematic, and a Japanese researcher was able to fool a system by using a gelatin-based fake finger (Lyon 2003: 71; Zuriek and Hindle 2004: 120). Even some within the security industry are uneasy about the rapid pace with which untested and poorly researched biometric technologies are being deployed (McMillan 2002).

Nevertheless, the appeal of biometric technologies may reside in their symbolic resonance rather than in any technical efficacy. As Loader (1999) has noted, the expanding market in security commodities, of which biometrics is a notable example, has a powerful symbolic component. The purchase of security commodities 'is not only a material act ... it is an emotionally-laden performance' (379–80). For the truncated nation-states of late-modernity, biometric technologies are potent signifiers of a reinvigorated sovereign power with the capacity to assert impermeable borders. Iris and fingerprint scanners, passport kiosks and smart cards are integral props in the theatre of statehood.

4.   SOVEREIGNTY, TECHNOLOGY AND THE BORDER

In recent decades, there has been an intensification of border and immigration controls in most western liberal democracies (Jayasuriya 2002). For example, Andreas (2000: 90) charts the intensification of policing the United States–Mexico border, an escalation that has included an infusion of personnel, fencing, technical hardware and surveillance devices. Pickering (2005: 123–38) also outlines similar developments in Australian border policing. The intensification of border controls is also evidenced in the increasing securitisation of airports. The 9/11 attacks, and earlier instances such as the TWA flight crash in 1996, have been instrumental in facilitating heightened security measures in airports, and in embedding airports in public consciousness as filters of risk (Adey 2004). As border posts, airports thus have substantial symbolic capital. As a recent report on Australian airport security noted 'perhaps as important as their contributions to transportation and the wider economy is the symbolic significance attached to airports. They embody the modern world in all its complexity, since few other places bring together our most advanced technological creations and the intricate interconnected systems we have devised to serve both those creations and ourselves' (Wheeler 2005: 5).

As highly symbolic nodes of modernity, airports become crucial platforms for the demonstration of the 'signifying practices' (Garland 1990) through which the power of the state to include and exclude is enacted. The centrality of securitising airports in the post 9/11 environment, then, has powerful signifying functions. Davis (2001: 45) suggests that airports may function as microcosmic spaces of wider security and surveillance trends, noting that 'the security regime of the airport departure lounges will likely provide a template for the regulation of crowds at malls, shopping concourses, sports events and elsewhere'. Biometric identification systems are integral elements of the intensified security regimes evident in airports (Zureik and Hindle 2004: 129). Examples include the SmartGate facial recognition system being trialed at Sydney Airport. The trial, which has been underway since November 2002, replaces face-to-passport matching normally done by a customs official with an automated process (Australian Customs Service 2004). Facial recognition systems are also being installed and tested in United States airports such as Boston's Logan International Airport and Dallas Fort Worth International Airport. Hand geometry technologies are also being used in New York, Miami and Los Angeles. In 2002, at least 30 airports were using some form of biometric technology to process passengers through immigration—and the number continues to increase to the point where it is becoming an established element of the international mobility infrastructure (Menghrajani et al 2002).

For nation-states, the engagement of biometric technology at physical borders bears a signification that neatly encapsulates the paradoxes of state sovereignty under conditions of globalisation. Biometric technology offers the possibility of rapid flows of capital and global elites through borders while simultaneously fortifying the border against unwanted intrusions from 'deviant' outsiders. The technology becomes instrumental in processes of global social classification in which 'low-risk' travellers are granted unimpeded access and mobility while 'high-risk' travellers from the global south, compelled to travel with limited or no documentation, are excluded and blocked. Registered traveller programs highlight this two-tiered system of mobility emerging in the post 9/11 context. Privileged passenger programs facilitate the rapid and unimpeded movement of elite travellers from the global north. Simultaneously those from the global south are increasingly blocked from entry. In a global economy where mobility is equated with participation, the consequences of this discrimination are enormously significant. In the United States, these systems of preferential mobility are encouraged in law. The *Aviation and Transportation Security Act 2002* provides that the Under Secretary of Transportation for Security may establish requirements to implement trusted traveller programs. Registered traveller programs are intended not only to provide selected travellers with expedited processing at border points, but also to 'target security resources to those travellers who might pose greater security risks' (General Accounting Office 2002).

Such systems have however been in place for some time. The United States Immigration and Naturalization Service Passenger Accelerated Service System (INSPASS), a hand geometry system used in seven US and two Canadian airports, has been in operation since 1993 (General Accounting Office 2003). Amsterdam's Schiphol Airport was the world's first airport to employ an automatic border control system using iris recognition technology for travellers. The 'Privium' system, installed in October 2001, is intended to fast track passengers carrying an iris data-embedded smart card through passport control (Woodward et al 2003: 295–6; Lyon 2003: 71). Similar projects have also been undertaken in other locations. At Tokyo's Narita airport, frequent customers of Japan Airlines are enrolled in a comparable system, as have been selected passengers at London's Heathrow airport and at Toronto and Vancouver (Bray 2003: 14). Biometric border control systems thus serve to exacerbate the trend identified by Bauman as 'the extraterritoriality of the new global elite and the forced territoriality of the rest' (2000: 221). Biometric technology is therefore both a powerful signifier and a formative element in the widening chasm between a small global elite possessed of mobility and capital and the many in the global south geographically confined and impoverished.

The signifying and political functions of biometric technology are also evident in its incorporation within the international passport system. Passports are the primary document for identifying, regulating and tracing mobile individuals. The passport is, as Salter suggests, 'a modern heuristic device which serves to link individuals to foreign policy, and according to which government agents classify travellers as safe or dangerous, desirable or undesirable, according to national, social or political narratives' (Salter 2004: 72). The spread of biometric passports has largely been dictated by United States legislation, and offers a tangible expression of that country's hegemonic power in the post 9/11 global order. Section 302 of the *Enhanced Border Security and Visa Entry Reform Act 2001* requires 'a visa waiver country, in order to maintain program participation, to certify by October 26, 2003, that it has a program to issue to its nationals qualifying machine-readable passports that are tamper proof and contain biometric identifiers'. Australia is currently introducing biometric passports, as is the United States and many countries in the European Union. The Australian Foreign Minister thus claimed that biometric passports would 'speed up movements through airport controls, boost aviation security and curtail identity theft. It should also prove invaluable in the fight against terrorism, people smuggling and other transnational crimes' (Downer 2003).

The dominant power of the United States is therefore instrumental in leading and setting the final standards for the global introduction of biometric passports (American Civil Liberties Union 2004c). The International Civil Aviation Organization (ICAO), the organisation governing international civil aviation, has been examining the issue of biometric passports since 1995. However, until recently, national and regional legislation protecting privacy and civil liberties mitigated against their adoption (International Campaign Against Mass Surveillance 2005: 9). In May 2003, the G8 countries (Canada, United Kingdom, France, Japan, Italy, Russia, Germany and the United States) entered into an agreement to implement a biometric passport system. Civil libertarians remain troubled that passports will utilise face recognition, not only among the least reliable of biometrics but also one that can be used at a distance to track individuals without their knowledge. Moreover, the passports are to include Radio Frequency Identification (RFID) tags. These are tiny computer chips that, when receiving a radio signal from an RFID reader, use that power to transmit the data they store. And in United States passports, this information would include name, date of birth, place of birth and a digital photograph and digital face recognition template (American Civil Liberties Union 2004c: 2). This raises enormous privacy and security issues, and significantly intensifies the potential for the surveillance and tracking of individuals.

The concern with biometric passports, then, resides on a number of fronts. As outlined by the International Campaign Against Mass Surveillance (2005: 8), biometric passports represent one avenue of obtaining 'nearly universal registration of everyone on the planet'. The potentially ominous ramifications of this development reside not in the documents themselves but in the possible databases linked to them and the tracking and classification potential they unleash. Evidence in relation to visa regulations and the tracking of 'non-citizens' is already demonstrated in the detention of hundreds of Muslim non-citizens in the wake of 9/11. United States authorities systematically registered and created dossiers on nearly every male over the age of 15 with origins in a list of countries (mostly Muslim) travelling in the United States. Individuals on the list were required to report to the government to be fingerprinted, photographed and questioned. Those who failed to register risked deportation and criminal penalties. This was carried out under the aegis of a program called the National Security Entry-Exit Registration System (NSEERS) (American Civil Liberties Union 2004b: 6).

The registration that occurred under NSEERS has been expanded, via a program called U.S.-VIST, to most visitors to the United States. A similar system in the European Union, the visa information system (VIS) is being developed to capture and store information—including biometric information—from all visa applications to European Union member states (International Campaign Against Mass Surveillance 2005: 5–6). The storage of this data and its linkage across databases will facilitate surveillance and monitoring on an unprecedented scale. The integration of biometric technologies into the international passport and visa system is then both a signification and realisation of new forms of power. The technologising of the border via biometrics betokens a renewed capacity of nation-states to police their boundaries. Technologised means of exerting control over movement form elements of 'processes of statecraft' (Devetak 2001: 197) whereby the sovereignty of the state is enacted through processes of inclusion and expulsion. These state symbolics have significant repercussions on the ground, as expanding databases facilitate new and powerful forms of cataloguing, coding and filing individual identities. Increasingly too, databases are globalised through the incorporation of biometric identifiers in the international passport and visa system, an architecture forged by the United States that opens up the possibility of a global identity system (Policy Laundering Project 2005).

5.   DIGITISING THE OTHER

Bigo (2002b: 2) has suggested that in the post 9/11 environment 'the proliferation of border controls, the repression of foreigners, and so on, has less to do with protection than with a political attempt to reassure certain segments of the electorate longing for evidence of concrete measures taken to ensure safety'. Questions of migration and mobility are thus interpreted increasingly as problems of security (Faist 2002). States of the global north have assessed the spectre of uncontrolled migration as a threat to sovereignty. Within this rhetoric, asylum seekers and refugees are increasingly cast, in Cohen's (2002) renowned formulation, as 'folk devils' in moral panics fuelled by law and order politics. The demonisation and criminalisation of asylum seekers has been accompanied by coercive measures such as indefinite detention and forced deportation. In the nation-states of the global north such coercive measures are elements of more sustained processes of criminalisation whereby the act of seeking asylum is itself constructed as a 'crime of arrival' (Weber 2002, citing Webber 1996).

Consequently, it is perhaps unremarkable that biometric identification systems have initially been deployed on asylum seeker populations, where they serve as technological signifiers of the securitisation of migration. Biometric identification systems involving fingerprinting those seeking asylum have become increasingly common and are in use in the United Kingdom, Netherlands and Australia (Woodward et al, 2003; van der Ploeg

2003: 87; Department of Immigration and Multicultural Affairs 2003). The United Kingdom's Home Office has adopted a biometric solution in the identification of asylum seekers. Asylum seekers are issued an application registration card (ARC) that carries a template of the bearer's fingerprints, as well as their photograph, name, date of birth, and nationality (Home Office, 2002). The card is designed to facilitate rapid identification of asylum seekers following initial processing at ports of entry or at the asylum seekers unit in Croydon. The objective of the card is to facilitate identification of asylum seekers by authorities. In so doing, the card firmly inscribes and secures a 'non-citizen' identity on individual asylum seekers. The system is designed not so much to facilitate access to services as to deny them, one stated purpose of the system being to counter fraud through the claiming of services under multiple identities (Woodward et al. 2003: 290.)

Biometrics technologies are accordingly mobilised within a larger 'tough on crime' style rhetoric that posits asylum seekers as fraudulent and criminal, justifying their exclusion from services. Biometric systems are discursively constructed as a technological buttress preserving community values against perceived external and 'alien' threats. United Kingdom Home Secretary David Blunkett (Home Office 2003) suggested that 'biometrics can play a big part in tackling illegal immigration and abuse of our asylum system and by embracing it we can reduce further the pull factor to the UK'. Blunkett was announcing a six-month pilot scheme, extending the biometric application of the ARC, whereby all visitors from Sri Lanka were required to provide a record of their fingerprint. The Sri Lankan pilot project was heralded as a resounding success, and biometric visa requirements have been stretched out to five African nations—Djibouti, Eritirea, Ethiopia, Tanzania and Uganda (Home Office 2004; Lettice 2004).

If anything, the introduction of biometric identification for asylum seekers in Australia is positioned within an even more vociferous climate of exclusionary law and order politics. In 2001, law and order issues were foregrounded during the Australian federal election coalescing around the question of immigration. On 26 August, a Norwegian vessel, the *Tampa*, arrived off the Australian coast carrying 400 primarily Afghani and Iraqi asylum seekers who had been rescued from a leaky vessel en route from Indonesia. The incident provided Prime Minister John Howard with an issue that seamlessly tapped deep-seated anxieties within the Australian elec- torate about invasion, outsiders and the defence of national sovereignty (McCulloch 2004a; Marr and Wilkinson 2003). The attack of 9/11, only two weeks after the arrival of the *Tampa* on Australian shores, facilitated the elevation of national security to the central election issue and conflated the identities of asylum seekers with potential terrorist threats (McCulloch 2004a).

The capacity of the Australian state to secure borders is thus replete with political symbolism. In media accounts, asylum seekers have been represented as deviant and diseased, threatening to infect the nation and undermine national sovereignty (Pickering 2001). Public narratives in Australia, as in other jurisdictions (Weber and Bowling 2004) have also configured asylum identities as 'illegal' 'fraudulent' and 'bogus'. Moreover, the security continuum identified by Huysmans (2000) in the European Union, linking border control, terrorism, international crime and migration, has also emerged strongly in the Australian context (Pickering 2005). The capacity of the Australian state to inscribe legitimate and illegitimate identities on those seeking asylum is therefore deeply implicated within a wider discourse of national security and sovereignty.

It is within this context that the Australian Parliament passed the *Migration Legislation Amendment (Identification and Authentication) Act 2004*. The legislation amended the *Migration Act 1958*, expanding the grounds for collecting biometric identifiers such as photographs, signatures and fingerprints. The stated purpose of this new legislation is to enhance the Department of Immigration, Multicultural and Indigenous Affairs' (DIMIA) capacity to 'establish and authenticate the identity of non-citizens at various stages of immigration processing, and on entry to and departure from Australia' (DIMIA 2004). The initiative is being generously funded by the Commonwealth Government, who have allocated $42.87 million to implement 'biometric technology for border security and identity management' (Bajkowski 2005). Facial recognition, iris scanning and fingerprinting are to form part of an overall strategy of identity management intended to 'strengthen identification processes' (DIMIA 2004). Asylum seekers are directly criminalised in the discursive construction of the initiative, through explicit reference to criminal activity. Departmental publicity for the measure notes that assembling a biometric database of asylum seeker details will 'improve Australia's border security. It will help to fight against the use of sophisticated techniques exploited by terrorists and criminals, to change identities and cross international borders' (DIMIA 2004).

Similar schemes also have been initiated in the European Union, United States and Canada. The countries of the European Union have established EURODAC, an automated fingerprint identification system. In the *Convention of Dublin 15 June 1990*, the member states of the European Union agreed that the first country where applicants arrived was to be responsible for their applications. This was to preclude one country passing asylum seekers on to another, as well as asylum seekers submitting multiple applications in different member states (van der Ploeg 1999a: 298). In 1991 European Union ministers responsible for immigration moved to establish a Community-wide system for the comparison of fingerprints of asylum applicants, while the agreement to build a central fingerprint database of asylum seekers was established in 1997 by the European Council. EURODAC was tested in 2002, and from 15 January 2003, asylum seekers' fingerprints have been taken whenever they seek asylum, whether inside or outside the European Union's borders. Fingerprints are then digitally transferred from member states to a central EURODAC unit for comparison against the existing database. Fingerprints of asylum seekers can be stored for up to ten years, or immediately erased if an applicant is granted nationality in a member state. In addition to asylum seekers, EURODAC is also a biometric database of 'persons who have crossed an external frontier of the Community in an irregular manner' (Europa 2003). These 'foreign nationals' have their biometric data retained for two years or immediately erased if they receive a residence permit or leave the territory of the European Union (Europa 2003).

EURODAC was justified by the European Union Council in terms of the need to accelerate decisions on asylum bids. Another powerful rationale behind the establishment EURODAC was a perceived need to stem 'asylum shopping' across member states and separate those categorised as 'legitimate' asylum seekers from other categories of migrant (Lodge 2004: 261). Across nation-states of the global north, then, biometric technology is being extensively deployed to demarcate and signify identities of 'non-citizens'. This process is intertwined with the wider securitisation of migration as a political issue and the attendant discursive criminalisation of migrant identities. International relations scholars have noted the significance of policing borders not only to preserve the integrity of the nation-state but as a marker and arbiter of state sovereignty overall. As Krasner (1999: 13) suggests, 'if a state cannot regulate what passes across its boundaries, it will not be able to control what happens within them'. Increasingly, the identity of the asylum seeker has been configured as a site on which state sovereignty is enacted. The capacity to establish legitimacy, confirm identity and expel those deemed 'illegitimate' has thus been a pivotal 'performance of sovereignty' (Devetak 1995; Pickering 2005).

The particular focus upon asylum seekers in biometric deployment is intertwined with the securitisation of migration and the criminalisation of persons seeking to move from the global south to the global north. The issuing of smart 'entitlement' cards and the targeting of 'illegal' migrants with biometric technologies serves to blend discourses of terrorism, organised crime and migration as a single coherent threat to national sovereignty. The need for biometric data incorporated into travel documents is most often cited as 'national security'—meaning security from 'illegal' migrants and terrorists (Thomas 2005: 16). However, in practice, such documents inscribe on those seeking asylum the identity of 'non-citizen'.

Fixing these 'non-citizen' identities through biometric documentation and 'entitlement' cards serves to heighten exclusion and reinforces the notion of migration as a problem of security. Subjecting asylum seekers to automated regimes of biometric classification also removes them from the potential discretion that can attend interaction with human agents. As such, nuanced judgements of justice, fairness and legitimacy may be replaced with automated processes (Norris, Moran and Armstrong 1998: 270; Lyon 2004: 2).

6.   MOBILE BORDERS AND THREATS FROM WITHIN

In their influential theorisation, Feeley and Simon (1994: 181–5) noted two characteristics of actuarial justice that resonate profoundly with the expansion of biometric identification systems. The first is the movement of exceptional powers—usually reserved for border areas such as airports and border posts—to interior national spaces. Another is the use of profiling in the interests and risk management and pre-emptive justice. Both these trends are encapsulated in the increasing number of nation-states implementing national identity card schemes in the wake of 9/11. As Lyon (2004: 1) notes, the importance of national identity card systems resides not in the issuing of the cards themselves but in the compilation of databases. He suggests these databases have the potential to become 'systems of social sorting, permitting extensive discrimination between different populations through modes of classification that may include ethnicity and religion'.

Schemes intended to discern citizens from non-citizens at the borders of nation-states through biometric passports and visas, and internally through asylum seeker and non-resident biometric registration and 'entitlement' cards are, through identity cards, extended to whole national populations. Establishing the identity of its citizens has of course been one of the key concerns of the modern nation-state (Higgs 2001; Torpey 2000). As Torpey (2000: 7) notes, states have sought this power for a large variety of reasons. These include enforcing military service, extracting taxation and labour, excluding, containing and monitoring 'undesirable elements', and monitoring the spatial and social composition of populations within the boundaries of the nation-state. Moreover, states have importantly sought this power in order to define who may move within and across their borders.

The logic of state power underpinning drives to secure and sort identities is frequently cloaked beneath arguments for administrative utility. The idea of using a single numerical identifier linked to numerous government databases appeals to bureaucratic efficiency and has been argued for both on the grounds of administrative ease and fraud reduction (Home Office 2004). National identity cards have been used in European nations for some time (Privacy International 1996). In 1987, Germany introduced a machine-readable identity card for citizens amidst considerable public resistance (Stalder and Lyon 2003: 80). 'Smart' identity cards differ from other paper-based precursors, however, in being electronically linked to centralised databases. The most significant developments in 'smart' identity cards are in Asia, where China, Hong Kong. Thailand, Malaysia and Singapore either have systems or are soon to institute them. All schemes are therefore instituted in nations that have authoritarian tendencies (Lyon 2004: 6). The potential of such schemes in terms of authoritarian control is concerning, but crises in more democratic nations have also sparked suggestions for national identification schemes over the past few decades. Arguments for an identity card surfaced in the United Kingdom following the IRA attacks of the mid 1990s and in Spain in response to ETA attacks (Lyon 2003: 73).

A major rationale being advanced for national identity schemes is their potential as a counter-terrorism measure. However, the efficacy of identity schemes in countering terrorism is highly questionable. A study conducted by Privacy International (2004) concluded that there was no evidence to support the assumed connection between identity cards and successful counter-terrorist measures. Of 25 nations that have experienced terrorist activity since 1986, 80 percent have national identity cards, one third incorporating biometrics. The report was unable to uncover a single instance where an identity card system was a significant deterrent to terrorist activity (Privacy International 2004). Moreover, the centralising tendency of databases could render concentrated biometric record systems themselves a target of terrorist attack. Mass biometric identification systems thus may increase vulnerability rather than reduce it (O'Neil 2005).

These pragmatic considerations nevertheless appear to be overridden by the assertion that identity cards will be a powerful tool in the 'war on terror', and moreover will be effective in combating transborder crime and 'illegal' migration. Often, also, the assertion is made that a significant number of nations already have national identity card systems. However, these are not always linked to centralised databases, and may have limitations on the transference on data between government agencies (Button 2005). The degree to which the palatability of identity cards has transformed in the post 9/11 climate is evidenced in the Australian case. A proposal for a national identity card in the form of the 'Australia Card' was raised in 1986 as a means of reducing tax evasion and fraudulent practices relating to social security claims. Although initially receiving some public support, opposition to the scheme due to its potential threat to civil liberties and concentration of state power solidified in a concerted campaign against the proposal. The

Australia Card Bill was introduced into parliament in October 1986. Later withdrawn due to a technical flaw, the Bill was never reintroduced, probably due to weight of public opinion opposed to the concept (Davies 1992: 30–43).

Despite the assumed political unpalatability of national identity cards in Australia, the issue is now firmly back on the public agenda. Senior Australian Federal Police officers have placed pressure on the federal government to institute an identity card scheme, arguing that it would be a valuable tool in preventing terrorism and identity theft (Riley 2004: 4). The Australian and British cases therefore offer examples of how arguments that identity cards will reduce terrorism, prevent fraud and assist in immigration control have been mobilised to make a previously politically unacceptable measure acceptable (Lyon 2004: 4). It is evident that there is a global trend towards 'smart' national identity cards with biometric identifiers. Arguments that identity cards prevent identity theft, terrorism and fraud elide the more significant role such modes of identification may play in processes of 'social sorting'. In a post 9/11 context, where the rule of law is progressively suspended in favour of sovereign power exercised through political force (Agamben 2005), previously unpalatable levels of surveillance are increasingly normalised.

National biometric identity cards are the most overt manifestation of an intensifying digital discrimination. The post 9/11 surveillance landscape is one where rising flows of abstracted personal data privilege some and discriminate against others; this is also increasingly carried out in advance of any offence. Identity cards are emblematic of the sharpening of sovereign power whereby control is increasingly exercised through universal surveillance stretched across the entire population (Lyon 2003: 81). United States' drives for a uniform global biometric passport are also tantamount to the creation of a 'global identity document' (Policy Laundering Project 2005). While the explicit motivation driving the concept of national identity cards may differ between jurisdictions, nevertheless, in all instances there resides the rationale of distinguishing between legitimate and illegitimate groups— between insiders and outsiders.

Digitised databases linked to individual identifiers thrust into view troubling vistas when their potential within the present 'state of exception' are contemplated. Post 9/11 racial profiling, once considered abhorrent within liberal democratic states, has increasingly been institutionalised as a domestic security measure (American Civil Liberties Union 2004b; Thobani 2003: 597). After 9/11, the paradox outlined by Agamben (1998: 15)— whereby the sovereign stands 'at the same time outside and inside the juridical order' but commanding 'the power to suspend the law'—has been explicitly demonstrated in relation to racial profiling. As Thobani (2003:

598) suggests, 'to make racial profiling an acceptable political technique of governance is to inscribe suspicion and illegality onto the bodies of people of color, making it possible, in this case, to round them up on the basis of nothing more substantial than their "looking" like Muslims'. The amplified and automated capacity to categorise and discriminate that attends biometric databases can only but deepen existing social divisions—already exacerbated through the racial profiling following the 'war on terror'. Indeed, national identity cards and the possibility of a global biometric identity document may presage nothing less than the total securitisation of the societies of the global north.

7.   SECURITY AND THE IDEAL SUSPECT

The heightened security fears following 9/11 have led to an unquestioning acceptance of high-tech solutions, of which biometric technology—which claims to authenticate and verify personal identity on the basis of physical characteristics—is the most notable. Initially deployed at the physical boundaries of the nation-state, biometric identification systems are progressively expanding across general populations. This expansion stretches the securitisation of the border into the internal spaces of the nation-state, intensifying processes of inclusion and exclusion. Within a generalised climate of fear post 9/11, an anxious public, eager for reassurance, has been willing to accept the efficacy of innovations such as iris scanning and facial recognition technology. Such acceptance has, of course, been aggressively promoted by biometric industry lobbyists and government experts who have been championing high-technology as the silver bullet in the 'war on terror'. But the claims of these advocates are successful also because they tap into the powerful faith in technology inherent in late-modern societies of the global north (Lyon 2003: 85).

The repercussions of this blind faith in technology are yet to be fully understood. But we may return to Agamben's (2004) warning that humanity itself becomes the dangerous class; in the globalised world of biometric surveillance every 'citizen' is reinscribed as an ideal suspect. As the notion of security infiltrates and seeps through the domains of public policy, the attraction of biometric technology escalates. The power to monitor, categorise and file biometric identifiers of citizens and strangers alike becomes a pivotal performance of statehood. Biometric technology is frequently justified by appeals to technical bureaucratic efficiency and to an increasingly pervasive discourse of security. But the consequences of this 'bio-political tattooing' may be great. Agamben (2004) suggests that the consequence is potentially the diminishment of the sphere of public participation, a situation in which 'the space we once upon a time called politics is ever more scaled down and tiny'. Humanity is then reduced to bare life —a biometric identifier—the ideal suspect subject to the shifting codes and categories of a sovereign rule outside normative law.

REFERENCES

Adey, P., 2004, Secured and sorted mobilities: examples from the airport, *Surveillance and Society*, **1(4): 500–519**.

Agamben, G., 2005, *State of Exception*, University of Chicago Press, Chicago.

Agamben, G., 2004, No to bio-political tattooing, *Le Monde* (10 January 2004); http://www.ratical.org/ratville/CAH/totalControl.html.

Agamben, G., 1998, *Homo Sacer: Sovereign Power and Bare Life*, Stanford University Press, Stanford, CA.

American Civil Liberties Union, 2004a, *The Surveillance-Industrial Complex: How the American Government is Conscripting Businesses and Individuals in the Construction of a Surveillance Society*, New York; http://www.aclu.org.

American Civil Liberties Union, 2004b, *Sanctioned Bias: Racial Profiling since 9/11*, New York; http://www.aclu.org.

American Civil Liberties Union, 2004c, *Naked Data: How the U.S. Ignored International Concerns and Pushed for Radio Chips in Passports Without Security*, New York; http://www.aclu.org.

Andreas, P., 2000, *Border Games: Policing the U.S.-Mexico Divide*, Cornell University Press, Ithaca.

Australian Customs Service, 2004, *Overview of SmartGate Trial*, Canberra.

Bajkowski, J., 2005, Budget 2005—winners and losers, *Computerworld* (11 May 2005); http://www.computerworld.com.au/index.php?id=918866272&eid=-255.

Bauman, Z., 2000, Social issues of law and order, *British Journal of Criminology*, **40(2): 205–221**.

Beckett, K., 1997, *Making Crime Pay: Law and Order in Contemporary American Politics*, Oxford University Press, Oxford.

Bigo, D., 2002a, Security and immigration: toward a critique of the governmentality of unease, *Alternatives*, **27: 63–92**.

Bigo, D., 2002b, To reassure and protect after September 11th, *Social Science Research Council Essays*; http://www.ssrc.org/sept11/essays/bigo.htm.

Biometrics Institute, 2005; http://www.biometricsinstitute.org.

Brake, M. and Hale, C., 1992, *Public Order and Private Lives: The Politics of Law and Order*, Routledge, London.

Bray, R., 2003, Eye to eye with airport security, *Financial Times* (1 April 2003) p. 14.

Button, J., 2005, On the cards, *The Age* (23 July 2005) p. 3.

Cohen, S., 2002, *Folk devils and moral panics: the creation of the mods and the rockers*, 3rd ed, Routledge, London.

Coleman, R. and Sim, J., 2000, You'll never walk alone: CCTV surveillance, order and neo-liberal rule in Liverpool city centre, *British Journal of Sociology*, **51(4): 623–639**.

Clarke, R., 2003, SmartGate: a face recognition trial at Sydney Airport, http://www.anu.edu.au/people/Roger.Clarke/DV/SmartGate.html.

Davies, S., 1992, *Big Brother: Australia's growing web of surveillance*, Simon & Schuster, Sydney.

Davis, M., 2001, The flames of New York, *New Left Review*, **12: 34–50**.

Department of Immigration and Multicultural and Indigenous Affairs, 2004, *Biometric Initiatives*, Fact Sheet 84 (30 September 2004); http://www.immi.gov.au/facts/84bio metric.htm.

Devetak, R., 1995, Incomplete states: theories and practices of statecraft, in: *Boundaries in Question*, J. Macmillan and A. Linklater, eds., Pinter Publishers, London, **pp. 19–39**.

Devetak, R., 2001, Postmodernism, in: *Theories of International Relations*, S. Burchill, R. Devetak, A. Linklater, M. Paterson, C. Reus-Smit and J. Tait, eds., Palgrave, New York, **pp. 181–208**.

Downer, A., 2003, Australia Leads the Way on Passport Biometrics, Media Release, FA 60 (4 June 2003); http://www.foreignminister.gov.au/releases/2003/fa060_03.html.

Downes, D. and Morgan, R., 2002, The skeletons in the cupboard: the politics of law and order in the new millennium, in: *The Oxford Handbook of Criminology*, M. Maguire, R. Morgan & R. Reiner, eds., 3rd ed, Oxford University Press, Oxford, **pp. 286–321**.

Doty, R., 1996, Sovereignty and the nation: constructing the boundaries of national identity, in: *State Sovereignty as Social Construct*, T. Biersteker and C. Weber, eds., Cambridge University Press, Cambridge, **pp. 121–147**.

Europa, 2003, 'Eurodac' system; http://europa.eu.int/scadplus/printversion/en/lvb/l33081.htm

Faist, T., 2002, Extension du domaine de la lutte: international migration and security before and after September 11, 2001, *International Migration Review*, **36(1): 7–14**.

Feeley, M. and Simon, J., 1994, Actuarial justice: the emerging new criminal law in: *The Futures of Criminology*, D. Nelken, ed., Sage, London, **pp. 173–201**.

Garland, D., 1990, *Punishment in Modern Society*, University of Chicago Press, Chicago.

Garland, D., 2001, *The Culture of Control: Crime and Social Order in Contemporary Society*, Oxford University Press, Oxford.

General Accounting Office [US], 2002, *Aviation Security: Registered Traveler Program Policy and Implementation Issues: Report to the Honorable Kay Bailey Hutchison, U.S. Senate*, GAO-03-253, Washington, DC.

General Accounting Office [US], 2003, *Border Security: Challenges in Implementing Border Technology: Statement of Nancy Kingsbury, Managing Director Applied Research and Methods*, GAO-03-546T, Washington, DC.

Giroux, H., 2002, Global capitalism and the return of the garrison state: rethinking hope in the age of insecurity, *Arena Journal*, **19: 141–160**.

Graham, S. and Wood, D., 2003, Digitizing surveillance: categorization, space, inequality, *Critical Social Policy*, **23(2): 227–248**.

Higgs, E., 2001, The rise of the information state: the development of central state surveillance of the citizen in England, 1500–2000, *Journal of Historical Sociology*, **14(2): 175–97**.

Home Office [UK], 2002, *Secure Borders, Safe Haven: Integration and Diversity in Modern Britain*, London.

Home Office [UK], 2003, Biometric technology to tackle immigration abuse, Press Release, 228/2003 (27 August 2003).

Home Office [UK], 2004, Increased use of biometrics to tackle asylum abuse, Press Release, 024/2004 (21 January 2004).

Huysmans, J., 2000, The European Union and the securitization of migration, *Journal of Common Market Studies*, **38(5): 751–77**.

International Campaign Against Mass Surveillance, 2005, *The Emergence of a Global Infrastructure for Mass Registration and Surveillance*.

Jayasuriya, K., 2002, 9/11 and the new 'anti-politics' of 'Security', *Social Science Research Council Essays*; http://www.ssrc.org/sept11/essays/jayasuriya.htm.

Jones, R., 2001, Digital rule: punishment, control and technology, *Punishment and Society*, **2(1): 5–22**.

Krasner, S., 1999, *Sovereignty: Organized Hypocrisy*, Princeton University Press, Princeton, NJ.

Lettice, J., 2004, UK plays asylum card to expand visa biometric scheme (21 January 2004); http://www.theregister.co.uk/2004/01/21/uk_plays_asylum_card/.

Lianos, M. and Douglas, M., 2000, Dangerization and the end of deviance: the institutional environment, *British Journal of Criminology*, **40(2): 261–278**.

Loader, I., 1999, Consumer culture and the commodification of policing and security, *Sociology*, **33(2): 373–392**.

Lodge, J., 2004, EU homeland security: citizens or suspects?, *Journal of European Integration*, **26(3): 253–279**.

Lynn, M., 2005, Security industry offers safe bet, *Investment Week* (22 August 2005).

Lyon, D., 2003, *Surveillance after September 11*, Polity Press, London.

Lyon, D., 2004, Identity cards: social sorting by database, *Internet Issue Brief No. 3*, Oxford Internet Institute, University of Oxford.

McCahill. M., 2002, *The Surveillance Web: The Rise of Visual Surveillance in an English City*, Willan, Cullompton.

McCulloch, J., 2004a, National (in) security politics in Australia: fear and the federal election, *Alternative Law Journal*, **29(2): 87–91**.

McCulloch, J., 2004b, Blue armies, khaki police and the cavalry on the new American frontier, *Critical Criminology*, **12: 309–326**.

McMillan, R., 2002, The myth of airport biometrics, *Wired News* (9 August 2002); http://www.wired.com/news/conflict/0,2100,54418,00.html.

Marr, D., and Wilkinson, M., 2003, *Dark Victory*, Federation Press, Sydney.

Menghrajani, V., Orantia, J., Pittlik, A. and Wolfsohn, A., 2002, Facing the Future: A Study on Biometrics, Unpublished paper, UTS Community Law and Legal Research Centre, Sudney.

Muller, B., 2004, (Dis)qualified bodies: securitization, citizenship and 'identity management', *Citizenship Studies*, **8(3): 279–294**.

Norris, C., Moran, J. and Armstrong, G., 1998, Algorithmic surveillance: the future of automated visual surveillance, in: *Surveillance, Closed Circuit Television and Social Control*, C. Norris, J. Moran and G. Armstrong, eds., Ashgate, Aldershot, **pp. 255–287**.

Norris, C. and Armstrong, G., 1999, *The Maximum Surveillance Society: The Rise of CCTV*, Berg, Oxford.

O'Neil, P., 2005, Complexity and counterterrorism: thinking about biometrics, *Studies in Conflict & Terrorism*, **28: 547–566**.

Pickering, S., 2001, Common sense and original deviancy: news discourses and asylum seekers in Australia, *Journal of Refugee Studies*, **14(1): 169–186**.

Pickering, S., 2005, *Refugees and State Crime*, Federation Press, Sydney.

Policy Laundering Project, 2005, Introduction: the problem of policy laundering; http://www.policylaundering.org/PolicyLaunderingIntro.html.

Privacy International, 1996, Identity cards: frequently asked questions; http//www.privacyinternational.org.

Privacy International, 2004, *Mistaken Identity: Exploring the Relationship Between National Identity Cards and the Prevention of Terrorism*, Interim Report, April, London; http://www.privacyinternational.org.

Riley, J., 2004, National ID cards urged in terror war, *Australian* (15 October 2004) p. 4.

Salter, M., 2004, Passports, mobility, and security: how smart can the border be?, *International Studies Perspectives*, **5: 71–91**.

Scheeres, J., 2002, Airport face scanner failed, *Wired News* (16 May 2002); http://www.wired.com/news/privacy/0,1848,52563,00.html.

Simon, J., 1997, Governing through crime, in: *The Crime Conundrum: Essays on Criminal Justice*, L. Friedman and G. Fisher, eds, Westview Press, Boulder, CO.

Stalder, F. and Lyon, D., 2003, Electronic identity cards and social classification, in: *Surveillance as Social Sorting: Privacy, Risk, and Digital Discrimination*, D. Lyon, ed., Routledge, London.

Thomas, R., 2005, Biometrics, international migrants and human rights, *Global Migration Perspectives, No. 17*, Global Commission on International Migration (GCIM), Geneva: http://www.gcim.org/gmp.

Thobani, S., 2003, Exception as rule: profile of exclusion, *Signs: Journal of Women Culture and Society*, **29(2): 597–600**.

Torpey, J., 2000, *The Invention of the Passport: Surveillance, Citizenship and the* State, Cambridge University Press, Cambridge.

van der Ploeg, I., 1999a, The illegal body: 'Eurodac' and the politics of biometric identification, *Ethics and Information Technology*, **1: 295–302**.

van der Ploeg, I., 1999b, Written on the body: biometrics and identity, *Computers and Society*, **29(1): 37–44**.

van der Ploeg, I., 2003, Biometrics and privacy: a note on politics of theorizing technology, *Information, Communication and Society*, **6(1): 85–104**.

Webber, F., 1996, *Crimes of Arrival: Immigrants and Asylum-Seekers in the New Europe*, Statewatch, London.

Weber, L., 2002, The detention of asylum seekers: 20 reasons why criminologists should care, *Current Issues in Criminal Justice*, **14(1): 9–30**.

Weber, L. and Bowling, B., 2004, 'Policing migration: a framework for investigating the regulation of global mobility, *Policing and Society*, **14(3): 195–212**.

Wheeler, J., 2005, *An Independent Review of Airport Security and Policing for the Government of Australia*, Commonwealth of Australia, Canberra.

Woodward, J., Orlans, N. and Higgins, P., 2003, *Biometrics: Identity Assurance in the Information Age*, McGraw Hill, Berkeley, CA.

Zuriek, E. and Hindle, K., 2004, Governance, security and technology: the case of biometrics, *Studies in Political Economy*, **73: 113–137**.

Chapter 6

BORDERS, BELONGING AND HOMELAND (IN)SECURITY

Mona J. E. Danner
Old Dominion University

Following September 2001, the United States engaged a war on terror that involved significantly tightening immigration procedures and border controls, and loosening legal standards related to surveillance and detention. Politicians and state agents vilified those who questioned the morality or legality of state actions in the war on terror. They argued that unprecedented threats to national security justified severe responses. Globalisation was implicated in the attacks and analysts wondered how global markets would be affected in the aftermath. The United States Government has long embraced neo-liberal economic policies that advocate increasing the role of the market under globalisation and shrinking the state. Yet, the manner in which the United States is fighting terrorism represents a dramatic expansion of the state. The new focus on 'homeland security' camouflages the extensive growth in the last four decades of the state control orientation and apparatus found in the criminal justice system and the military. The 9/11 attacks, and manipulation of attendant fear of the 'other', serve as an opportunity for the state to respond with a control-oriented security strategy with the goal of controlling potentially problematic populations increasingly marginalised in the global economy.

1.   GLOBALISATION AND 9/11

'Globalisation' refers to the intensification of the historical process of 'increasing interaction across national boundaries that affects many aspects of life: economic, social, cultural and political' (United Nations Economic and Social Commission for Asia and the Pacific 1999). Technological

111

S. Pickering and L. Weber (eds.), Borders, Mobility and Technologies of Control, 111–122.
© 2006 *Springer. Printed in the Netherlands.*

advancements in communications (especially the internet), mechanisation and transportation increase the automation, speed, ease, geographic reach, and breadth of exchange. They make possible expanded production, distribution, and consumption of all known commodities including goods, services, capital, information, and labour, thereby 'enabling individuals, corporations and countries to reach around the world farther, faster, deeper and cheaper than ever' (Friedman 1999: 40). Globalisation also represents a political process as state managers and elites make choices about how new technologies are used, the extent to which state policies and practices are made subject to international institutions and organisations, and borders are protected (Kerr and Sweetman 2003).

Fundamentally, economic globalisation is about the ascendancy of the neo-liberal economic agenda emphasising markets over governments and requiring liberalised trade and foreign investment policies, decreasing state involvement in regulating national economies and providing social services, and increasing privatisation of government activities and flexibility in labour markets. The loss of spatial and temporal limits brought on by globalisation results in a more connected and interdependent world as borderless trade and investment increase both the ability and the competitive need to do business internationally (Wichterich 2000). Taken together, neo-liberal economic policies make it possible to do so as they decrease barriers to the movement of global capital.

However, neither globalisation's benefits nor costs have been evenly distributed. The deindustrialisation and wage stagnation begun in the 1970s in the United States and other industrialised countries continued into the 1990s with increased corporate downsizing and job outsourcing. The capitalist logic of searching for ever cheaper labour and fewer regulations exacerbated the widening gap between the rich and poor in wealthy countries without closing it in the developing world. As a result, major anti-globalisation protests and global justice campaigns emerged in the United States in 1999 in Seattle, followed several times each year during national political party conventions, and in conjunction with the meetings of the World Economic Forum, the World Bank and International Monetary Fund, World Trade Organization, G20, G8 and European Union.

The attacks that occurred in the United States on 11 September 2001 represent another act of resistance to globalisation. They signalled rejection of United States economic, military, and political hegemony. They were an 'in your face' aggressive pushing back against western cultural 'pollution,' from the perspective of religious fundamentalists. Yet the event itself is less enduring than the response to it.

Technological advancements in the distribution of video images made the second plane crash into, and the ensuing collapse of, the World Trade Center towers immediately visible again and again around the world. Neither the Pentagon nor the Pennsylvania field where the fourth plane crashed elicit the same emotional reactions as does the World Trade Center. The images were so striking and repeated so often that the site itself has become a much-visited shrine. It is also a testament to the contradictory nature of globalised capitalism, as an event which so challenged its necessary conditions can be so easily commodified and marketed. Everything 9/11 sells everywhere, from newspapers to t-shirts, music, art, and politicians as well as public policies, patriotism and fear (Heller 2005). These responses united people and magnified feelings of belonging to the nation.

2. BORDERS AND BELONGING

Although *what* happened on 11 September remained incomprehensible for days, *who* had done it became quickly known: 'Muslim extremists' and 'Islamic fundamentalists.' The popular rhetoric was that 'they' gained entrance to the United States because generous immigration policies made student visas easy to get, the trusting United States nature made border controls lax, and outdated legal restrictions made capturing terrorists difficult. The dark side of globalisation came home to the United States, contained in darker-skinned bodies spewing hatred of America founded in an evil religion. 'They' came and moved freely around a country where they didn't belong.

The question of belonging looms large in the response to 9/11. On 12 September, Noam Chomsky (2001) wrote about the choice faced by the United States Government: to try to understand the conditions creating the terrorists and attempt to ameliorate those conditions, or simply to demonise and try to crush the individuals and ideas involved. The United States chose the latter, hardening the borders—physically as well as psychically—to further separate 'them' from 'us' in order to secure the state. While being careful in its language not to indict all Muslims and Arabs, in its actions, the United States practiced a policy of racial profiling and detained thousands, ultimately deporting many of them for not belonging.

But who belongs in a globalised economy? Capitalists, patriots and compliant workers are always welcome. Problematic populations—criminals, protesters and immigrants—are not particularly welcome, but can be useful if for no other reason than to define boundaries. Even though belonging, by definition, implies being part of or connected to, in a capitalist economy, belonging applies less to people than to products, except when the products *are* people, treated as commodities to be marketed. By marketing 'them' as demonic and dangerous, the state diverts attention away from deteriorating social conditions that surface with the advancement of the neo-liberal economy. In the face of supposedly weak physical borders, national psychic borders are strengthened, as citizens define themselves as separate from, and superior to, immigrants.

Even as a globalised world expands international awareness, groups feeling themselves threatened promote nationalism. Immigration represents the most easily identifiable face of globalisation for many in the United States. Anti-immigrant views have always existed and been fuelled by xenophobia and racism, especially in times of crisis. It is within this context that borders are hardened and border crossers are suspect, threatened, and demonised.

Until 9/11, the United States rhetoric was that its borders were open to people from other nations to escape political repression, to study, work or be reunited with their families, albeit in controlled and politically acceptable numbers, carefully selected to aid the nation and not to cost it (or at least not to cost the politicians supporting immigration). For all nations, immigration policies are about accepting or rejecting specific groups. Immigration represents an especially ambivalent endeavour within the United States. Although a nation born of immigrants, United States policy demonstrates a clear preference for white Anglo-Saxon Protestants, and an increased suspicion of groups as they diverge from that norm. Only when the *next* immigrant group was even *more* different did bigotry and discrimination lessen for the immediately preceding group. Historically, native United States citizens—in reality second-generation or later immigrants—considered new arrivals dirty and dangerous, criminal and sometimes treasonous. Following 9/11, immigrants were equated with terrorists, though not for the first time (Gerstle 2004). Simply put, the popular rhetoric about many immigrants has long been that they do not really belong in the United States, and when present anyway, their movements need to be closely controlled.

3.   CONSEQUENCES OF A CONTROL-ORIENTED STATE SECURITY STRATEGY

The consequences of a control-oriented state security strategy include decreased civil rights, increased fear and the sense of insecurity, and staggering costs. On the ground in the United States, homeland security has translated as an attack on immigrants and suspicion of immigrant rights, especially Arab and Muslim immigrants. It has also initiated a heightened attack on and criminalisation of dissent. Both immigrants and dissenters sit on the border of legitimacy in the United States, suspected as lacking patriotism, not belonging, and as terrorist-sympathisers, if not potential terrorists. As such, they are much like prisoners, and the state's view of and response to them parallels its treatment of offenders. The increased scrutiny of these populations helps alleviate pressures on the state under globalisation and the intensification of the state security apparatus emphasises national security to the neglect of human security. It also runs counter to those advocating shrinking the state to promote market globalisation since the manner in which the United States is advancing national security represents a dramatic state expansion. In reality, fighting terrorism is simply an extension of the old role of controlling populations, both outside and within state borders, through either the military or the criminal justice system. The arrival of foreign terrorism to United States shores increased the state commitment to control populations, both immigrants and citizens, and those engaged in civil dissent became especially suspect. Actually, the war on terror's emphasis on 'homeland security' simply camouflages the extensive growth in the last four decades of the state control orientation and apparatus found in the criminal justice system and the military.

3.1   Fearing Freedom

Interrogation of the control-oriented security strategy reveals the state's fear of freedom. Crime control in general, and homeland security and the war on terror more specifically, mean increased surveillance of citizens and immigrants, decreased civil rights, including the use of secret courts and trials, decreased acceptability of dissent, and increased imprisonment and detainment. In the aftermath of the attacks on the World Trade Center and the Pentagon, the Bush administration pushed through Congress the *USA Patriot Act 2001* and, later, the *Homeland Security Act 2002*. Both laws are actually a long-desired conservative laundry list of changes to civil rights guarantees.

The United States Government justifies increased surveillance of citizens and immigrants because it might help detect terrorist activities before they occur. However, the surveillance methods employed and suggested represent a significant incursion of civil rights and innocent people are harmed. Hundreds of Arabs and Muslims were arrested and detained, held, tried, imprisoned and deported in secrecy in the weeks following 9/11. The Federal Bureau of Intelligence's (FBI) terrorist watch list was released to government agencies and private corporations; its numerous errors resulted in the harassment of people with absolutely no involvement in terrorist activities (Davis 2002). The Pentagon's Total Information Awareness program, a proposed electronic surveillance program, would have eventually enabled the government to track people's daily activities, including their use of libraries, email and the internet, telephones, credit cards, and the contents of their medical records. The program was disbanded following public outcry regarding excessive surveillance; however, private companies continue to amass significant quantities of data about citizens which are regularly accessed by the government (American Civil Liberties Union 2004b). Until the attacks, 'probable cause' was the legal standard required to initiate intelligence surveillance of United States citizens; now, a far lower standard is required and information learned can be turned over for unrelated criminal prosecution. Previously forbidden 'sneak and peek' searches in which government agents search homes without notice are now allowed. Government officials may now listen in on previously confidential attorney–client conversations without notice. In contrast to the increased surveillance and decreased civil rights of citizens, the new laws protect private industries from scrutiny if they are part of the 'critical infrastructure' of national security, even if their actions endanger public safety.

The expansion of the state in controlling populations has also led to attacks on the acceptability of civil dissent. The Attorney-General of the United States vilified as lacking patriotism those who questioned the morality or wisdom of the war—either on terrorism or on Iraq—and accused them of aiding terrorists (Ashcroft 2001). United States colleges and universities have been considered relatively safe spaces for civil dissent, in large part because of their commitment to academic freedom. The new state emphasis on homeland security, however, has made college campuses an important place for government surveillance. A university police officer on the University of Massachusetts, Amherst campus was recruited to work with the FBI's Anti-Terrorism Task Force as part of his campus job. This affiliation led to the questioning of a faculty member about his political views and organisational affiliations, even though no specific suspicious activity was reported (this is just one of many examples) (American Civil Liberties Union 2003). Universities are also more sensitive to public opinion and academics can no longer assume university support for their research and free speech practices, including writing critical of the government and participation in anti-war teach-ins.

Political advocacy groups are identified as potential terrorists and put under surveillance by federal, state and local police. Since 9/11, the FBI's Joint Terrorism Task Force has collected thousands of files on a wide variety of advocacy organisations including the American Civil Liberties Union, Greenpeace, United for Peace and Justice, People for the Ethical Treatment of Animals and the American-Arab Anti-Discrimination Committee. The Denver, Colorado police department, like other local law enforcement agencies, maintained files on local peace and justice groups. Nearly four years after 9/11, Muslim groups are still subject to surveillance and their members to interviews resulting in deportations (American Civil Liberties Union 2004b).

State actions taken as part of homeland security are extraordinarily punitive, as demonstrated by the United States war on crime and drugs. Now in its fourth decade, with no end in sight and little decrease in drug use or the problems associated with drug use, this war has resulted in the incarceration of two million people in prisons and jails, more than a fourfold increase in just 20 years. Another 4.9 million adults are under some other form of correctional supervision, such as probation or parole (United States Department of Justice 2004). Over 182,000 of those imprisoned are women and another one million women are on probation or parole (Harrison *et al.* 2004; Glaze and Palla 2004). In the 1980s, the rate of women's imprisonment increased nearly twice as much as that of men's, and 34 new women's prison units were opened (Immarigeon and Chesney-Lind 1992). African-Americans, who account for 13 percent of the population, are 45 percent of those incarcerated (Beck and Karberg 2001); 25 years ago, they were 35 percent of those locked up (Maguire *et al.* 1993: 618). Black men are seven times and black women are over 4.5 more likely to be imprisoned than are white men and women (Harrison *et al.* 2004); the expansion of mandatory and increased sentences for drug law violations accounts for much of the increase (Mauer 1990). The rate of imprisonment of African-American men is growing faster than their rate of college admission (Ziedenberg and Schiraldi 2002). The numbers of black women imprisoned for drugs has increased more than three times that of white women (Bush-Baskette 1998). Nearly all of those behind bars are poor.

United States practices and politics about crime control are being reproduced in the homeland security and war on terror arenas. The war on crime and drugs led to increased surveillance and traffic stops of African-Americans and Latinos, a practice known as racial profiling. Racial profiling is now evident in the war on terror as immigration law is selectively enforced on the basis of nationality, race, and ethnicity (American Civil Liberties Union 2004a). Middle Eastern and Muslim men and women are routinely stopped and called in for questioning by local and federal law enforcement and immigration authorities. The slightest technical visa violations can lead to imprisonment and deportation and even legal immigrants are detained for minor offences and technical violations. Punitive practices in American prisons are reproduced at Abu Ghraib and Guantánamo Bay. Just as the 1996 Prison Litigation Reform Act denied access to the courts for inmates charging abusive treatment, so too does the Bush administration continue to argue that detainees have no rights to civilian court oversight (Herbert 2004). As state authority expands with the focus on crime control, homeland security and the war on terror, civil rights shrink for immigrants, minorities and dissenting civilians, and do not even exist for detainees and enemy combatants.

4.   STAGGERING COSTS OF CONTROL

The global economy was humming along quite well in the 1990s and early 2000, at least in the United States and to the great benefit of corporations and stock holders. The economic boom brought on by new technologies was so dramatic that during the 1990s the United States federal budget went from deficits to surpluses for the first time in 27 years (Congressional Budget Office 2005: 134) and rates of unemployment and poverty declined to their lowest levels in more than 20 years (Bureau of Labor Statistics 2005, Census 2005). The growth of the internet and preparation for 'Y2K' fueled the dot-com bubble of the 1990s which finally burst in late 2000, leading to a recession. By May 2001, the Bush admini- stration and a Republican Congress had passed massive tax cuts with most benefits going to the wealthy.

The economy initially remained depressed in response to 9/11 and the anthrax scares as uncertainty and fear loomed. While consumers curtailed air travel and unnecessary expenditures, the federal government, however, began a security spending spree that first focused on the homeland and then quickly spread to the wars in and reconstruction of Afghanistan and Iraq. The White House estimated that the United States spends $100 billion per year on homeland security, not including costs associated with the military (Office of Homeland Security 2002: 63). Simply establishing the new Department of Homeland Security was expected to cost $3 billion (Congressional Budget Office 2002). The United States Conference of Mayors estimated that cities would spend more than $2.6 billion on additional security costs by the end of 2002, an amount that increased by $70 million per week with the war in Iraq and heightened security alerts (United States Conference of Mayors 2003). Since 9/11, the military has received nearly $200 billion in supplemental appropriations and now spends $6 billion per month just to maintain its presence in Iraq and Afghanistan as well as anti-terrorist activities in the United States; defence now claims over 50 percent of discretionary outlays (Congressional Budget Office 2005: 6, 140). Not surprisingly, the flow of this much money this quickly with inadequate oversight has resulted in a significant degree of waste and fraud (Higham and O'Harrow 2005; Marek 2005).

The consequences of the cost of homeland security and the war on terror mirror those associated with crime control. It costs over $22,000 per year to imprison a person in the United States (Stephan 2004). The enormous and costly prison construction program undertaken during the 1990s meant that prisons represented 'the only expanding public housing' in the United States (*The Nation* 1995: 223). And at the beginning of 21st century, the costs associated with maintaining these facilities and incarcerating citizens, especially geriatrics, as 'lifers' age, are quickly dwarfing the costs of construction. As a result of increased incarceration, state budget spending on corrections has grown at six times the rate of spending on higher education and states now spend more money building prisons than colleges. Decreased state support for higher education has meant increasing costs for students and their parents, at the very time that more women and minority men have entered college (Ziedenberg and Schiraldi 2002).

The growing cost of homeland security and the wars, coupled with the economic downturn, have resulted in increased deficits which the Bush administration has used to justify additional cuts to governmental budgets. Social service programs to benefit the poor, most of whom are women, are those most frequently targeted. The United States Conference of Mayors (2004) identified homeland security and defence costs as further endangering social services including programs aimed to ease hunger and homelessness. Education and health care also face cuts while criminal justice, along with defence, remains quite safe.

Structural adjustment programs (SAPs) are most commonly associated with the global south. Conservative rhetoric about government inefficiencies and high taxes in the 1980s camouflaged the beginnings of structural adjustment in the United States. By the mid-1990s as the growth of the internet accelerated globalisation, it became clear that the federal government was following the tenets of structural adjustment as far as reducing the role of the state in maintaining social services. Dramatic state expansion has occurred, however, in the crime control, homeland security and war on terror arenas. This maintenance of national security comes at the cost of human security as the numbers of poor, homeless, hungry and uninsured Americans continue to rise.

5. GLOBALISATION, HOMELAND (IN)SECURITY AND JUSTICE

Questions surrounding borders, mobility and technologies of control need to consider the responses to 9/11 in understanding recent United States actions to limit mobility and control various populations. In short, 9/11 represents a unique political opportunity for the state to respond more forcefully than would otherwise be possible to those whose economic marginalisation makes them potentially problematic. Immigrants are suspect, but so are red-blooded blue-collared Americans battered by the forces of glo-balisation whose circumstances may propel them into the ranks of criminals or protesters. Redirecting attention away from their economic insecurity towards fear of foreigners represents a way to co-opt citizens into accepting a control-oriented state security strategy. Homeland security is not just about protecting 'us' from immigrants who belong outside the borders, but also from citizen dissenters residing within.

Problematic populations grow and become more ominous as human security is threatened. The United Nations identifies seven categories of threats to human security: economic, food, health, personal, environmental, community and cultural, and political insecurity (United Nations Develop-ment Programme 1999). As globalisation has ever more quickly torn down the borders of space and time, human insecurity has increased throughout the world. Prior to the 1980s, many workers in the United States had been beneficiaries of an increasingly global economy. Since then, economic insecurity has increased, economic justice is lacking and income inequality is growing. Corporate profits and the salaries of chief executive officers (CEOs) are soaring while the median income of workers continues to fall. Since 1990, average CEO compensation has increased 300 percent, while average production worker wages have increased only five percent and average minimum wage worker income has actually declined six percent; the CEO:worker pay ratio is now 431:1. The control-oriented state security strategy has been particularly profitable for defence contractors and their CEOs whose pay increased 200 percent from 2001 to 2004 alone (Anderson et al. 2005). During that same time, the United States poverty rate and the number people without health insurance increased and real median earnings fell; household incomes remained stagnant or fell for the fifth year in a row for all but the wealthiest 20 percent (Census 2005).

Rather than respond to the economic insecurity faced by many Americans, the Bush administration has used fear inspired by 9/11 to build support for its unilateral war in Iraq and on terrorism. Billions of dollars have been spent on restricting the borders and on a variety of advanced technologies for surveillance and control. Activating these technologies requires laws permitting their use which, in turn, requires mobilising public opinion to gain their acceptance. The 9/11 attacks gave the state the opportunity to enhance technologies increasingly necessary to control potentially problematic populations. In arguing that national security can only be achieved with restrictions on civil and human rights for detainees, immigrants and protesters, the United States counts on capitalists and patriots to remain compliant.

Thanks to Nancy Wonders, who encouraged the beginning of this chapter, and to Kara Hoofnagle, who helped finish it.

REFERENCES

American Civil Liberties Union, 2003, *Freedom Under Fire: Dissent in Post-9/11 America*, New York.

American Civil Liberties Union, 2004a, *Sanctioned Bias: Racial Profiling Since 9/11*, New York.

American Civil Liberties Union, 2004b, *The Surveillance-Industrial Complex: How the American Government Is Conscripting Businesses and Individuals in the Construction of a Surveillance Society*, New York.

Anderson, S., Cavanagh, J., Klinger, S., and Stanton, L., 2005, *Executive Excess 2005: Defense Contractors Get More Bucks for the Bang, 12th Annual CEO Compensation Survey*, Institute for Policy Studies and United for a Fair Economy, Washington, DC.

Ashcroft, J., 2001, *Testimony before the Senate Judiciary Committee* (6 December 2001).

Beck, A. J. and Karberg, J. C., 2002, *Prison and Jail Inmates at Midyear 2000*, U.S. Department of Justice, Washington, DC.

Bureau of Labor Statistics, 2005, *Annual Average Unemployment Rate, Civilian Labor Force 16 Years and over (Percent)*, Washington, DC; http://www.bls.gov/cps/prev_yrs.htm.

Bush-Baskette, S. R., 1998, The war on drugs as a war against Black women, in: *Crime Control and Women: Feminist Implications of Criminal Justice Policy*, S.L. Miller, ed., Sage, Thousand Oaks, CA, **pp. 113–129**.

Congressional Budget Office, 2002, *Cost Estimate: H.R. 5005 Homeland Security Act of 2002 As Introduced on June 24, 2002*, Washington, DC.

Congressional Budget Office, 2005, *The Budget and Economic Outlook: Fiscal Years 2006 to 2015*, Washington, DC.

Census (U.S. Bureau of the Census), 2005, *Income, Poverty, and Health Insurance Coverage in the United States: 2004*, Washington, DC.

Chomsky, N., 2001, A quick reaction, *Counterpunch* (12 September 2001). http://www.counterpunch.org/chomskybomb.html.

Davis, A. 2002, FBI's post-sept.11 'watch list' mutates, acquires life of its own, *The Wall Street Journal* (19 November 2002) pp. A1, A10.

Friedman, T. L., 1999, A manifesto for the fast world, *The New York Times Magazine* (28 March 1999) p. 40.

Gerstle, G., 2004, The immigrant as threat to American security: a historical perspective, in: *The Maze of Fear: Security and Migration After 9/11*, J. Tirman, (ed.,) The New Press, New York, **pp. 87–108**.

Glaze, L. E. and Palla, S., 2004, *Probation and Parole in the United States, 2003*, U.S. Department of Justice, Washington, DC.

Harrison, Paige M. and Karberg, J.C., 2004, *Prison and Jail Inmates at Midyear 2003*, U.S. Department of Justice, Washington, DC.

Heller, D. (ed.), 2005, *The Selling of 9/11: How a National Tragedy became a Commodity*, Palgrave Macmillan, New York.

Herbert, B., 2004, America's Abu Ghraibs, *The New York Times* (31 May 2004) p. A17.

Higham, S. and O'Harrow, R. Jr., 2005, Contracting rush for security led to waste, abuse, *Washington Post* (22 May 2005) p. A1.

Immarigeon, R. and Chesney-Lind, M., 1992, *Women's Prisons: Overcrowded and Overused*, National Council on Crime and Delinquency, San Francisco, CA.

Kerr, J. and Sweetman, C., 2003, Women reinventing globalisation, *Gender and Development* **11(1): 3–12**.

Maguire, K., Pastore, A.L., and Flanagan, T.J., (eds.,) 1993, *Sourcebook of Criminal Justice Statistics 1992*, U.S. Department of Justice, Washington, DC.

Marek, A.C., 2005, Security at any price? Homeland protection isn't just job 1 in Washington; it's more like a big old government ATM, *U.S. News & World Report* (30 May 2005) **pp.** 22–30.

Mauer, M., 1990, *Young Black Men and the Criminal Justice System: A Growing National Problem*, The Sentencing Project, Washington, DC.

The Nation, The prison boom (20 February 1995).

Office of Homeland Security, 2002, *National Strategy for Homeland Security*, U.S. Government, Washington, DC.

Stephan, J.J., 2004, *State Prison Expenditures, 2001*, Bureau of Justice Statistics, Washington, DC.

U.S. Conference of Mayors. 2003, *The U.S. Conference of Mayors Survey on Cities' Direct Homeland Security Cost Increases Related to War/High Threat Alert*, Washington, DC.

U.S. Conference of Mayors, 2004, *Hunger and Homelessness Survey*, Washington, DC.

U.S. Department of Justice, 2004, *Almost 6.9 Million on Probation or Parole or Incarcerated in U.S. Prisons or Jails* (25 July 2004).

United Nations Economic and Social Commission for Asia and the Pacific, 1999, *Economic and Social Survey of Asia and the Pacific, 1999*, United Nations, New York.

United Nations Development Programme, 1999, *Human Development Report 1999: Globalization with a Human Face*, Oxford University Press, New York.

Wichterich, C., 2000, *The Globalized Woman: Reports from a Future of Inequality*, P. Camiller, trans., Zed Books, London.

Ziedenberg, J., and Schiraldi, V., 2002, Cellblocks or Classrooms?: The Funding of Higher Education and Corrections and Its Impact on African American Men, Justice Policy Institute, Washington, DC.

Chapter 7

CONTROL, PROTECTION AND NEGLIGENCE
Border security in the western Balkans

Alice Hills
Leeds University

Borders dominate the security agenda in the western Balkans, a region of traditional smuggling routes, organised crime and corruption. Political and ethnic discontents focus on its disputed borders, and criminal gangs and illegal migrants cross them. Current border control is ineffective.

A dramatic increase in uncontrolled migration and illegal trafficking brought these issues to the fore in the late 1990s, when improving the region's border control became a priority for the European Union. At its Zagreb summit of November 2000, the European Union identified a need to develop effective border management in the region, and for existing systems to adopt its functional standards. By 'border management' was meant the processes and procedures associated with border checks, which take place at authorised crossing points, and border surveillance, which is carried out on the so-called 'green' (that is, land) borders between authorised crossing points.

Despite the European Union's action, functional border security remains neglected by the academic community. Borders are discussed in terms of globalisation, identity politics, visa regimes, illegal trafficking, and uncontrolled migration, rather than border management, with the result that a significant aspect of state behaviour is incompletely understood.[1]

In this chapter, I argue that a more nuanced understanding of the changing nature, form and location of states' responses to borders is possible when evaluated in terms of the agents managing border security: border guards. The term 'border guards' is often used interchangeably with 'border police', however, I will use the former here. Border control is about law enforcement, as well as the protection of borders, and most states in the European Union's sphere of influence categorise their guards as police; but the word 'guards' emphasises that border guards are ideally independent and

123

S.Pickering and L.Weber (eds), Borders, Mobility and Technologies of Control, 123–148.
© 2006 Springer.Printed in the Netherlands.

specialist multi-purpose police, subordinated to ministries of the interior but not forming part of a national police force.[2]

I evaluate state dependence on borders as markers of territory, and inclusion and exclusion, in terms of the guards who exercise state authority at and around the border, and how they experience and understand that authority. I discuss how governments and guards understand the predicament insecure borders and international pressures pose for them. In this way, I assess the extent to which changes in the rationale underpinning border security are reflected in guarding priorities, structures and practices. I conclude the chapter by arguing that while the European Union's vision of regional order requires control, filtering and exclusion to be balanced by facilitation and communication; this demands a degree of political will and institutional capability that is often lacking in the Balkans. In other words, states may regard borders as territorial markers, but social realities, vested interests, and the resilience of security structures ensure that borders retain their subversive potential.

There is no simple correlation between changes in the meaning of borders and guarding practices; current developments result from a mix of political, ideological, functional and cultural variables. The dynamics of guarding in the western Balkans are shaped by political imperatives (primarily those of the European Union and national elites); security threats (uncontrolled migration and organised crime); and socio-economic challenges (corruption, poverty, and chronic under-development). The precise balance between the variables depends on context. Changes in rationale have had a positive effect in relation to countries actively wishing to develop close relations with the European Union—many recent developments in regional border management are explicable as political gestures, or in terms of the burden-shifting logic informing European Union policy-making—but much remains the same.

This conclusion is reached through four stages. The first introduces the major variables shaping regional border security, while the next three focus on the strategic choices made by Bosnia Herzegovina, the Republic of Macedonia (hereafter Macedonia), and Albania in the face of pressure from international organisations and domestic vested interests. This approach acknowledges the importance of regional dynamics but avoids the possibility of producing too narrow and specific an explanation of why and how states exercise their authority on borders. Bosnia Herzegovina is a European protectorate, which makes the assumptions underpinning its system explicit, while Macedonia illustrates the tensions between new and more entrenched security problems, and Albania shows what happens when the state neglects border control.

1.   BORDER INSECURITY

There is no one answer as to why states exercise authority at and around the border in the western Balkans, or as to how guards understand borders, but strong patterns are identifiable. These are the result of the regional security environment, the nature of guarding, and the European Union's emphasis on regional cooperation.

1.1   Security Environment

Many security threats are present on the region's borders. Not only are caches of arms and ammunition hidden along borders that are isolated by bad roads, mountains and rural poverty, but also, disputes about the location of boundaries or border crossings are frequently used to obstruct political settlements. Macedonia, for example, faces external challenges resulting from the uncertain status of Kosovo and from the refusal of neighbouring states to recognize Macedonia's own identity. In April 2003, Prime Minister Crvenkovski argued that calls for changing borders or exchanging populations are a 'direct call for ethnic war' (International Crisis Group, 2003b: 29), while, on 25 December, Defence Minister Buckovski said that resolving Kosovo's final status depends on the satisfactory delineation of Macedonia's borders.[3] Significantly, the death of President Trajkovski of Macedonia in a plane crash on the mountainous border between Bosnia Herzegovina and Croatia on 26 February 2004 was immediately perceived as a potential threat to national security, resulting in heightened patrol along Macedonia's borders.

Easy assumptions about state understanding of the meaning of borders are, however, of questionable value, for regional politics are overshadowed by widespread corruption and personal ties; national and regional criminal networks are adept at exploiting the foibles or greed of politicians, busi-nessmen and security officers (International Crisis Group, 2003a). In truth, the smuggling of migrants, drugs, cigarettes, cars and weapons, together with trafficking in women and, to a lesser extent, children, affects all countries. Negligence on the part of guards remains a major obstacle to effective border control, but this is not necessarily seen as problematic by the governments or guards concerned.

In contrast, the European Union takes the matter very seriously, for the Balkans is the main gateway for illegal goods and migrants into western Europe. Accurately quantifying the scale of the problem is impossible, but several thousand illegal migrants probably pass through countries such as Bosnia Herzegovina each month. The situation has improved since 2000, when the International Organisation for Migration (IOM) estimated that more than 50,000 illegal migrants passed through Bosnia Herzegovina on their way to the European Union in the first ten months of the year, but it remains serious. In particular, crime and uncontrolled migration threaten the European Union's goal of regional integration, which is based on a series of inclusionary and exclusionary policies the enforcement of which depends on effective border management. As a result, the promotion of effective and politically acceptable styles of guarding in the states bordering the European Union has become one of its strategic priorities.

1.2   Guarding

Border guards police migration, demonstrate sovereignty, and often represent an important source of state budgetary income, but until recently their role has been seen as of technical interest only. At best, guarding has been understood as a craft in which skills are acquired through experience, and which are limited to those in the same occupation. At worst, guards have been seen as the poor relations of a despised police. Police studies has neglected guards, while the literature on border management has focused on the changing nature of borders, the need for international cooperation, apprehensions, measures to combat trafficking, and the means for making border control more effective.[4]

This situation is changing as a result of the European Union's strategic agenda and international concern over transnational crime and illegal migration. But the role of guards is more significant than this suggests, for they operate at the intersection of a number of functional, political and theoretical concerns that reflect and affect the exercise of state authority. They occupy a significant space on the security spectrum because their operational environment requires a range of activities, from militarised units to documentation centres, and they have both military and police functions and roles. Being border forces, often working in dangerous environments, they have a traditional affinity with military units. At the same time, managing trafficking and migration is essentially a policing task that requires enforcement skills. In practice, most accept the European Union principle that guards should fulfil an independent and specialised role that emphasises policing responsibilities at the expense of combat-related capabilities.

Border guarding tends to be subsumed under policing, but the role played by guards and the nature of their task are more significant than this suggests. On the one hand, international reform programs invariably advocate an independent and specialised role for guards that emphasises policing responsibilities at the expense of combat-related capabilities. This reflects the criminalisation of, for example, uncontrolled migration. Further, managing migration and human trafficking is essentially a policing activity—responding to alien smuggling involves border guards working with alien police, criminal police, other government agencies, non-government organisations, and international organisations. On the other hand, the possibility of confronting armed gangs in sparsely populated border zones means that guards often act as paramilitary units. Indeed, the operational demands of managing green borders (that is, between legal crossing points) ensures that even police-oriented border services require a rapid-reaction response that depends on military-style discipline. The result is that most guards are technically police, even if some are really interior troops. Whatever the case, their tasks range from customs duties to militarised units.

Such roles are not exclusive, but they are indicative of the political significance attached to such challenges, and of tensions in contemporary guarding. One result is that parallel lines of action have developed at the multilateral level. They are symbolised here by the differing approaches to border security adopted by the European Union and the North Atlantic Treaty Organisation (NATO). The European Union emphasises civilian control in the context of European integration, whereas NATO speaks of protection and employs military-based surveillance. The result is that border security performs several distinct functions. It must control, because the Balkans is a gate to the European Union for illegal trafficking, but it must also protect internationally-desirable but disputed or volatile borders.

Border guards thus occupy a significant space on the security spectrum. They have police and military functions and roles that involve close working relationships (and rivalries) with police and military forces, not least because the geographic border is also the psychological and professional border between police and military roles and duties. They often represent a multi-functional enforcement authority.

This means that even the most ineffective national authorities are expected to work with international organisations such as EUROPOL, the International Border Police Conference (IBPC, Budapest), the European Union's Centre for Information, Discussion and Exchange on the Crossing of Frontiers and Immigration (CIREFI), and the International Civil Aviation Organisation, Facilitation Division (ICAO FAL-Panel), as well as networks of border liaison officers. They are also expected to cooperate with the Schengen authorities; that is, with member states of the European Union, all of whom are now (with some partial exceptions) covered by the Schengen agreement and convention. The agreement, which committed Germany, France, Belgium, Luxembourg and the Netherlands to developing a common area of security and justice free of internal borders checks, was signed at Schengen, Luxembourg in 1985. Its provisions were implemented by a convention signed in 1990, though technical challenges meant that they were not put into practice until the mid 1990s. The convention's key points concern the harmonisation of provisions for entry into the Schengen area by non-European Union citizens, asylum, dealing with cross-border drug trafficking, and cooperation on police operations and judicial matters.

Such agencies are important for a variety of reasons. In particular, their number suggests that guarding cannot be understood as a purely functional matter, least of all in the European Union's sphere of influence, because borders continue to play a central symbolic role in European politics. Indeed, Andreas' (2000: x) argument that the intensification of policing on the European Union's borders has less to do with deterring illegal trafficking and migration than 'recrafting the image of the border and symbolically reaffirming the state's territorial authority' is particularly pertinent with regard to the impact of the European Union on regional border management.

1.3   Schengen's Space

The attention focused on border management (as opposed to the delineation of borders) reflects two linked trends which shape regional under-standing of the purpose of state authority on the border. The first is that effective border control is of direct concern to the European Union, while the second follows from the ambition of the region's states to be recognised as part of Europe, or, better still, to become European Union members.

Improving border management is a fundamental element in the European Union's security strategy. It puts pressure on regional governments to improve their record of fighting transnational crime while monitoring their progress and assisting them to implement effective border security through the CARDS (Community Assistance for Reconstruction, Development and Stabilization) program. CARDS is the cornerstone of the European Union's policy in the region. It is implemented nationally but aims to provide regional coherence through the development of common approaches and technical specifications. This suggests that whether or not the European Union is intent on burden shifting is of less immediate functional conse-quence than its conviction that effective security requires a degree of mutual trust based on a shared understanding of what is necessary. In practice, most countries accept CARDS assistance because they want good relations with the European Union, rather than with their neighbours. Most are conse-quently in the process of developing strategies for border management. Further, their anticipatory planning is invariably based on the Schengen principles.

Guidelines for the European Union's preferred model of border management were laid down in the Schengen *acquis* which was integrated into the European Union framework in 1999 (when the Treaty of Amsterdam came into force).[5] Schengen addresses the legal basis for action, as well as the definition and demarcation of borders, border crossing procedures, the aim and content of border checks, details of acceptable travel documents, and visa policies and practices. According to Schengen, border security is a matter of law enforcement, not national defence; crossing the external border at a point other than an official border post without special permission is illegal. Security is to be delivered by a professional, specialist, multi-purpose border police, with its own dedicated and unified command chain, rather than by military troops or conscripts; border police are to be answerable to a ministry of the interior rather than a ministry of defence. The policing methods used must be understandable to those crossing borders, and the officers concerned must be accountable to legislatures, specialised parliamentary committees, and other executive authorities. The *acquis* is supplemented by the *Schengen Catalogue,* which provides political guidance as to what is politically acceptable to the European Union. It is made up of recommendations and best practices, rather than legally binding documents, and sets out the EU's understanding of the best way for countries to reach European Union standards (2002: 2).

Achieving anything like Schengen standards demands a significant administrative capacity. It requires a coherent national strategy, and the creation of a specialised and trained force of guards, with adequate financing and resourcing, and dedicated command and communications structures. It means that the function of guarding must not be fragmented amongst authorities, guards should not be the target of political disputes, and political debates (concerning, for example, the location of a border) should not be allowed to disrupt normal border control. None of this is easily achievable in the Balkans.

Despite this, the desirability of the European Union's stated aims and objectives are widely acknowledged. The obligations associated with Schengen's standards may apply only to member states, but in practice they form the basis of a European standard of border management to which countries in the western Balkans aspire. Bosnia Herzegovina's system, for example, reflects, or is compatible with, European Union standards, although most countries (Macedonia and Albania in this case) are only now considering the strategies and measures required to develop one. Even so, most senior guards accept (or at least acknowledge) that it is desirable to use European Union standards as the basic criterion for their country's future development.

In practice, European Commission proposals to assemble a common corpus of legislation are widely tracked, with the result that European standards of border management are now emerging (see European Commission 2002). Even Macedonia and Albania know that European Union proposals will introduce certain mandatory 'good practices' in the existing *Common Manual for External Borders*, and that these will exert political pressure on their border standards. They cannot ignore European Union specifications for legal frameworks and procedures. Nor can they dismiss as politically irrelevant the European Union's introduction of cooperation mechanisms. But Schengen standards are demanding, and there are naturally differences of understanding and acceptance across the region (to say nothing of resources and capacity), especially in relation to operational notions such as service. This is most noticeable in relation to the guidance and assistance elements of the European Union's ideal model. Guards within the European Union's direct sphere of influence are trained in the rights and protection of asylum seekers, and in commonality, none of which makes sense to the average guard at a check point on Macedonia's border with Serbia. Organisational differences, meanwhile, include the role of specialist mobile units. Thus, Bosnia Herzegovina has specialist mobile units capable of supporting regular units whereas Macedonia does not, the reason being that such units require a high degree of operational flexibility and logistical support.

Despite this, regional progress has been made towards a common understanding of what is required by the European Union; problems have been acknowledged, as has the need to develop appropriate cooperative measures. Even Albania, with its notoriously low levels of border security, is developing links with its neighbours, as is evidenced by the opening of a number of border crossings in late 2003. It is keen to show that it actively patrols its border with Macedonia.

1.4   Compatibility

The means by which compatibility with Schengen's standards is to be achieved includes CARDS programs, 'integrated border management', and assistance from organisations such as the International Centre for Migration Policy Development,[6] the Organization for Security and Co-operation in Europe and the Stability Pact.

The influence of the European Union results from it being the single largest donor to the region, which ensures that senior guards in the region take CARDS very seriously. In late 2000, for example, the European Union adopted a six-year CARDS program with an overall budget of €4.6 billion. In turn, the Justice and Home Affairs projects funded by the various CARDS's national programs underwrite specific projects intended to provide guidance, improve the capacity of border guards and customs officials, and strengthen regional cooperation structures. CARDS also supports the influential stabilisation and association process, which is intended to assist countries reach closer integration.

The management model promoted by CARDS is that of integrated border management, which is seen as a tool for increasing the trust and cooperation necessary for transferring Schengen-style border security to south-east Europe, and as a means by which the European Union can deepen its defences.[7] According to the *Schengen Catalogue* (2002: 9, see also 11–15), the integrated border security model refers to:

> the system covering all aspects of border policy. This system is spread over four complementary tiers (filters) which are: activities in third countries, countries of origin and transit, bilateral and international cooperation, measures at the external borders and further activities inside the territory.

The term integrated border management is also used descriptively to refer to cooperation, coordination, and the integration of the various processes, procedures and actors involved in delivering Schengen-style border security. Three types of inter-agency cooperation are thought to be especially useful: coordinated processing at border crossings (together with a clear understanding as to who checks what and sequencing); integrated information technology systems that include intelligence from guards, national police, and customs; and the acceptance of joint responsibilities.

1.5   Common Assumptions and Principles

When allied to the special environment and culture in which the border task is performed, the role played by the European Union ensures that guards share a common vocabulary. Border security, for example, is widely understood as comprising tasks and missions such as the provision of security filters and cross-border cooperation. Procedural issues are often unsatisfactory (few countries keep records of aliens applying for a visa or residence permit) but bilateral agreements, for example, are generally seen as an important way of dealing with removal, repatriation and readmission. Schengen's insistence of information exchange and national and local liaison officers is accepted too. In other words, the need for regional cooperation is accepted. Indeed, a survey conducted in 2003 by the Geneva Centre for the Democratic Control of Armed Forces suggests that most countries regard cooperation as critical for the development of effective national and regional border security.[8] Furthermore, the means by which this is to be achieved are invariably thought to include joint border-surveillance systems, joint assessment systems, joint training centres, networks of liaison officers, and a common terminology. This represents a common regional understanding that is explicitly shaped by Schengen principles and which shapes the exercise of state authority.

A degree of unanimity now exists regarding the organisational and functional variables needed for effective border security, yet significant differences remain. An explanation as to how and why border services differ is to be found in variables such as legacy issues (the inheritance of war or specific traditions), geo-political factors, organisational choices, social realities, and functional imperatives, rather than the meaning of borders as such. Of the various factors, European Union initiatives are probably the most positive influence and social realities the most negative. Even so, the balance between the variables is more nuanced than this suggests because tensions exist at a number of levels. There is, for example, a disconnection between certain international and regional assumptions. Those resulting from the role of NATO are particularly significant; NATO plays a subordinate role in regional border security but continued insecurity (and NATO's links to the United States) means that it cannot be dismissed. As a result, two key themes underlie the international assessment of border security in the western Balkans: control and protection.

1.6   Control and Protection

The need for control is invariably taken as self-evident, but that for protection is more controversial. Control is a relatively uncontroversial law enforcement matter. Certain internationally desirable borders (such as that between Macedonia and Serbia) remain, however, controversial; they require protection by military or paramilitary forces. The European Union and NATO are technically partners in the region, but their roles are not equal because the level of risk is not uniform. Context matters; European Union-style border police cannot operate against gangs—30- or 40-strong and armed with missile launchers and Kalashnikovs—in the triangle between Serbia, Kosovo, Macedonia and Albania. The result is, as Jonas Widgren, the then director of the International Centre for Migration Policy Development, noted in 2002, that two parallel lines of action exist at the multilateral level.[9] The European Union emphasises control, while NATO is preoccupied with protection. The European Union speaks of the need for 'sound' border control in the context of the region's integration into European Union structures, whereas NATO is primarily concerned with military-based protection and surveillance.

Military methods of guarding are undoubtedly different to those promoted by the European Union. Troops are not trained or equipped to perform police tasks, yet NATO remains involved in many border-related activities. Indeed, the United Nations Interim Administration Mission in

Kosovo justified its inclusion in border security talks in 2003 on the basis that it provides an interim administration for Kosovo. And it was the North Atlantic Council that promoted the conference on border management and security in Ohrid in May 2003 that was hosted by Macedonia and supported by the European Union, Stability Pact, and the Organization for Security and Co-operation in Europe. Indeed, Ohrid's focus on border management and anti-trafficking operations in Albania, Macedonia, and Serbia and Montenegro/Kosovo (rather than demarcation issues) is indicative of NATO's priorities. At the same time, Ohrid reaffirmed the need for a regional approach to border security, and local and regional ownership.

NATO's role can be seen as representing a temporary complementarity before full European Union standards of civilian authority and tight co-ordination can be applied. This is not problematic as such, and European Union officials usually argue that integrated border management (IBM) can accommodate a military role in such circumstances. Not only is it accepted that ideals may need to be temporarily adjusted in politically sensitive areas, but also, some officials claim that this will offer a firm basis for further cooperation in border security. The position of the European Union and European Commission is that such an arrangement is both realistic and acceptable as a means for achieving security. Nonetheless, the reintroduction of a military presence is seen within the region as a retrograde and destabilising move: the European Union advocates border security as a civilian task yet promotes the role of the military when it suits its own interests.

In practice, trends, options, and issues of convergence and divergence in border management are best seen in terms of specific regional examples, which also illustrate the strategies, options, and problems typically limiting the exercise of state authority on borders.

2.   BOSNIA HERZEGOVINA

The State Border Service (SBS) of Bosnia Herzegovina is important here because its creation, formal objectives and organisation reflects the international community's understanding of state border requirements.

The initial impetus behind the creation of the SBS is difficult to identify, but it seemingly owed much to the determination of the then special representative of the United Nations' Secretary-General, Jacques Klein.[10] Klein was convinced that Bosnia Herzegovina, as a new country with porous borders, required a service that could control its borders, thereby preserving its sovereignty, territorial integrity, political independence and 'international personality'.

Klein's aggressive approach to state building reflected that of the international community. The requirement for a Bosnia Herzegovina state border police was first raised at the December 1997 Peace Implementation Council in Bonn, and the drafting of preliminary legislation took place in the following months. The high representative finally imposed a border service directorate designed to enforce Bosnia Herzegovina law on the SBS in January 2000, after the repeated failure of Bosnia Herzegovina's State Parliament to promulgate the resultant *Law on the State Border Service*. The State Parliament ratified it in the summer of 2001, a number of SBS units were inaugurated in the following months, and a training centre was opened. By 2002, staff levels were approximately 1400, divided between a head-quarters and 15 units. By 2003, there were approximately 2400 police, 10 percent of whom perform administrative duties.

The creation of the SBS also resulted from the international community's determination that the new service should be a showcase for an autonomous multi-ethnic police. Indeed, this desire has consistently shaped its development; witness the successful proposal by the office of the high representative in 2004 that the SBS, together with a new State Investigation and Protection Agency (SIPA) and local police forces, should be merged into a single national police structure, to be monitored at state level. International commitment to the SBS's success ensured that the United Nations Mission in Bosnia Herzegovina border service department would control the SBS's development and management, that the service's integrated border control management model is based on European Union standards, and that its equipment and training reflects international standards and approaches. The SBS inherited little in the way of resources, so extensive equipment and training programs were needed; pre-war Bosnia Herzegovina did not have an international border or border force, so the new guards had no experience of controlling international borders, identifying forged documents, or dealing with illegal immigration. Many countries, including Austria, Germany, Hungary, Italy, the Netherlands, Sweden, Switzerland, the United Kingdom and the United States, gave bilateral financial assistance, donations, and training programs.

The SBS's formal organisation and objectives reflect the philosophy of such donors, for whom democratic (that is, Schengen-style) border management is a normative priority, a legitimising principle, and an organising device. Assistance is seen as a tool to ensure that Bosnia Herzegovina has the working structures and capacity needed to function as a country, meet the challenges of transnational crime, grasp the opportunities offered by the European Union's stabilisation and association process, and deter illegal migrants. In other words, the service fulfils multiple objectives.

2.1   Strategic Options

The SBS strategy is designed to achieve four major objectives. Firstly, Schengen-type border control in terms of security and increased awareness; secondly, harmonisation with European Union border control and customs regulations; thirdly, to curtail illegal migration to western Europe; and lastly, to control border security while contributing significantly to the effective collection of customs and excise revenue by channelling goods to customs points and diverting traders to legitimate crossings where duties can be levied.

The two fundamental themes shaping the service's development are security and state building. The first theme, security, is critical. Bosnia Herzegovina is a springboard to the European Union for illegal migrants and organised crime, and the SBS is intended to act as a filter mechanism for the European Union's own security. The function was accordingly defined as including the supervision of state border and airport security, control over state border crossings, discovering and preventing indictable offences and apprehending the persons committing them, and investigating border-related criminal offences within the border jurisdiction (up to ten kilometres from the border); the offences are mainly those of organised crime, illegal migration, trafficking and corruption. It was always thought essential that the new service should possess operational flexibility, mobility, strong investigative and intelligence capabilities, and a proficient information technology network and data server. Ambassador Klein consequently stressed the need for international cooperation, which meant that importance was attached to information exchange, readmission agreements, joint control zones, joint patrols, and joint intelligence and investigation between Bosnia Herzegovina and its neighbours.

Secondly, the service represents an experiment in both state and institution building. International assistance to Bosnia Herzegovina's institutions ensured that it has the working structures and capacity needed for it to function as a viable country. To this can be added pressures from both the international community and the entities for a 'professional' and multi-ethnic institution. This is reflected in the service's budget and its guards' conditions of service. By early 2003, the total deployment budget was $US28.3million, of which 61 percent was for salaries, 15 percent for allowances, 11 percent for operating costs, and 13 percent for capital budget. Salaries range from €648 per month for the director and his deputies, to approximately €240 for the most complex jobs performed by officers with low educational standards. It also explains the service's distinctive management model. The Border Service Directorate (BSD) is at the apex of the model, with the Chief of the Border Service Department reporting directly to the commissioner of the United Nations Police Task Force (IPTF) or his equivalent. The SBS Directorate meanwhile consists of three equal directors, one from each ethnicity, who are appointed for a period of four years (the first appointments were made in 2000), with the directorship rotating between the three every eight months. (This helps get round the problem that so far Bosnia Herzegovina's state institutions have been weak when compared with entity administrations of the Federation and Republika Srpska). The director and his two deputies report to the Council of Ministers on political issues and work closely with the chief of the service. They also supervise the internal control unit of the SBS, which deals with disciplinary matters.

2.2   Assessment

The importance of border security is clearly recognised in Bosnia Herzegovina. The return of nationalist parties to power in the general elections of July 2002, for example, implied an awareness of the importance of strong borders. And at a regional conference in Sarajevo in October 2003, Deputy Security Minister Mektic underlined this by emphasising Bosnia Herzegovina's determination to adopt European standards regarding border security: 'We are absolutely determined to fight against terrorism, organized crime and especially drugs smuggling, human trafficking, illegal migration, etc' (OHR BiH Media Round-up 2003).

The success of the SBS is unsurprising, given the political capital and resources invested in it. The service is expensive but it is amongst the most advanced border systems in the region and its creation is a major achievement. It has enhanced the authority of the state, and increased its revenues, making a real contribution to securing financial resources for the budgets of both the state and the entities. It has had an impact on uncontrolled migration too, thereby acting as a filter mechanism for the European Union. In 2000, for instance, nearly 25,000 people passing through Sarajevo airport were unaccounted for (the figure can probably be doubled because Sarajevo was thought to be the starting point for thousands of immigrants from Iran, Turkey, Bangladesh, China and Sri Lanka), but within 12 months of controls being put in place, the figure had dropped to 9000. On balance, significant progress has been made (Tuzla Night Owl 2003).

Even so, vested interests are problematic. New security agencies are always vulnerable to sabotage, manipulation, or co-option by the agents or structures whose interests are threatened. Not surprisingly, various attempts were made to use entity votes and ethnic control of key areas to sabotage or subvert the SBS; the Bosniac nationalist Party of Democratic Action (SDA) argued that electoral losses in 2000 mattered little provided it retained control of key positions in the border and intelligence services (Hylton 2002: 161). The ability of international organisations to deal with this is limited, although the monitoring of appointments, financing and training by international officers helped the service avoid compromising its formal functions and legal framework.

Even so, SBS has yet to escape from its social and political environment. It has adopted several strategic documents authored by international groups, but has then failed to implement them. The notion that it exists to enforce the law rather than the wishes of the government of the day means little because ideas such as personal accountability are absent from the existing police culture. Corruption, low quality recruits and incompetence are real problems. So too is the service's powerlessness in the face of well-organised smuggling operations enjoying political protection. Similarly, the SBS cannot touch the most profitable forms of organised crime in Bosnia Herzegovina (human trafficking and smuggling) because they are a regional rather than local problem, and regional cooperation leaves much to be desired. Dealing with the minority communities that dominate border areas is particularly difficult, for their interests are threatened by an effective centralised border service. Similar considerations apply to the ethnic groups' militaries and intelligence agencies (which are to be unified). International pressure for specific forms and standards of border management are, as ever, offset by social and regional realities.

3.   MACEDONIA

In contrast to the state border service of Bosna Herzegovina's civilian nature, Macedonia's border system is militarised. The Macedonian–Yugoslav border was not marked during Milosevic's time, but a demarcation agreement was signed after his fall in October 2000, and Macedonian security forces began to patrol the border. This threatened the interests of organised crime in Kosovo, and soon led to Macedonia's security forces clashing with protection units linked to the smuggling chains that ran from Macedonia into Kosovo, Montenegro, Albania, and Bosnia Herzegovina, and on into western Europe (International Crisis Group, November 2002). Indeed, the conflict of 2001 began when Macedonian troops tried to impose border controls in Tansuševci, a smuggling village bordering Kosovo. Insurgents and criminal gangs quickly took advantage of the security vacuum in the border regions between Macedonia, Albania, Kosovo, Serbia and Montenegro. Large tracts of Albanian dominated areas were soon beyond state control, and certain villages became notorious as transit points for illegal goods, and as recruiting and training bases for Albanian extremists. High levels of illegal migration and human trafficking on the country's northern and eastern borders made matters worse. In addition, Macedonia became a trans-shipment point for heroin from south-west Asia and cocaine from Latin America, although drugs, weapons, tobacco and alcohol are smuggled in most of the country.

Macedonia's borders are porous and unsafe, its border regions poor or corrupt according to European Union norms, and the scale and intensity of armed confrontations on its borders is significant. NATO units patrol in the northern border area, and Macedonia's own border brigade is fully integrated into the military chain of command. Border security units from the under-resourced and ineffective regular police are only present at official border crossings, while the customs service is unarmed and reliant on the police for protection. Not surprisingly, much of the wider European Union debate about border control is prompted by the insecure state of Macedonia's borders.

3.1   Strategic Options

Macedonia's strategic options are limited. It can continue to place poorly trained military forces and ineffective police on its insecure borders, or it can gain international credibility by reforming its border system in the light of Schengen standards. Elements of both options are evident, although Macedonia's formal objectives are dictated by its strategic priority of achieving European Union membership; President Trajkovski signed Macedonia's formal application to join the European Union the day before his death. Macedonia is therefore in the process of reforming its existing system of border security along the lines advocated by the *Schengen Catalogue*.[11] The goal is to develop a specialised multi-purpose police force by means of integrated border management.

This strategy results from a number of conflicting trends. The first is the dominant role of Macedonia's military in border matters. Ministers argue that the main task of the army is to maintain Macedonia's borders and ensure its territorial integrity; this is only to be expected in the circumstances. Regional security challenges may be shifting from military to criminal threats, but boundaries are blurred when the criminals concerned are heavily armed gangs. Responsibility for border security is, accordingly, split between the Ministry of Defence, which is responsible for surveillance of the green and blue border by means of its conscript-based Border Brigade, and the Ministry of the Interior's Border Crossings Sector (BCS). The BCS, which is responsible for formal border checkpoints, consists of police officers that are posted to border crossing points on a rotational basis (there are approximately 6000 uniformed officers in the police, and 16 border police stations). A degree of cooperation exists between the BCS and other agents with an interest in border-related matters, such as customs and health services, but relations between the police and military are bad; police at border crossing posts often have no information on the green borders running alongside checkpoints.

The second trend results from the focus of the international community moving from military-oriented peacekeeping operations to confronting organised crime. Echoing this, Prime Minister Crvenkovski argues that the main threat to stability is no longer armed conflict, but criminality; Macedonia must therefore develop a police-based response. But neither law enforcement nor criminalisation are straightforward in Macedonia, not least because anecdotal evidence suggests that many of the senior police involved in border management are corrupt, as are those further down the chain. Vested interests play a significant part in developments too. Political infighting at the governmental level is intense, and senior officers are promoted, moved sideways, sacked or retired (according to their political skills and connections) more frequently than is the case in most European Union forces.[12] No doubt most senior officers wish to have the best of both worlds, whereby opportunities for personal gain are combined with the status associated with Schengen's professional guards.

Macedonia's priority remains national security ('the protection of the state border line'), but its goals now include developing coherent national standards, and the transformation of the existing surveillance regime based on the Army of the Republic of Macedonia (ARM) into a law enforcement agency of specialised border police. The chosen strategy is best seen in terms of Macedonia's project for integrated border management, a major element within which was a CARDS's project intended to enhance the operational capacity of the new service within the existing organisational framework. This would effectively fulfil immediate needs at the same time as developing the new organisational structure and operational capacities necessary for compliance with European Union standards (for details, see European Agency for Reconstruction, 2003).

3.2   Assessment

The current government broadly accepts the reforms promoted by international donors, but many of the programs associated with reform will take years to complete. Meanwhile, the situation in Macedonia represents a real challenge to Schengen's standards. In particular, the factors subverting reform must be addressed. Organised crime, guns, and entrenched corruption shape the environment in which reform is to occur, and to this may be added social deprivation, ethnic tensions, and political and economic instability. Such factors affect both the operational environment of guarding, and guards as individuals and as a group.

Organised crime is arguably the single biggest threat to security and stability in Macedonia. The gangs concerned are adept at exploiting the weaknesses of members of the government and security forces, which in turn protect them (International Crisis Group, November 2002). The seriousness of organised crime is intensified by the easy availability of guns (Quin 2003). Corruption, meanwhile,

> especially at high levels of government, is endemic. It has evolved from passive exploitation to active coercion and acquired the capacity not only to retard economic progress but also to feed organised crime and, in turn, political and communal instability. In effect, the state has come to function in important respects as a 'racket', while the racketeers thrive in a culture of impunity (International Crisis Group, August 2002: 1).

The system encourages autocratic administration, inefficiency and the politicisation of the security services, including those responsible for border security.

The extent to which the Macedonian state depends on borders as a marker of territory is thus complex. There is no national security strategy as such, and both military and police are inexperienced and inappropriately trained. Macedonia's smuggling interdiction capabilities are limited, while the Border Brigade's doctrine is outdated, its tactical capabilities weak, and it has little ability to gather intelligence or conduct threat assessments. But this situation arguably has more to do with a fundamental lack of political will than inadequate resources. International organisations are prepared to fund reform because they cannot afford to ignore Macedonia's border vulnerabilities. Thus, the European Commission allocated €3.3 million from its year 2001 budget for police reform, with about half the amount being disbursed. Separately, the European Commission (through the European Agency for Reconstruction) implemented a major program for integrated border management (including customs as well as the proposed border police) involving some €14 million over the past four years. The Ministry of Interior, however, is seemingly unwilling or unable to cooperate.

3.3   Ohrid Conference

Old and new style border management collide in Macedonia. In particular, the role played by its military reflects wider European controversies concerning the appropriate balance between police and military roles in border management: the European Union sees border management in Macedonia as an inherently civilian task on which it should lead, while NATO insists that it is sometimes better placed to handle it (International Crisis Group 2003b: 8). The dispute came to a head when NATO officials accused the European Union of sabotaging the conference that NATO had initiated on border security and management in Ohrid, on the Albanian border, in May 2003.

The conference was called to develop a coherent and concerted approach to border security in the western Balkans. It addressed border management and anti-trafficking operations in the region, especially where, for exceptional reasons, military units are temporarily involved in border security and interdiction operations. And it focused on the need for common political goals, objectives, principles and procedures, especially during transitional periods; that is, before the military withdraw and specialised police take responsibility, or where military units are involved in protection or interdiction operations. Its aim was the transfer of control to appropriate civilian authorities as soon as possible. But although Schengen standards clearly require border security to be the responsibility of the new border police, some NATO officials argued that Macedonia's northern border still requires a military presence: Kosovo's status is unresolved, armed extremists enter the province, and ARM are currently involved in 'combat positions' in the crisis regions. Nonetheless, this may not be a real problem. Some senior European Union officers insist that both may be appropriate according to context, while others promote the role of paramilitary units on the basis of France's experience of using gendarmerie. NATO, meanwhile, continues to provide advice on the military aspects of reforming and restructuring border security.

Both approaches are probably appropriate according to context. Certainly most guards accept the need for a rapid reaction force, and proposals for such a unit in Macedonia won some support from the international community; NATO was particularly keen. The unit's personnel would be mainly military, with some police elements, and the ARM, in 'cooperation' with the police, would control it. NATO justifies this as consistent with the overall framework for reforming ARM—at the expense of a civilian border police.

4.   ALBANIA

The capacity and desire of the Albanian state to assert its authority at the border are low, and Schengen standards mean little in a society with no tradition of respecting the law and an administrative culture developed for a repressive state.

Albanian border security is in theory conventional. Border police, whose task is not shared with the army, staff all border checkpoints (though the specialised mobile groups replacing the old static units are to be 'fused' with military units).[13] Authority for border security flows from the Ministry of Public Order, which delegates police duties to the State Police Directorate, and thus to the Central Border Police Directorate (which is part of the State Directorate), and down to local border directorates. The law on the state police charges the Central Directorate with controlling the state border, and adhering to Albania's multinational border regimes and readmission agreements. All relevant regulations are contained in the law on surveillance and control.

In reality, Albania's record is extremely poor. Attempts by Albania's corrupt governments to address the country's dishonest security services, high unemployment, decayed infrastructure, and deeply rooted criminality have been ineffective, while the activities of Albanian organised crime are notorious across Europe. Levels of trafficking in arms, contraband, and illegal migrants are high, and Albania is a major trans-shipment country for heroin and cocaine. Albanian border management is marked by inefficiency, corruption, lethargy, and a non-functioning structure. There is no separate, fixed, or formal border police. Indeed, the system barely functions. There are separate border policing units inside the state police structures, and there is a specific recruitment policy, but border police do not have their own resources or career paths. The border police may have a fixed number of staff (about 1680), but officers are rotated between the various state police units and none are specialists. Most trained officers were trained under the old regime, but more than half the police have not been trained at all.

As a result, Schengen standards mean little to the untrained generalists, while the few who have received training from international projects do not use their training because they are moved between units. National and local databases in forged documentation are not available. Appropriate legislation exists but even senior officers find difficulty in identifying the relevant laws and legislation; officers rarely have knowledge of, let alone access to, the existing regulations. Add harsh weather and poverty to an almost total lack of resources and the realities of Albanian border management become only too clear, as the small, dark and broken-down premises of many of Albania's border crossings show.

4.1   Strategic Options

The past decade in Albania has been marked by political and economic instability, violence, and the rise of organised crime, but Albania's small western-trained elite is increasingly concerned about its image abroad, and the government has begun talks with the European Union on a stabilisation and association agreement (similar to those signed with Croatia and

Macedonia). Much border-related legislation has been reformed in recent years, but this has not been part of a coherent strategy. There are signs that this situation is changing. In January 2004, for example, after the deaths of a number of illegal immigrants trying to reach Italy, the government introduced a number of reforms aimed at fighting organised crime, and reducing corruption amongst police and customs officials, allowing it to claim that 2004 was to be a decisive year in the fight against trafficking. Nevertheless, the European Union's member states remain concerned about the government's commitment to improving law enforcement and reducing the pervasive corruption; poor border security has been one of the greatest obstacles to Albanian membership of NATO and the European Union (Hope 2002).

The strategic options available are limited but sharp. Albania wishes for better relations with the European Union, which cannot ignore Albania's non-existent border security; the numbers of illegal migrants transiting through Albania means that Albanian migration, border control and asylum policies urgently need to be aligned with European Union standards. In March 2003, prompted by bad international publicity, the government for-mally accepted that it must develop a strategy for reform (using the framework of integrated border management). At that time, a two-phase reform strategy for border control was submitted to the Ministry of Public Order by the International Centre for Migration Policy Development. The 150-page report, *Upgrading the Border Guarding System of Albania Along European Standard,* outlined a radically new border control system whereby Albania can achieve a degree of compliance with Schengen's standards. This has, however, yet to be developed.

4.2   Assessment

The Albanian Government is now keen to show that it patrols its borders effectively and is committed to fighting organised crime and uncontrolled migration, but its exercise of authority faces many obstacles. These include geography, centralisation, policing standards and social realities. Thus, Albania's coastal location and proximity to Italy ensures that trafficking remains a major problem. The government's attention, meanwhile, is focused on Tirana, not Albania's border regions; the north is neglected and effectively untouched by economic and social progress evident elsewhere (International Crisis Group, February 2003: 10). Policing standards are very low. The border police are not part of the national police as such, but it is difficult to believe that they have avoided the factionalism, corruption and inefficiency characterising it and Albania's other security forces.

Above all, social realities obstruct policing in a society where key social issues include the growth of organised crime, corruption and poverty. Guarding is, moreover, a dangerous business because large numbers of arms and ammunition are in circulation or are hidden in border regions. The government initiated a number of high profile measures, but such projects merely displace crime as the gangs concerned move elsewhere. Further, the current government (like its predecessor) pays little attention to organised crime's links to guards, customs officials and politicians. This is unlikely to be seriously addressed by a society in which all forms of business are conducted on the basis of personal connections; conventional notions of criminalisation have little meaning. Tellingly, Transparency International's latest reports have no chapter on Albania because it is unable to identify a sufficiently broad-based, or impartial network. Given these factors, effective guarding is unlikely.

The obstacles to reform in Albania are consequently serious. Against this it may be argued that much has been achieved in the decade since the collapse of the one-party state, most of it without outside intervention. Indeed, the International Centre for Migration Policy Development believes that Albania's border management is 'in a transitional development process'.[14] But what has not changed is the political elite's seeming inability or unwillingness to take corruption and illegal trafficking seriously. Similar considerations apply to the senior security officers whose opportunities would be threatened by reform. Indeed, an effective or efficient border system is probably not in the interests of either group. As a result, reform strategies have been implemented and negotiations with the European Union on a Stabilisation and Association Agreement begun, but reform has yet to take place. It is noteworthy that Albania's border laws, like much of its legislation, now consist of a mix of imported foreign standards that are difficult to enforce.

5.   CONCLUSION: CONTINUITY AND DISCONTINUITY

How and why neighbouring border systems differ is best explained in terms of the political skills and vested interests of the senior officials and officers involved, the social realities of corruption, poverty, and underdevelopment, and the geographical proximity of the countries concerned to the European Union; Schengen's influence appears to decrease with geographical distance. National systems and practices reflect the complex bargaining, vested interests and social realities involved in the exercise of state security.

Each country is, of course, unique, yet common patterns of functional development are identifiable, and many of the assumptions underpinning regional explanations and practices are shared. This is particularly noticeable amongst senior officers, many of whom know each other. To what extent, therefore, can a regional consensus regarding the exercise of state border authority be identified? To what extent has the significance of borders become blurred, or security become de-territorialised?

5.1 Shared Assumptions

Most border forces in the region face similar problems; illegal trafficking is a regional, rather than national, issue. They probably share a defensive culture comparable to that of the public police too. Each aspires to develop national strategies accommodating Schengen's requirements, each has the same formal core mission, and each shares a broad understanding of what border security entails. Additionally, regional cooperation is seen as crucial for the development of effective border security, and as a way forward for both individual countries and the region as a whole. The development of common regional standards based on Schengen principles is accordingly emphasised, as are closer ties with Brussels and non-European Union third countries, together with the exchange of border-related information, the creation of a regional-level risk assessment system, joint operations along common borders, and a network of liaison officers.[15] Most senior guards think that intra-regional ties, as well as those between the region and the European Union and third countries, should be strengthened as a matter of urgency. The European Union, meanwhile, supports the development of integrated border management in each country, as well as regional cooperation mechanisms. Many countries in the Balkans confront challenges similar to those of European Union applicant and candidate countries, and the standards, as embodied within the Schengen *acquis* and *Catalogue*, are consequently seen as providing a means for measuring the convergence of regional border services to appropriate functional standards.

Whether such developments mean that the meaning and exercise of state authority on borders has blurred is, however, questionable. For there are sharp political limits to cooperation, even if this is glossed over by the vocabulary employed by many senior guards. Organised crime may challenge the significance of borders, but security has yet to be de-territorialised— witness the importance attached to border control in Bosnia Herzegovina and Macedonia.

5.2   Subversive spaces

The extent to which changes in the political rationale or meaning of
border security have been prioritised over the functional transformation of
the policing structures and institutions delivering it is, however, difficult
to assess. To some extent the search for an answer to this question is
unprofitable, for it is impossible to disentangle the tight links between the
European Union's political project, its response to security threats that are
not amenable to military solutions, the region's strong desire to be part
of Europe, the inherent resilience of security organisations, the strength of
vested interests, and social realities. What is clear is that developing a
regionally appropriate model of border security has been a priority for the
European Union in recent years and pressure has been brought to bear on
countries in the western Balkans to adopt not only the European Union's
functional standards, but also its understanding of democratic governance.
Regional systems are expected to adhere to or reflect Schengen's precepts.
Additionally, Schengen itself is attractive to the region's border guards as it
is seen to offer a means to enhance their status. This is because Schengen's
complex rules must be implemented by a specialist, skilled, and autonomous
police adhering to 'European' standards, rather than by the poor relations of
a despised public police. Most senior officers therefore accept the general
principle that while border security ultimately serves national interests,
Schengen standards represent an international functional benchmark.

Border security matters, then, for political, practical, and theoretical
reasons. Trends in border management are indicative of both the continuing
importance of borders as territorial markers, and of the extent to which
managing cross-border challenges requires the integration of international,
regional, national and sectoral interests. Further, guards exercise state
authority at the intersection of a number of topical concerns, where many
contemporary problems pose themselves with peculiar intensity. They
manage the interface of military and police powers, external and internal
security, and conventional and new security threats. Even so, pronoun-
cements by senior officers are often spoilt by the actions of their juniors.
Border standards adapt to local norms, and the transferability of Schengen-
style border management to the region is less certain than the European
Union might wish.

Thanks are due to the International Border Security Advisory Board of the Geneva Centre
for the Democratic Control of Armed Forces (DCAF), in whose company much of the
research for this paper was conducted, November 2001–March 2003: Aare Evisalu, Arto
Niemenkari, Andrus Öövel, Jürgen Reiman and Zoltan Szabo. Parts of this chapter
appeared in Hills (2005).

[1]   For an exception, see Andreas (2003).

[2] Decisions as to whether guards should be referred to as a 'force' or a 'service' have more to do with politics than functional standards.

[3] BBC Monitoring/KosovaLive website, quoted by Centre for South East European Studies; http://www.csees.net/news.

[4] Major omissions include the systematic analysis of comparative data. See International Organization for Migration (2000: 79).

[5] The Schengen *acquis* lays out the written rules and commonly accepted standards for border management within the Schengen sphere. See Niemenkari (2002).

[6] The International Centre for Migration Policy Development (ICMPD) is an inter-governmental organisation based in Vienna; http://www.icmpd.org.

[7] For integrated border management, see European Commission (2002).The European Agency for Reconstruction is an independent agency responsible for managing the main European Union assistance programs in Serbia and Montenegro, and Macedonia.

[8] Personal communication, Geneva, March, June 2003.

[9] Statement by Jonas Widgren (ICMPD) on behalf of the Border Guard Task Force of the Stability Pact, Bucharest, 6 June 2002.

[10] This section is based on a series of personal communications, discussions and interviews with Jacques Klein, his advisers, SBS officers, and Boznia Herzgovena officials, February 2002–March 2003.

[11] The material used in this section is based on interviews and discussions in Helsinki, Kassel and Geneva, April 2002, June 2002 and March 2003.

[12] The relationship between criminals and politicians raises disturbing questions. See, for example, European Stability Initiative.

[13] The information in this section is based on interviews, discussions and private correspondence with Albanian officers and officials, April 2002–March 2003.

[14] Personal communication, Geneva, March 2003.

[15] This section is based on material presented at three DCAF workshops, Geneva, January–March 2003.

REFERENCES

Andreas, P., 2000, *Border Games: Policing the U.S.–Mexico Divide*, Cornell University Press, Ithaca.

Andreas, P., 2003, Redrawing the line: borders and security in the twenty-first century, *International Security*, **28(2): 78–111**.

Community Assistance for Reconstruction, Development and Stabilization,

European Commission, 2002, IP/02/661, Commission proposes integrated management of the EU's external borders to secure the area of freedom, security and justice (7 May 2002) Brussels.

European Commission, .*Multi-annual Indicative Program 2002–2004: CARDS Assistance Program to the Western Balkans,* annexed to the European Commission's Regional Strategy Paper 2000–2006; http://www.ear.eu.int/agency.

European Agency for Reconstruction, 2003, *FYR Macedonia Annual Program 2003*; http://www.ear.eu.int/macedonia/fyrom-alc2f3g4.htm.

European Stability Initiative, *Ahmeti's village*, http://www.esiweb.org/pages/rep/rep_mac_02.htm.

European Union, 2002, *Schengen Catalogue. External Border Control, Removal and Readmission: Recommendations and best practices*, Brussels.

Hills, A., 2005, *Border Security in the Balkans: Europe's Gatekeepers*, Adelphi paper No. 371, Oxford University Press for IISS, London.

Hope, K., 2002, Albania: crackdown follows EU pressures, *Financial Times*, 18 December.

Hylton, J, 2002, Security sector reform: BiH Federation Ministry of the Interior, *International Peacekeeping*, **9(1): 161**.

International Crisis Group, 2002a, *Macedonia's Public Secret: How Corruption Drags the Country Down*, Balkans Report 133 (August 2002).

International Crisis Group, 2002b, *Moving Macedonia Toward Self-Sufficiency: A New Security Approach for NATO and the EUICG*, Balkans Report 135 (November 2002).

International Crisis Group, 2003a, *Albania: State of the Nation*, Balkans Report 140 (March 2003).

International Crisis Group, 2003b, *Macedonia: No Room for Complacency*, ICG Europe Report 149 (October 2003).

International Organization for Migration, 2000, *Migrant Trafficking and Human Smuggling in Europe: A Review of the Evidence with Case studies from Hungary, Poland and Ukraine*, Geneva.

Niemenkari, A., 2002, *EU/Schengen Requirements for National Border Security Systems*, DCAF Working Paper 8 (March 2002); http://www.dcaf.ch/publications/Working_Papers/08.pdf.

OHR BiH Media Round-up (27 October 2003); http://www.ohr.int/ohr-dept/presso/bh-media-rep/round-ups.

Quin, D., Jovanovski, V., et. al, 2003, *Armed to the Teeth: Disarming Civilians in Albania, Kosovo and Macedonia Means Making them See Guns are a Threat to Security, not a Guarantee*, Investigative Report 470, November; http://www.IWPR.net/Balkans.

Tuzla Night Owl, 2003, The State Border Service is making great results (11 November 2003) 8:321; http//www.tfeagle.army.mil.

Chapter 8

STATE CRIME BEYOND BORDERS
Europe and the outsourcing of irregular migration control

Penny Green
University of Westminster

Europe's sea borders are in a process of fortification, which is increasingly taking place extra-territorially. European Union member states for a number of years have been developing partnerships, and regional agreements with third countries, in a concerted effort to contain irregular migrants and asylum seekers in regions of origin or transit countries. According to a major report by Oxfam, some 90 percent of asylum seekers are now forced to enter the European Union irregularly because circumstances preclude the obtaining of visas and travel documentation required for regular entry (Oxfam 2005: iii).

In late 2004, the European Commission sent a technical delegation to Libya with the intention of 'initiating dialogue and cooperation with Libya on migration issues'. Despite a number of human rights concerns arising from the mission, the Home Affairs Council in June 2005 supported the 'need for a comprehensive and integrated approach to migration in the Mediterranean which encompasses dialogue and cooperation with Libya' (Council of the European Union 2005).

In this chapter, I examine the outsourcing of irregular migration control by the European Union. Focusing on the partnership agreement between Italy and Libya and the broader European strategy that it heralds, I chart developments within European asylum policy which resonate strongly with Australia's vilified 'Pacific solution'. In doing so, I argue that these developments will further increase the vulnerability of asylum seekers to criminal practices and omissions by states and their agents (Green and Ward 2005).

S. Pickering and L. Weber (eds.), Borders, Mobility and Technologies of Control, 149–166.
© 2006 *Springer. Printed in the Netherlands.*

1.   THE DEVOLUTION OF IRREGULAR
IMMIGRATION CONTROL

Since the 1990s, Europe has been working consistently to divest itself from the immediate responsibility of protecting, processing and accepting asylum seekers and refugees. During the 1990s, it used the carrot of European Union membership to encourage candidate states to act as a bulwark against irregular migration in Eastern Europe. As Hayes and Bunyan (2003: 72) explain '[v]isa requirements, bilateral readmission agreements between EU and candidate countries, EC funding and technical assistance to immigration and border police authorities, declarations that central and eastern European countries are safe for the return or protection of refugees, and the condition that accession candidate countries must implement the EU Justice and Home Affairs acquis in full before they can be considered for full accession' comprised the incentive and conditions package that resulted in the creation of what is now widely described as a 'buffer zone'.

Later, the idea of devolving the control of irregular immigration was to be extended even further. The idea of exporting European responsibility for refugee protection to nations of origin and transit well beyond the close borders of the European Union was first mooted by Britain. Explicitly inspired by Australia's extra-territorial 'Pacific solution' and driven by the stated desires to reduce the number of asylum seekers entering Europe and to strengthen the external borders of the Union, the Cabinet Office together with the Home Office issued a policy document in March 2003, *New International Approaches to Asylum Processing and Protection.*[1]

The British proposal (supported by both the Dutch and Danish governments) was two-pronged—the first involved regional protection zones which were to be established in regions where conflict or disaster had created significant internal displacement. The zones were to provide accommodation and protection until such time that the internally displaced or refugees could return to their homes of origin. The second prong, transit processing centres more blatantly embodied the government's anti-asylum message. These centres were, as Baldaccini (2005: 3) has argued, 'unambiguously holding camps' to be established just outside Europe's borders to which asylum seekers and other irregular migrants caught attempting to enter the United Kingdom and other European Union countries would be sent. Here in the camps (managed, it was envisioned, by the International Organization for Migration) claims for asylum would be processed and successful applicants resettled in Europe on a 'burden-sharing basis'. Those unsuccessful were to be repatriated to their country of origin or provided with temporary protection until it was safe for them to be returned (Home Office 2003a). The point being that irregular migrants would not be able to enter Europe until a successful application for asylum had been processed and approved outside the European Union. Oxfam (2005: iv) describes the transit processing centres as a 'dangerous idea ... discredited on grounds of legality, morality and practicality'. In June 2003, the European Union rejected the United Kingdom's proposals arguing that rather than shifting the asylum burden outside the European Union, sharing the 'burden' was more consistent with the first phase in the development of a common European asylum system. However, over the past two years, the emphasis on refugee 'protection' has been couched increasingly as an 'external' problematic and in subsequent debates, the European Council has shown considerable interest in the regional management component of the United Kingdom proposals. This 'interest' was formalised with the European Council's adoption of The Hague Programme in November 2004 which has as its pivot 'migration partnerships'. While clothed in the language of refugee protection and sympathy for overstrained developing countries, European Union 'migration partnerships' with third countries are primarily concerned with establishing border controls which contain irregular migrants in countries of origin or transit regions and with establishing agreements on return and readmissions. It is now not difficult to envisage the resurrection of the United Kingdom's proposed transit processing centres given that regional management has 'come to define the EU's external approach to immigration and asylum' (Baldaccini 2005: 3).

The European Union neighbourhood policy focuses on countries closer to Europe—specifically those regarded as problematic because of the transit opportunities they present for irregular migration (that is, those countries bordering Europe in the south and east: Algeria, Egypt, Morocco, Tunisia, Libya, Israel, Jordan, Syria and the Palestinian Authority; Ukraine, Moldova, Belarus, Armenia, Azerbaijan and Georgia).

In relation to the external dimension of asylum and migration, The Hague Programme outlines European Union policy priorities as: 'prevent and combat illegal immigration, inform on legal channels for migration, resolve refugee situations by providing better access to durable solutions, build border-control capacity, enhance document security and tackle the problem of return' (Annex 1, 14292/04: 20). In order to pursue these aims, the European Council is encouraging partnerships with third countries, countries and regions of origin and countries and regions of transit and on the development of a return and re-admission (removal and repatriation) policy (Annex 1, 14292/04: 21). Migration partnership, while avowedly designed to tackle both migration flows and issues of refugee protection capacity within partnership countries, have demonstrably not been about refugee protection, rather, the focus has singularly been on immigration control. As Baldaccini (2005: 16) argues, these partnerships, '[i]n return for trade and aid concessions ...

attempt to establish a series of concentric circles in which states outside the EU play an ever-increasing role in assisting the application of the EU migration management priorities'.

The idea of European Union Regional Protection Programmes (RPPs) was endorsed by The Hague Programme in 2004 and the European Commission has been tasked with their development. Essentially, RPPs are to complement migration partnerships by encouraging self-reliant refugee protection, administration, reception and local integration schemes in countries of origin. Effectively, European Union member states will be able to remove asylum seekers to any country willing to accept them without any consideration of the merits of the asylum claim and without adequate safeguards, despite the implicit breaches of the Geneva Convention involved.[2] According to Baldaccini (2005: 10), member states have considerable latitude in setting down rules under which the presumption of safety can be challenged in individual cases and they will not be obliged to obtain assurances that the third country concerned will process the claim'.

As the United Nations High Commission for Refugees (UNHCR) has warned, the 'safe third country' provisions of the directive should not result in 'any precipitous initiatives to declare such countries safe in the absence of acceptable protection safeguards'.[3] It is not difficult, however, to imagine RPPs becoming an excuse for denying asylum claims in European Union member states and for the justification of wide-scale returns to countries which in reality may be far from 'safe'.

In addition to RPPs and neighbourhood partnership agreements, the Council also wants an end to internal border controls within Europe with a concomitant strengthening of surveillance and control over the external borders of the European Union (under the authority of national border authorities) (Annex 1 14292/04: 23).

What this actually means is developing a multi-pronged European strategy of exclusion which involves the interception of asylum seekers before they reach the borders of the European Union; in countries of transit, to halt further movement and to process asylum claims; and in regions of origin, to increase protection capacity and establish 'orderly entry' mechanisms; and in the refugee's country of origin, to negotiate readmission/return.

2.   GENERAL OVERVIEW

Despite strong evidence that asylum claims to most European Union countries are declining,[4] the number of refugees and other 'persons of concern' to the UNHCR has dropped by 18 percent in the past three years to 17.1 million, and the rate of removals for failed asylum seekers has increased, many European governments are taking increasingly restrictive measures to control the asylum process (UNHCR 2005). As a result, asylum seekers are becoming increasingly vulnerable to state crimes (perpetrated by both European Union and third country states) as the humanitarian principles underlying the Geneva Convention in respect of refugee protection are steadily eroded. Migration management and control underpins the European neighbourhood policy while improving refugee protection is barely paid lip service. Liz Fekete (2005: 5) locates this erosion of humanitarian protection in the development of a common European asylum policy:

> In the EU the shift from protecting refugees to protecting states can be seen most clearly in the development of a common asylum policy based on set targets both to reduce the numbers of asylum claims and to increase removals of failed asylum seekers.

The attempts to establish a common European asylum policy—an agenda for harmonisation set in the Treaty of Amsterdam 1997—have resulted in the establishment of standards set below many of the member states' own domestic standards which sometimes did not even conform to the minimum standards required by international law (European Council on Refugees and Exiles 2004).

It is estimated that around 4000 asylum seekers or irregular migrants drown at sea every year as they attempt to flee conflict, persecution and poverty. Around 2000 of these drownings are estimated to occur in the Mediterranean Sea as desperate people risk dangerous sea crossings in the hope of finding their way to western Europe (Pugh 2005; Moorehead 2005). According to Pugh, around a third of those who begin these perilous voyages die en route. They depart from Libya, Tunisia or Morocco, having already journeyed thousands of miles from sub-Saharan Africa, or countries such as Iraq, Bangladesh and Palestine. According to a report in the *European Race Bulletin*, those attempting to reach Europe as irregular migrants almost always rely on the services of traffickers or smugglers for at least some part of their journey (Fekete 2003a: 3; Morrison 2000).

3.   FROM LIBYA TO LAMPEDUSA, RETURN

A focus on one neighbourhood partnership foreshadows the vision Europe seeks to develop as a union and demonstrates the nature of state criminality and human rights abuse taking place as a result of increasingly exclusionist approaches to European asylum policy.

Despite the earlier rejection of the United Kingdom's proposed transit processing centres, the European Union has moved purposively toward introducing elements of Australia's infamous 'Pacific solution' to irregular migration. Following its political and diplomatic 'rehabilitation', Libya is set to become for the European Union what Nauru is for Australia—both a buffer and a filter between the rest of Africa and Europe—a zone of exclusion wherein hundreds of thousands of irregular African migrants en route to Europe may soon be held in refugee camps. It will be in Libya (and possibly later in Morocco, Mauritania, Algeria and Tunisia) that European 'offshore processing' will take place.

Until 2004, Libya was the only north African country which did not share a formal agreement with the European Union on tackling irregular migration. As a result, and combined with Gaddafi's pan-Africanist policies, it became a magnetic transit destination for refugees across Africa and the Middle East (*The Guardian* 2004). According to Libyan officials, up to two million irregular migrants have found their way to the Libyan coastline in the hope of finding passage to western Europe. With the assistance of people smugglers north and south of the Sahara, these migrants pay small fortunes (up to $US 2000 each) to be transported in overcrowded and often woefully unseaworthy wooden vessels or rubber dinghies to the outposts of western Europe. Italy, with its 7600 kilometres of coastline, and its close proximity to north Africa, has in recent years become the first country of arrival for more asylum seekers or irregular immigrants than any other member of the European Union (Moorehead 2005: 55)

According to the UNHCR, over 5000 irregular migrants have lost their lives attempting to make the crossing to Italy in the past decade. It is the small Italian island outpost of Lampedusa—the main island in the Pelagie Archipelago, 200 kilometres south west of Sicily—geographically only 275 kilometres from Libya, which has been the focus of Italian irregular migration control and the harbinger of a wider European strategy of exclusion and state crime. The route between Libya and Lampedusa has become—despite its treacherous waters—a preferred crossing point for thousands of Africans attempting to reach Europe. In July 2004, almost 800 boat migrants arrived on Lampedusa; in December of the same year, over 700 irregular migrants were intercepted off the coast of Lampedusa on five different vessels; in March 2005, over 1000 irregular migrants arrived within 48 hours; in May of the same year, over 600 arrived in Lampedusa, and within 24 hours a further 100 were intercepted to the south of the island. Despite the continual arrival of thousands of irregular migrants each year, detention facilities on the island are designed for only 190 people (Migration News Sheet (MNS) August 2004; January, April, May 2005). When the investigative journalist Fabrizio Gatti, in the guise of a Kurdish asylum seeker rescued from the island's waters, was placed in Lampedusa's detention centre, he reported on the extreme overcrowding, lack of sanitation and the demeaning and sometimes violent treatment meted out to refugees in the centre. In direct contradiction of Italy's Interior Minister, Guiseppe Pisanu's, assurances to the European Commission that a hearing before a justice of the peace was always carried out to validate all detentions on Lampedusa, Gatti reported that no such hearings took place during the period of his detention for any of those detained with him (Gatti 2005).

4. ITALY AND LIBYA—A PARTNERSHIP AGREEMENT

In July 2003, Italy and Libya signed a bilateral agreement aimed at combating irregular migration from Libya to Italy (Migration News Sheet May 2004). The Italian partnership agreement with Libya follows in the wake of Italy's Anti-landings Decree (2003) which, in response to a 33 percent increase in landings by sea, grants the Italian police special powers to intercept and turn back boats before they enter Italian waters and provides for the extended presence of the Italian navy in international waters for the purpose of stopping and searching vessels suspected of involvement in people trafficking. Italy, as part of its 'permanent liaison' with Libya, has also financed a program of repatriation flights from Libya to countries of origin (which have included conflict zones such as Eritrea) and a detention camp for illegal migrants (with a further two such camps to be financed in southern Libya) (Trucco 2005: 1).

A further agreement between Silvio Berlusconi and Colonel Gaddafi, signed on 25 August 2004, committed Libya to sealing its southern border with Niger, readmitting the *extracomunitari* sent back from Italy, and repatriating foreigners who had entered Libya from the south. In return, Italy lobbied the European Council to lift the arms embargo placed on Libya in 1986. For many years, Libya had argued that European Union sanctions on arms sales had hampered any efforts it might make in controlling irregular migration. Its inability to purchase high speed vessels, radar equipment, night-time surveillance equipment and so on limited its capacity to control its own borders. Italy's Interior Minister, Giuseppe Pisanu, had warned that if Europe refused to lift sanctions in September 2004, Rome would resume military cooperation with Tripoli to control irregular migration by sea, regardless (MNS September 2004). Libya's declaration that it would no longer pursue weapons of mass destruction, its willingness in 2004 to pay compensation to the victims of a terrorist attack in Berlin, intense lobbying from Berlusconi, a United States decision to lift sanctions, and the European priority to control asylum seeking finally led to the European Union formally lifting sanctions against Libya in October 2004. That Libya might use European Union weapons and technology against irregular migrants in ways incompatible with international law was not a consideration for the European officials involved in the decision.

The Italian-Libyan agreement was couched in guarantees given by Berlusconi that 'no-one would be deported to the Sahara, detention camps would not be built in the desert and deportations would only be carried out by air.' The same report, however, provides evidence that foreigners inside Libya have been targeted by the Libyan security service' in 'dawn house-to-house raids, of people seized in the street or outside workplaces, and of tens of thousands herded into the Al Gatrun detention camp in the desert, and taken to the Sahara' (quoted in Gatti 2005).[5]

This exclusion operation has targeted foreigners from across sub-Saharan Africa including Senegal, Mali, Nigeria and Cameroon. These foreigners had been invited to work in Libya and during the years of the western embargo, Gaddafi abolished entry visas for them. Following Gaddafi's Italian agreement, the situation for these guest workers is now precarious. Gatti (2005) reported that '[o]ver 100,000 are believed to have already been captured or persuaded to leave. 14,000 were thrown out into the desert in February alone, loaded onto the 72 lorries that crossed the border'. According to the *Red Crescent*,[6] since the Libyan deportations began, at least 106 people have died during these repatriations through the desert from Tripoli to Libya's southern borders. Gatti (2005) reported that the dead included those deported from Lampedusa. The worst incident saw 50 immigrants crushed to death when their overloaded lorry overturned on the treacherous pass of Tumu on the Libya–Niger border.

Italy has on number of occasions violated the *non-refoulement* principle of the 1951 Geneva Convention and has consistently flaunted its own asylum and immigration laws in order to control irregular migration from Libya. In the first week of January 2004, over 1500 irregular migrants were summarily deported by the Italian authorities to Libya without any judicial review. Further deportations from the detention centre in Lampedusa continued throughout 2004 and into 2005 (with around 1000 collective expulsions to Libya in October 2004 alone) despite widespread condemnation by human rights non-government organisations. Moreover, when 37 African irregular migrants were rescued by the humanitarian ship *Cap Anamur* from their sinking ship in August 2004, the Italian authorities arranged for diplomats from several of the countries of origin to see them in spite of clear indications that they were seeking asylum. According to the UNHCR, 'Exposing possible refugees to a representative of the government that may be responsible for their flight is contrary to basic refugee protection principles. (MNS 2004: 13). When the claims of 36 of the asylum seekers were examined by the five-member central commission which processes refugee claims in Italy, it recommended that 22 of the Africans be allowed to remain on humanitarian grounds. Despite this recommendation, the Italian authorities proceeded with expelling all 36 (MNS August 2004).

In May 2005, the European Court of Human Rights asked Italy to suspend the expulsion of 11 irregular migrants to Libya. The case, presented by a team of Italian lawyers, is part of a wider campaign contesting the legality of Italy's collective expulsion of irregular migrants to Libya. (Networking Human Rights Defenders [FIDH] 2005).

Playing the anti-terror card, Guiseppe Pisanu argued that the mass expulsions were necessary as part of the fight against terrorism, 'that obliges us to be particularly vigilant about the clandestine immigrants coming from the Horn of Africa, where al Qaeda is well established, and those from the sub Saharan zone where Islamic extremism is undergoing rapid growth' (cited in MNS November 2004: 12).

The European Parliament has also expressed disapproval of Italy's policy of collective expulsions to Libya,[7] but Italy's negotiated agreement with Libya continues to be seen as an opportunity to push back Europe's borders and to contain what has been described as the 'refugee crisis' within the borders of Africa.

5.   EUROPE AND THE ESTABLISHMENT OF CAMPS

Motivated by Italian negotiations with Libya, the President of the European Commission met with Colonel Gaddafi in Brussels in April 2004. At this meeting, Gaddafi offered to cooperate with the European Union in combating terrorism and irregular migration by sea in return for European investment in Libya's oil and tourism industries (MNS May 2004).

Led by Germany's Minister of Interior, Otto Schily, and his Italian counterpart, Giuseppe Pisanu, serious consideration is now being given to a strategy which would involve the creation of immigration 'gateways' established outside Europe, that is, the effective 'outsourcing' of asylum decision-making and processing to Libya and possibly Morocco, Algeria and Tunisia. Officers in camps established in north Africa would determine an applicant's right to asylum and refuge would be sought as near to the applicant's country of origin as possible. For Schily, refuge in Europe would be an exception. Pisanu presented the envisaged processing detention camps as a 'kind of job centre' from which European countries could select immigrants according to preferred destination and which would act as a counter against trafficking gangs. While traffickers south of the Sahara could not be controlled, Pisanu argued that it was possible to assume responsibility for the organisation of 'decent maritime transport for accepted immigrants' (MNS November 2004). Only Spain and France have voiced their opposition to the establishment of camps ('humanitarian reception centres' in the words of the European Commission) in third countries, such as Libya (MNS November 2004). The United Kingdom has remained supportive but silent on the proposed camps.

While Morocco has rejected the plan[8] (*El Pais*, quoted in MNS November 2004) and Algeria 'cannot accept having a camp on a Maghreb country's territory where illegal immigrants will be cooped up waiting for their papers to be processed in a European country'(Official News Agency, cited in MNS November 2004). Libya's own response has been ambivalent. While working closely on the repatriation scheme and border control with Italy, Gaddafi, in an interview with Italian Radio (RAI), declared that his country could not be 'the coastguard of Europe' and 'Libya alone cannot stop millions of people coming from Africa' (MNS January 2005: 5). Earlier, Shoukri Ghanem, the Libyan Prime Minister, had argued that camps for illegal immigrants in 'certain countries' would not resolve the problem for Europe; instead, he argued that irregular migrants must be helped 'to remain where they are' by creating local employment opportunities in countries of origin. (MNS December 2004: 4).

In a letter to the European Minister delegate of Foreign Affairs and Immigration, dated 1 June 2005, Peer Baneke, the General Secretary of the European Council on Refugees and Exiles, warned of the dangers and consequences of negotiating a framework of cooperation with Libya which would include returns from the European Union.

> Morocco, Libya, Algeria and Tunisia are countries people flee from. In Libya, hundreds of critics and dissidents of the Gadaffi dictatorship have disappeared. Many have been tortured or executed. The fundamental freedoms are restricted and the death penalty applies for a whole series of minor offences (Kopp 2004).

In their *Freedom in the World* annual assessments, Freedom House has consistently rated Libya as offering the very least freedom in terms of political rights and civil liberties.[9] The organisation Human Rights Watch report that asylum seekers and irregular migrants (particularly sub-Saharan Africans) living in or in transit through Libya have been attacked by police, arbitrarily detained in sub-standard conditions, or expelled to countries such as Somalia and Eritrea where their safety can in no way be guaranteed (Human Rights Watch 2004).

According to Human Rights Watch:

> Given Libya's terrible treatment of migrants and asylum seekers, the EU's offshore processing centres would likely violate the right to seek asylum. The EU would be shifting responsibility for migrants and asylum seekers to a developing country with a poor human rights record.

Similarly, Amnesty International has argued that Libya, as a state party to the Organization of African Unity (OAU) *Convention Governing the Specific Aspects of Refugee Problems in Africa*, has violated its *non-refoulement* principle several times with the forcible return in July and August of 2004 of hundreds of Eritreans, many of whom Amnesty International believe were detained incommunicado under harsh conditions in a secret detention centre (Amnesty International 2005).

6.   BORDER CONTROL

Fekete (2003b: 3) has argued that the central purpose of the European Union Council's border control programme (which grew out of the Seville Summit, June 2002) 'is to create as many barriers to refugee movement, in as many different countries and regions, as possible and, in the process, extend the EU's zone of influence over border controls'. As a result, there has been a steady erosion of the humanitarian obligations laid on governments by the Geneva Convention to protect those fleeing persecution. Contrary to international law, and Article 31 of the Geneva Convention, the European Union's border control programme penalises those who use illegal means to enter a country for the purpose of seeking asylum. Moreover, the act of seeking asylum through irregular means becomes not only criminal but implicates the irregular migrant in the international organised crime of trafficking. According to the European Council on Refugees and Exiles 'the fact is that EU member states have made it nearly impossible for asylum seekers to gain access to the EU in regular ways' (2005; see also Fekete 2004: 75).

Australia has provided both a very specific blueprint and a 'moral' precedent for the European challenge to the Geneva Convention. Australia's raft of border protection legislation,[10] which followed the dramatic rescue of 433 asylum seekers by the Norwegian freighter *MV Tampa*, and the Australian Government's subsequent refusal to allow the asylum seekers onto Australian territory, has led to a permanent naval blockade in Australia's territorial waters. Boats carrying asylum seekers or irregular migrants detected in Australian territorial waters are intercepted and escorted to international waters. At the same time, under the *Migration Amendment*

(Excision from Migration Zone) Act 2001, small Australian islands and territories on potential trafficking routes between Asia and the Australian mainland were excised so as not to be considered part of Australia for the purposes of migration. Just as the 'Pacific solution' and the legislation which enshrines it was designed to prevent irregular migrants from entering Australian territory or from seeking refugee protection on one of Australia's outlying islands or territories, so can the arrangement which Italy has fostered with Libya be understood.[11]

At their June 2005 meeting, European Union ministers of justice and the interior expressed their 'utmost concern about the human tragedies that take place in the Mediterranean as a result of attempts to enter the EU illegally' (MNS July 2005). While the European Union's Justice and Home Affairs Council argues that its desire to establish cooperative arrangements with Libya is motivated by the humanitarian disasters described above and the desire to prevent further loss of life, the evidence suggests overwhelmingly that these tragedies are a consequence of precisely the strategies of repressive border control which the European Union is seeking to reinforce with its Libyan dialogue. When the worst post-war tragedy at sea involving the drowning of 283 irregular migrants took place off Sicily in December 1996 the European Commission was silent. So too were the Commission's member states, all of whom failed to express concern at this appalling loss of life. Without bodies washed up on European beaches, this tragedy remained an open secret among the fisherman of the Sicilian island of Portopalo who recovered body parts in their fishing nets for years afterwards (MNS July 2005). It is therefore somewhat disingenuous for the European Commission to argue that its attempts to negotiate asylum control arrangements with Libya is being driven by humanitarian concerns. The fact that Libya has become a transitionary *mecca* for potential illegal migration to Europe far outweighs any officially expressed justification for current bilateral negotiations.

According to Statewatch, the tragedies such as those described above 'only become commonplace after the adoption of restrictive immigration policies … which force would-be migrants to seek alternative, illegal and often life-threatening ways to travel to their destinations' (Statewatch News Online 2005). By blaming the drowning of thousands of irregular migrants instead on 'poorly managed migration flows' the myth which sustains European Union immigration policy allows it to negotiate arrangements with Libya, formally satisfied by Libya's stated commitment to fulfil its international obligations with regards to the protection of refugees, and to respect the principle of *non-refoulement*.

Certainly, Italy's own practice of the mass repatriation of irregular migrants without an opportunity to apply for asylum, and its refusal to allow UNHCR officials to meet with those repatriated, does not auger well for the thousands of would-be asylum seekers at the heart of these developments (MNS August 2004).

7.   EXPORTING THE BORDER

Within the context of The Hague Programme, and following pressure from a range of European states, but particularly those in the southern Mediterranean (Italy, Malta, Cyprus), the European Commission sent a technical mission to Libya to develop a plan of cooperation and assistance in respect of irregular migration emanating from the north African country. Despite underlining that cooperation between the European Union and third countries must be guided by 'principles of full respect of human rights, the rule of law and the demonstration by those countries of a genuine commitment to fulfil their obligations under the Geneva Convention of Refugees', the fact that Libya fails to conform to the majority of these principles has proven no barrier to the initial stages of the process. In June 2005, European Union member states formalised cooperation with Libya over a range of immigration issues but voiced reservations such that the 'extent and development such a cooperation will depend on Libya's commitments on asylum and human rights' (MNS July 2005: 7).

The agreement includes a training program for Libyan border guards and police officers involved with irregular immigration; the development of a joint risk analysis in respect of illegal migration toward Libya and the European Union; the possibility of intensified cooperation around migration management; and, significantly, to provide assistance for the upgrading of existing centres for irregular migrants to increase Libya's capacity to hold those awaiting passage to western Europe (MNS July 2005). According to Gatti (2005), Alfredo Mantovano, Deputy Leader of the National Alliance, reported with a degree of satisfaction, 'from a certain point of view Libya is a de facto member of the Schengen area … the first political effect of these agreements is that Libya is taking back the *clandestini* against whom it has been unable to conduct an exclusion operation'.[12] According to the Migration Service News, 'It is no secret that north African countries with perhaps the exception of Libya which wants something quite different in return, are rather reluctant to make use of their limited resources to assume the role of border guards on behalf of the EU and prevent irregular migrants from heading for western Europe' (MNS September 2004: 4).

8.   STATE CRIME AND THE 'MEDITERRANEAN SOLUTION'

The important question when assessing the criminality of states in relation to asylum policy and practice is not so much the potential illegality of states in these processes but the extent to which state activities in relation to refugees and forced migrants can be understood as deviant and subject to sanction by audiences external to the state's own formal legal mechanisms (Green and Ward 2004; Pickering 2005; Grewcock 2006 forthcoming). Across the board, leading transnational human rights non-government organisations (including Human Rights Watch, Amnesty International, Oxfam and the European Council on Refugees and Exiles) have condemned the European Union's proposed outsourcing of asylum processing and management.

In an earlier paper co-authored with Grewcock, I argued that the European response to irregular migration was primarily an issue of state identity based on restricted entry and the development of a European state apparatus. The evidence I have presented in this chapter around the development of neighbourhood partnership agreements strongly reaffirms that analysis. The European project has involved increasingly restrictive immigration policies which exclude refugees; a policy emphasis on 'border protection'; an increased use of military-style policing the border; increasing levels of cooperation between different state agencies and different states; a focus on trafficking as an aspect of transnational organised crime, analogous to drugs or terrorism; and a desire to 'externalise border control' by imposing and enforcing restrictions on entry before there is a physical possibility of crossing the border, including the creation of buffer zones in neighbouring states (Green and Grewcock 2002). European asylum policy has continued to be built upon principles of exclusion (often widely condemned by transnational civil society) while the excluded are reconstructed as threats to a 'common understanding' of what Europe is. In the process, traditional protections and rights accorded to asylum seekers and refugees have been seriously eroded. The anticipated outsourcing of asylum processing and 'protection' to a country such as Libya, where no framework of refugee protection even exists, is a dramatic but logical extension of the European project.

European Union member states have obligations to those seeking asylum from persecution under the 1951 convention as well as under the European Convention for Human Rights, yet as one of the world's leading refugee non-government organisations has reported (Oxfam 2005: 16), rather than honour these obligations:

member state's actions, both in negotiating EU legislation, and in taking unilateral measures, have repeatedly shown that the overriding concern of member states is to reduce the numbers of asylum seekers on their territory.

As Green and Grewcock have argued, 'the failure by states to positively embrace the right to asylum and attempts by states to systematically minimize any responsibilities they hold in relation to those seeking asylum, have resulted in the systematic and organised breach of human rights' (2002: 88), which can usefully be defined as state crime.

Italy, as I have discussed, has violated the *non-refoulement* principle of the 1951 Geneva Convention. Thousands of irregular migrants have now been repatriated en masse from Italy to Libya without being given the opportunity to apply for asylum and at the same time denied access to the UNHCR. In addition, many have been exposed by the Italian authorities to officials from potential countries of origin deemed unsafe by the UNHCR.

More specifically, the 'war' against irregular migration itself results in systematic crimes perpetrated by state agents policing borders as the example of the treatment of detainees in Lampedusa's detention centre and the practice of violent expulsion and deportation in Libya demonstrate. This 'war' forces many seeking asylum into the hands of exploitative organised crime networks, which increasingly offer the only hope of escape for those fleeing repression, terror, discrimination or civil conflict (Kyle and Koslowski 2001). As such it ensures organised crime networks expand and flourish. The state has, therefore, actively encouraged the growth of organised trafficking by restricting all legitimate means of seeking asylum. As 'legitimate' avenues for the seeking of asylum have been closed, irregular migrants have been increasingly forced into perilous clandestine journeys such as those across the Mediterranean Sea during which thousands have met their deaths. There is little doubt that European asylum policies have actively contributed to the increasingly dangerous routes irregular migrants are now forced into taking. While European Union member states have invested heavily in strategies designed to control irregular migration, the impact has been to block 'safe and legal ways for asylum seekers to access protection in EU member states, forcing them into dangerous situations' (Oxfam 2005: 34).

If the European Commission pursues the outsourcing of its asylum obligations; if it continues to advance neighbourhood and regional partnership agreements with third countries in pursuit of this organisational goal; and if it continues to develop militarised border control arrangements with countries such as Libya, then irregular migrants will become increasingly vulnerable to an even wider range of state abuse and organised crime than is currently experienced. With the aim of consolidating a European identity, and facilitated by state organisational crime, what we might well call the 'Mediterranean solution' may soon eclipse the exclusionary practices of Australia in the Pacific.

I am very grateful to Liz Fekete from the Institute of Race Relations for sharing with me valuable insights on this topic.

[1] Available from http://index.homeoffice.gov.uk/nstory.asp?itemid=424.

[2] Under the directive on minimum standards on procedures for granting and withdrawing refugee status: Article 27 Doc 14203/04.ASILE 64, 9 November 2004 (adopted Spring 2005).

[3] United Nations High Commissioner for Refugees, Mr. Ruud Lubbers, Talking Points for the Informal Justice and Home Affairs Council, Luxembourg (29 January 2005); http://www.unhcr.ch.

[4] Europe as a whole (44 countries including countries of the former Soviet Union and former Yugoslavia) saw asylum applications decline by 21 percent between 2003 and 2004 (UNHCR 2005).

[5] Translated by Imogen Forster for the Institute for Race Relations (10 August 2005); http://www.irr.org.uk/2005/august/ak000011.html.

[6] Red Crescent is a branch of the Red Cross organisation operating in a Muslim country. The crescent-shaped emblem replaces the red cross.

[7] See European Parliament, resolution Lampedusa (14 April 2005) P6_TA-PROV (2005) 0138.

[8] *El Pais* (1 October 2004) cited in *Migration News Service* (November 2004: 4).

[9] http://www.freedomhouse.org/ratings/index.htm.

[10] Including *Migration Amendment (Excision from Migration Zone) Act 2001* (Cth), *Migration Legislation Amendment Act 2001*(Cth) and *Border Protection (Validation and Enforcement Powers) Act 2001* (Cth).

[11] For detailed discussion of Australia's 'Pacific solution', see Pickering (2005); Marr and Wilkinson (2003).

[12] On 14 June 1985, the Federal Republic of Germany, France, Belgium, Luxembourg and the Netherlands signed the Schengen Agreement (Schengen being a place in Luxembourg) on the gradual abolition of checks at their common borders. On 19 June 1990, the *Convention Implementing the Schengen Agreement* was signed. Its key points relate to measures designed to create, following the abolition of common border checks, a common area of security and justice. Specifically it is concerned with:

- harmonising provisions relating to entry into and short stays in the Schengen area by non-European Union citizens (uniform Schengen visa);
- asylum matters (determining in which member state an application for asylum may be submitted);
- measures to combat cross-border drugs-related crime;
- police cooperation (hot pursuit);
- cooperation among Schengen states on judicial matters.

REFERENCES

Amnesty International, 2003, *UK/EU/UNHCR Unlawful and Unworkable: Amnesty International's Views on Proposals for Extra-territorial Processing of Asylum Claims* (June 2003) London; http://web.amnesty.org/library/pdf.IOR610042003ENGLISH/$File/IOR6100403.pdf.

Amnesty International, 2005, *Urgent Action: Italy / Libya*; http://www.amnesty.ie/content/view/full/3613/.

Baldaccini, A., 2005, EU partnerships under the Hague Programme: trading immigration controls for refugee needs, *Justice*; http://www.justice.org.uk/inthenews/main.html.

Betts, A., 2003b, *The Political Economy of Extra-territorial Processing: Separating 'Purchaser' from 'Provider' in Asylum Policy*, New Issues in Refugee Research, Working Paper 91, UNHCR, Geneva.

Betts, A., 2004, The international relations of the 'new' extra-territorial approaches to refugee protection: explaining the policy initiatives of the UK government and the UNHCR, *Refuge* (March 2004).

Council of the European Union, Brussels, 2005, *Note from the Presidency to the Council. Subject: Draft Council Conclusions on Initiating Dialogue and Cooperation with Libya on Migration Issues*, doc no 9413/1/05 REV1 (27 May 2005); http://www.statewatch.org/news/2005/ jun/01eu-libya.htm.

European Council on Refugees and Exiles, 2004, *Broken Promises—Forgotten Principles: An ECRE Evaluation of the Development of EU Minimum Standards for Refugee Protection, Tampere 1999– Brussels 2004*, June 2004; http://www.ecre.org.

European Commission, 2004, *Technical to Libya on Illegal Immigration 27 Nov–6 Dec 2004*, Report 7753/05 DGHI, Brussels

European Council, 2004, *The Hague Programme*, annexed to the Presidency Conclusions, Brussels:European Council, 4 and 5 November, para. 1.6.1.

Fekete, L., 2005, *The Deportation Machine: Europe, Asylum and Human Rights*, Institute of Race Relations, London.

Fekete. L., 2003a, Death at the border—who is to blame?, *European Race Bulletin*, 44 (July 2003).

Fekete. L., 2003b, From refugee protection to managed migration: the EU's border control programme, *European Race Bulletin*, 43, April.

Gatti, F., 2005, Sahara: the last journey of the damned, *L'Espresso*, 24 March.

Green, P. and Ward, T., 2005, *State Crime: Governments, Violence and Corruption*, Pluto Press, London.

Green, P. and Grewcock, M., 2002, 'The war against illegal immigration: state crime and the construction of a European identity, *Current Issues in Criminal Justice*, Special Issue: Refugee Issues and Criminology, **14(1): 87–101.**

Grewcock, M., 2006 forthcoming, Forced Migration and State Crime, unpublished PhD thesis, University of New South Wales.

Hayes, B. and Bunyan, T., 2003, Migration, Development and the EU Security Agenda in: *Europe in the World: Essays in Foreign, Security and Development Policies*, Bond, London.

Hayter, T., 2000, *Open Borders: The Case Against Immigration Controls*, Pluto Press, London.

Home Office [UK], 2003a, *New International Approaches to Asylum Processing and Protection*; http://index.homeoffice.gov.uk/nstory.asp?itemid=424.

Home Office [UK], 2003b, Home Secretary statement on zones of protection, Press Release (27 March 2003) London; http://index.homeoffice.gov.uk/nstory.asp?itemid=424.

Human Rights Watch, 2004, Libya blocks visit by rights group—torture, political trials, treatment of migrants remain major concerns, Press Release (7 December 2004).

Kevin, T., 2004, *A Certain Maritime Incident: The Sinking of SIEV X*, Scribe Publications, Melbourne.

Kopp, K., 2004, *Magazine for Development and Cooperation*; http://www.inwent.org/E+Z/content/archive-eng/11-2004/foc_art4.html.

Kyle, D., and Koslowski, R., eds., 2001, Global Human Smuggling: Comparative Perspectives, Johns Hopkins Press, Baltimore.

Marr, D. and Wilkinson, M., 2003, *Dark Victory*, Federation Press, Sydney.

Mathiesen, T., 2005, Lex vigilatoria—towards a control system without a state? in: *Essays for Civil Liberties and Democracy in Europe*, European Civil Liberties Network.

Migration News Sheet, 2004, 2005, *Monthly Bulletin on Immigrants, Refugees and Ethnic Minorities*, Migration Policy Group; http://www.migpolgroup.com/topics/2054.html.

Moorehead, C., 2005, *Human Cargo: A Journey Among Refugees*, Chatto and Windus, London.

Morrison, J., 2000, *The Smuggling and Trafficking of Refugees: The Endgame in European Asylum Policy*, UNHCR.

Noll, G., 2003, *Visions of the Exceptional: Legal and Theoretical Issues Raised by Transit Processing Centres and Protection Zones*, working paper; http://www.ecre.org.eudevelopments/debates/nollresponserev.pdf.

Oxfam, 2005, *Foreign Territory: The Internationalisation of EU Asylum Policy*, Oxford.

Pickering, S., 2005, *Refugees and State Crime*, Federation Press, Sydney.

Pugh, M., 2005, Drowning not waving: boat people and humanitarianism at sea, *Journal of Refugee Studies*, **17(1): 50–69**.

Statewatch News Online, 2005, *EU/Libya: Full steam Ahead, Without Pausing to Think*; http://www.statewatch.org/news/2005/jun/01eu-libya.htm.

The Guardian, 12 August 2004.

Trucco, L., 2005, Lampedusa—a test case for the subcontracting of EU border controls, in: *Essays for Civil Liberties and Democracy in Europe*, European Civil Liberties Network; http://www.ecln.org.

United Nations High Commissioner for Refugees, 2004, *The European Union, Asylum and the International Refugee Protection Regime, UNHCR's Recommendations for the New Multiannual Programme in the Area of Freedom, Security and Justice*, September.

United Nations High Commissioner for Refugees, 2005, *Asylum Levels and Trends in Industrialized Countries, 2004*, Population Data Unit/PGDS, Geneva.

Ward, K., 2004, *Navigation Guide: Regional Protection Zones and Transit Processing Centres*, The Information Centre about Asylum and Refugees in the UK, Oxford.

Webber, L., 1995, *Crimes of Arrival*, Statewatch, London.

Chapter 9

THE GENDER OF CONTROL
Violence against women on the United States-Mexico border

Jan Carpenter
Northern Arizona University

The story of enforcement of the United States–Mexico border over the last ten years is one of militarisation in which the war has shifted from urban to rural areas and the enemy/victim is increasingly female. Recent United States border policies and technologies of control have created a more hostile and violent environment for women without achieving the stated goal of reducing the number of illegal immigrants into the United States. Instead, border policies function to appease competing interest groups and as selective enforcement mechanisms enacted against women. On the Mexican side of the border, social control mechanisms operate against women in a similar fashion, in men's attempts to regain stability and power in times of rapid change.

The trend, beginning in the 1970s and through to the early 1990s, was toward Mexican immigrants' settlement in the United States rather than the earlier pattern of temporary or seasonal labour practices (Chang 2000: 5). Settlement tends to result in the empowerment of Mexican women migrants as they gain economic strength and are able to renegotiate patriarchal domestic relationships (see Sassen 1999 and Hondagneu-Sotelo 1994). In reaction to the perceived costs of settlement by Mexican women and families, United States border policies and militarisation of technologies of control reduced the options and increased the dangers for women wanting to immigrate to the United States.

In the 1990s, women began working in Mexican factories called *maquiladoras*, resulting in increases in their domestic and economic empowerment (see Lim 1990 and Nanda 1997). At the same time, the number of rapes and murders of women factory workers multiplied along the border. In this chapter, I propose that violent methods of social control used against women on the Mexican side of the border mirror the violence of

United States border policies and technologies of enforcement. Mexican women are the primary targets of drastic technologies of control on both sides of the border in efforts to reproduce traditional hierarchical relationships during times of rapid social and economic change.

In the first section of this chapter, I provide an overview of United States–Mexico border policies and their effects on the demographics of immigration. Next, I discuss the militarised rape by United States border agents and the rape and murder of women on the Mexican side of the border. In the final section, I provide concluding remarks.

1.   BORDER POLICIES

In response to the shortage of labour caused by World War II, the United States enacted the Bracero program as a temporary measure to allow Mexican men into the United States, primarily as seasonal agricultural workers. The Bracero program was in force from 1942 to 1964 and provided the American economy with a source of cheap labour that imposed few obligations on the United States in terms of social services or support. The costs of raising and educating these workers were incurred in Mexico, as were all the social costs of their families.

In the 1970s, more Mexican women and families migrated and began to settle permanently in the United States. By 1988, research indicated that women had become the majority of 'settled' undocumented Mexican immigrants (Chang 2000: 5). With the change in the gender of immigrants came a shift in United States rhetoric against immigration. No longer was the 'immigration problem' one of Mexican men stealing jobs from American workers; the problem was Mexican women, who were portrayed as 'idle, welfare-dependent mothers and inordinate breeders of dependents' (Chang 2000: 4). In response, in part, to media images of Mexican women pouring into the United States to have their babies and soak up social services, and costing United States taxpayers billions each year, in 1994, California passed Proposition 187 which cut off many public benefits to undocumented immigrants. The policy prevented undocumented children from receiving a public education and blocked women immigrants from claiming benefits to which they had previously been entitled, including prenatal and preventative health care such as immunisation (Chang 2000: 1). Governor Pete Wilson found that his appeals to eliminate medical, education, and welfare benefits to illegal immigrants produced political rewards in the form of his increased approval ratings. This so-called 'Wilson effect' did not go unnoticed by other political figures as immigration increasingly became a hot issue during an election year (Ellingwood 2004: 31).

In 1994, President Bill Clinton announced Operation Gatekeeper which focused border control efforts on busy urban corridors, starting with San Diego. Operation Gatekeeper provided the San Diego border patrol with $45 million to amass its forces along a border fortified with 'floodlights, fences, and an assortment of hardware such as buried sensors, night-vision goggles and military-style infrared scopes capable of distinguishing human forms in the darkness' (Ellingwood 2004: 35).

The result was a dramatic drop in apprehensions of illegal immigrants in the San Diego area. Democratic Senator Dianne Feinstein stated that, 'Operation Gatekeeper has really been an unprecedented success. What it tells me is it's a myth that the border cannot be enforced. It can be enforced' (quoted in Ellingwood 2004: 89). What Senator Feinstein did not mention was that, although the border was enforced in her political arena, during the five-year period that apprehensions were down in San Diego, they increased along the rest of the United States–Mexico border (Ellingwood 2004: 90).

Along with increased immigration came increased human rights violations and deaths as immigration moved from the urban areas to the more dangerous deserts and mountains. The Organization of American States filed a petition charging that the United States had overstepped its right to protect its border. As Ellingwood (2004: 68) points out:

> Operation Gatekeeper has steered this flow of immigrants into the harshest, most unforgiving and dangerous terrain on the California-Mexico border. The United States has done this knowing that the policy would dramatically increase the number of illegal border crossers who die and without taking adequate steps to prevent these deaths.

New United States border policies such as Proposition 187 and Operation Gatekeeper are not gender neutral. Chang (2000: 4) suggests that such effects are not unintended, that 'immigration from the Third World into the United States doesn't just happen in response to a set of factors, but is carefully orchestrated—that is, desired, planned, compelled, managed, accelerated, slowed, and periodically stopped—by the direct actions of US interests, including the government as state and as employer, private employers, and corporations'. She states (11) that the objective of border policies is:

> to capture the labor of immigrant men and women separate from their human needs or those of their dependents. In essence the goal of these laws and 'reforms' is to extract the benefits of immigrants' labor while minimizing or eliminating any obligations or costs, whether social or fiscal, to the 'host' US society and state. While it is easier to extract cheap labor from independent men through temporary worker programs

by recruiting single men, ensuring that they remain single, and ultimately ousting them once they have served their purpose, it is more difficult to accomplish this extraction from women who bear and care for children.

In California, Proposition 187 showed its framers' obvious intention to target Mexican women and children. By denying education and health benefits to children and prenatal care to women, the proposition made life more difficult for women immigrants. Operation Gatekeeper has accomplished the same goal in a much more subtle manner. By moving immigration routes from urban areas to remote, dangerous sites, the 'immigration problem' has not only been removed from the public eye (at least in more populated areas) it has also turned immigration back into a form that favours young, fit men and discourages women and children.

Though the stated goal of the United States southwest border strategy is to deter illegal immigration, 'the data suggest little or no reduction in the number of migrants, only a reduction in female undocumented migration relative to male undocumented migration. This implies that since the Southwest border strategy went into effect in 1994, settlement has decreased relative to temporary labor migration' (Brownell 2001: 80). As a result of Operation Gatekeeper, United States politicians look tough on immigration and have been able to benefit United States employers with a de facto Bracero program without incurring the wrath of American workers who see such a program as costing them their jobs. United States employers prefer temporary undocumented workers rather than those who are settled because they can pay temporary workers less in wages (Brownell 2001: 81). Without appearing to do so, the United States border policy has specifically targeted women and children immigrants; for the benefit of United States employers and politicians, Operation Gatekeeper has accomplished those precise results.

2.   RAPE ON THE BORDER

While Operation Gatekeeper changed the demographics of Mexican illegal immigration to the detriment of women and families, United States border policies have resulted in a militarisation of the border that provides an environment conducive to militarised rape. Until 1982, federal law prohibited cooperation between the army and civilian law enforcement. Since that time, changes in laws have allowed the United States–Mexican border to become militarised in two key ways: military units have been introduced and integrated in the border region and the border patrol has been modified 'to resemble the military via its equipment, structure, and tactics'

(Falcon 2001: 32). Enloe reports that this militarisation involves 'cultural, institutional, ideological, and economic transformations' (Falcon 2001: 32). Evidence of this militarisation is seen in the transfer of the Immigration and Naturalization Service (INS) from the Department of Labor to the Department of Justice (Falcon 2001: 32).

The militarisation of the United States–Mexico border that began in the 1980s was stimulated by the 'war on drugs' which added drug enforcement to the mission of the United States border patrol. Before that time, the military was largely removed from domestic law enforcement duties (Dunn 2001: 8). Dunn reports that, '[t]he recent shift toward a military role in the border region has gone largely unexamined by scholars and has occurred with little awareness or public debate'. Despite the killing by a marine of a United States teenager herding goats along the border near Redford in Texas, lawmakers continue to support the deployment of military troops along the border, passing three authorising Bills in the United States House of Representatives in the years 1997 to 2000 (Dunn 2001: 8). The militarisation of domestic law enforcement has significant human rights, and specifically gendered, implications.

According to Falcon (2001), rapes along the United States–Mexico border have been systematic and have taken the form of militarised rape against a racialised enemy. Rape in areas such as Bosnia and Rwanda has been recognised as a war crime, the purpose of which is not sex but power and the dehumanisation of women (Falcon 2001: 31). Falcon proposes that two types of militarised rape are occurring along the United States–Mexico border. First, national security rape used as 'an instrument for bolstering a nervous state' and secondly, systematic mass rape which is 'an instrument of open warfare' (2001: 33). These types of institutionalised, militarised rapes are characterised by the following conditions: a regime preoccupied with national security; the belief that security is a military problem; national security policy in the hands of a masculinised policy elite; and male domination of the police and national security apparatuses (Falcon 2001: 33).

While rape has always occurred along the border, especially as a 'price' for entry into the United States, the militarisation of the border contributes to the ideology of immigrant women as a racialised enemy in the United States national environment of 'us versus them.' Due to the lack of accurate data on the number of rapes along the border, it is impossible to conclude whether the incidence of rape has increased. However, the militarisation of the border has occurred and turning the United States–Mexico border into a 'war zone' creates a climate conducive to changing the nature of the power relationship between border agents and illegal women immigrants. According to Falcon (2001: 42), '[f]actors contributing to the prevalence of militarised border rape include unaccountability, abuse of power, ineffective hiring protocols, minimizing human rights standards, and a culture of militarization'.

On 3 September 1993, border patrol agent Larry Selders stopped two men and two women in Nogales, Arizona. The four had illegally crossed the border to go shopping. Agent Selders let the men go and detained the women in his border patrol vehicle. He informed the women that he would not take them to the border patrol station for processing and deportation to Mexico if they had sex with him. They refused. Selders let one of the women go, and allegedly drove off alone with the other woman and raped her. The women reported the crime, and on 25 July 1994, Selders entered a plea of no contest on a reduced charge of 'attempted transporting of persons for immoral purposes ... while married' (Falcon 2001: 36). He received a one-year sentence and was paroled after six months. A federal grand jury later indicted Selders with one count of civil rights violations, two counts of bribery and two counts of harboring undocumented people. He received a 14-month sentence for violation of civil rights but was given credit for time served. The woman received an award of $753,045 for the rape, which her attorney argued 'could have been prevented if Selders had been held accountable for previous acts of violence against women. Three other women testified ... that Selders had attacked them. ... Since Selders was a government employee at the time, the US government paid the monetary reward' (Falcon 2001: 36).

In May 1990, Immigration and Naturalization Service (INS) officer James Riley was charged with 'forcible rape with the use of a firearm, kidnapping and rape under the color of authority' for allegedly kidnapping a woman from a bar and raping her in his home (Falcon 2001: 36). Even though, as a member of the INS Employee Sanctions Unit, it was not a part of Riley's job to patrol for undocumented people, he told the woman she was under arrest because she did not have legal documents to be in the United States. Riley was also charged with eight other felonies involving four other women. He was found guilty of false imprisonment and acquitted of kidnapping and rape charges (Falcon 2001: 37).

On 16 December 1989, border patrol agent Santiago Esteves stopped a young woman and asked her for her immigration papers. He let her go, but later looked for the woman at her workplace and then found her at a shopping centre. She agreed to go with him. He took her to his home and allegedly told her that she had to have sex with him. He took out two guns. She testified that Esteves 'force[d] an object into her vagina, placed his hands on various parts of her body, orally copulated her, and forced her to have intercourse with him' (Falcon 2001: 39). Esteves was convicted of felony rape charges and received a 24-year sentence for which he served less than three years. Esteves was also accused of sexual misconduct involving two other women, but was not convicted of any crime.

In November 1996, border patrol agent Charles Vinson pleaded guilty to a charge of 'oral copulation under color of authority while armed with a firearm' (Falcon 2001: 38). The undocumented victim was attempting to reunite with her husband and son. Vinson had previously been removed from a horse patrol after he was accused by fellow border patrol agents of conducting aggressive and improper searches of women (Falcon 2001: 37).

The rapes reported in this paper represent a sample of crimes against undocumented women which resulted in conviction of border patrol or INS agents. It is reasonable to assume, given that they are in the United States illegally and that women often tend to be hesitant to report rape, that most undocumented women who are raped do not report the crime. Human rights groups report that sexual abuse of immigrant women by United States border patrol agents is rampant, and the 'system to hold Border Patrol agents accountable for such acts is weak at best' (Luibheid 2002: 121). Luibheid states that the way that rape cases have been handled by the INS shows that the organisation is 'institutionally complicit in making rape possible and negligent in its response to incidents of rape and sexual assault (127).

In her analysis of rape on the border, Luibhied (2002: 130) concludes that:

> Since rape is a technology for (re)producing hierarchical social rela-tionships, it reconstructs borders. These borders are not reducible to the nation's territorial borders, however. Instead, they involve social, economic, political, psychological, and symbolic borders within the United States that connect to sexuality, gender, race, and class inequities. Yet at the same time, the reproduction of these internal borders arti-culates with practices for controlling the territorial border. ... The interaction between the reproduction of the territorial and internal border is evident at two levels, in instances of rapes of undocumented women. First, as technology for reproducing social borders, rape inscribes undocumented women within US-based hierarchies of gender, sexuality, race, and class. But second ... undocumented women have almost no mechanisms available to protest or contest these inscriptions, especially when rape is perpetuated by Border Patrol agents. The fact that raped undocumented women have virtually no mechanisms for protest means that rape is also a site for the inscription of documented versus undo-cumented status as salient. Therefore, rape at the border by the Border Patrol is a site for the reinscription by the state of the social body as stratified by gender, sexuality, race, class, and legal status.

Border patrol agents who have raped women have tended to release them into the United States rather than return them to Mexico. The act of rape by border agents has not tended to function as a strategy to literally enforce national borders by keeping undocumented women out, but rather to keep them 'in their place' in terms of social, racial, gender, and national hierarchies. Like the rape of women in the former Yugoslavia and in Rwanda, women's bodies become the location for violent struggles for power in times of uncertainty, fear, and ethnic hatred.

In Mexico, various statistics indicate that only 17 out of every 100 abused women report the crime and that 95 percent of reported cases of sexual abuse go unpunished (Cevallos 1998: 2). In the case of a number of rapes on the Mexican side of the border, it is much easier to count the crimes because the women were murdered after they were raped. In Juarez, more than 300 women have been murdered in the last 11 years, and 70 are still missing. Many have been sexually assaulted, strangled, mutilated, and dumped in the desert (Katzarova 2004: 8). While initial reports stated that the women were prostitutes, many were *maquiladora* workers. Arrests have been made, but the rapes and murders continue. As recently as April 2004, another woman's body was found in the desert. Evidence indicates that there are multiple perpetrators (Gomez 2004: 31). Organisations such as Amnesty International and the Mexican National Human Rights Commission have criticised Mexican authorities for 'inadequate forensic work, faking evidence, coercing confessions and mistreating victims' families' (Burnett 2004: 14).

The city of Juarez in Mexico has 1.3 million inhabitants and 380 *maquiladoras* (Burnett 2004: 13). It is the country's fourth largest city (Balli 2003: 108). Roughly half the population are transients who come from all over Latin America hoping to cross the border into the United States. Many stay and find work in the *maquiladoras* (Hewitt et al. 2003: 119).

Reporters have latched on to the story of the Juarez murders. In an article entitled 'Death Comes to the Maquilas: A Border Story,' Nathan (1997: 18) reports that:

On a scorching day in August 1995 in Ciudad Juarez, Mexico, a trash picker combing an illegal dump site discovered the half-naked corpse of a young woman. Police eventually identified her as Elizabeth Castro, a 17-year-old from a poor neighborhood who had last been seen alive downtown a few days earlier. Since then in the same desert area—just a few miles south of El Paso, Texas eleven more female bodies have been found. Most were adolescents as young as 14. All were slender and dark-skinned, with shoulder-length hair. Many bodies are too decomposed to determine the cause of death, but the better-preserved victims were raped and strangled or stabbed. Most were partly unclothed, with their underpants torn. Some had their wrists bound; on some, a breast was mutilated or severed. Of the victims police have identified, all came from impoverished families. Last spring, seven more bodies turned up in another desolate part of town. Again, they were half-naked, bound and mutilated.

In an article entitled 'Girls Who Find New Roles in Mexico Also Face Danger,' La Franchi (1999: 6) reported on the 'Jack the Ripper-style' sex murders:

> The corpse of one of the first such victims, Alma Chavira Farel, was found in early 1993. An autopsy revealed she had been strangled and raped 'por las dos vias'—a Mexican euphemism for vaginally and anally. During the next several months, eight more young women were similarly murdered. The pattern continued in 1994 and 1995. By summer of that year, bodies were being discovered every few days, buried in or strewn around desert trash dumps near the city.

There are many theories about the murders. One relative of a murder victim points out that, '[t]he female workers in the *maquiladoras* are not the whole story. A certain percentage of the victims are young girls between the ages of 10 and 12. Victims also include students and young women [in] other businesses' (Diaz 2003: 14). The executive director of the Coalition for Justice in the Maquiladoras, Martha Ojeda, states that: 'The murders go beyond Juarez. There are also cases in Nogales, Tijuana, and Tamaulipas' (Diaz 2003: 14). In Chihuahua City, 15 young women have disappeared and nine corpses were found between 1999 and 2003 (Guillermoprieto 2003: 83).

The murders have been hypothesised to be tied to the drug trade, to Satanic sacrifices, to organ trafficking, to the police (Burnett 2004). Diana Washington Valdez (2005) has written a book on the murders, and has accused young members of prominent Juarez families of killing young women 'simply for the sport of it' (Burnett 2004: 12). Journalists, activists, and sociologists have developed the following theory to explain the murders (Balli 2003: 111):

> The story tells that when the immigrants came to Juarez from the countryside, they brought with them traditional Mexican ideas about gender. Women were to stay home, obey their husbands, and raise the children. But when wives and girlfriends and daughters began earning their own paychecks, they tasted a new independence and savored it. They bought nice things for themselves. They went dancing. They decided when bad relationships needed ending. In many cases, because

unemployment rates for men were higher, women even took on the role of breadwinner in their families. The men saw their masculinity challenged and lashed out. Their resentment, uncontained by weakened religious and community bonds, turned violent, into a rage that manifested itself in the ruthless killing of women.

Officials have concluded that 178 of the Juarez murders are the result of domestic violence, not a serial killer or unknown assailants (Lydersen 2003: 5). The founder of Juarez's only domestic violence resource center, Esther Chavez Cano, sees the murders 'as part of the larger picture of machismo and oppression of women in Juarez … domestic violence increases, alcoholism increases. The men don't have work and they feel like they are supposed to be the supporters of the family, so they are frustrated, and they abuse' (Lydersen 2003: 5).

While it is impossible to point to any one reason for all the murders of young women along the border, there is convincing evidence that the rape and murder of many of these women represent men's attempts to reassert dominance and traditional gender relationships. Women's empowerment sometimes comes at a very high cost.

3.   CONCLUSION

Mexican women in recent years have begun to increase their domestic and economic power by settling in the United States and by working in Mexican factories. To state that many women find that immigration and wage labour provide them with opportunities to challenge repressive social controls and to improve their lives is not to suggest that the life of a female illegal immigrant or factory worker does not come with significant costs, nor that immigration or factory work is the answer to Mexican women's problems. It does, however, emphasise the gendered nature of social changes on the border and provides a framework for discussing the technologies of control used against women.

Mexican women's crossing of national and social boundaries has resulted in restrictive and violent policies and practices against them on both sides of the border. United States border policy has shifted the entry routes to the United States to dangerous and remote locations, producing a de facto return to the Bracero program that tends to encourage migration of young, fit male workers and exclude women and families. Politicians and employers reap the benefits of a policy biased against Mexican women and families without appearing to do so.

As a result of the policy of militarisation of the United States border, women's bodies have become subject to militarised rape in a hyper-masculinised climate of nationalism and fear. Men are using rape on both sides of the border as a technology of control designed to terrorise and subordinate women in attempts to reproduce traditional hierarchical relationships.

REFERENCES

Balli, C., 2003, Cuidad de la muerte, *Texas Monthly*, **31(6): 108**.

Brownell, P., 2001, Border militarization and the reproduction of Mexican migrant labor, *Social Justice*, **28(2): 69–83**.

Burnett, J., 2004, Chasing the ghouls: The Juarez serial murders and a reporter who won't let go, *Columbia Journalism Review*, **42(6): 12–15**.

Cevallos, D., 1998, Serial rapes and murders on border with US, Interpress Service News Agency (11 August 1998); http://ipsnews.net.

Chang, G., 2000, *Disposable Domestics: Immigrant Women Workers in the Global Economy*, South End Press, Cambridge, MA.

Diaz, K., 2003, The border-murders mystery: Someone is killing young women along the US-Mexico frontier, *Hispanic*, **16(10): 14**.

Dunn, T., 2001, Border militarization via drug and immigration enforcement: Human rights implications, *Social Justice*, **28(2): 7–31**.

Ellingwood, K., 2004, *Hard Line: Life and Death on the US-Mexico Border*, Pantheon Press, New York.

Falcon, S., 2001, Rape as a weapon of war: advancing human rights for women at the US-Mexico border, *Social Justice*, **28(2): 31–51**.

Gomez, J., 2004, Death toll: 300 women and counting, *Lesbian News*, **29(11): 21**.

Guillermoprieto, A., 2003, A hundred women, *The New Yorker*, **79(28): 83**.

Hewitt, B., Macias Aguayo, A., Bard, A., and Sheff-Cahan, V., A wave of murders terrorizes the women of ciudad Juarez, *People*, **60(8): 4**.

Hondagneu-Sotelo, P., 1994, *Gendered Transitions: Mexican Experiences of Immigration*, University of California Press, Berkeley.

Katzarova, M., 2004, Letters from Juarez, *Nation*, **278(12): 8**.

LaFranchi, H., 1999, Mexican evolution for women's rights, *Christian Science Monitor*, **91(134): 6**.

Lim, L., 1990, Women's work in export factories: the politics of a cause, in: *Persistent Inequalities: Women and World Development*, I. Tinker, ed., Oxford University Press, Oxford.

Luibheid, E., 2002, *Entry Denied: Controlling Sexuality at the Border*, University of Minnesota Press, Minneapolis.

Lyderson, K., 2003, The disappeared: in Juarez's maquiladoras, murders of women continue, *In These Times* (9 June 2003).

Nanda, M., 1997, History is what hurts: A materialist feminist perspective on the green revolution and its ecofeminist critics, in: *Materialist Feminism: A Reader in Class, Difference, and Women's Lives*, R. Hennessy and C. Ingraham, eds., Routledge, New York, **pp. 363–394**.

Nathan, D., 1997, Death comes to the maquilas: a border story, *Nation*, **264(2): 18–23**.

Sassen, S., 1999, *Guests and Aliens*, New Press, New York.

Chapter 10

LAW AND ORDER ON THE BORDER IN THE NEO-COLONIAL ANTIPODES

Kerry Carrington
University of New England

The principles of enclosure within borders and the segregation of populations who belong from those who do not are the foundations of the sovereignty of the modern state. Border control measures deployed in the neo-colonial antipodes that arise from such conceptions of territorial sovereignty and statism consequently bear many similarities to the disciplinary technologies of population control used around the world as devices for assigning citizens to competing nation-states and expelling those who do not otherwise belong. In an increasingly troubled 21st century, destination countries like Europe, the United Kingdom and Australia have increasingly intensified their efforts to tighten their borders, assert their sovereignty and expel 'non-citizens'. In this respect, Australia has emulated the border protection practices of the United States and the United Kingdom, but not in every respect. In some senses, Australia has the dubious honour of leading the world, rather than vice versa, in border protection measures and technologies which historically have been the mechanism for 'white' nation building and protecting the continent's pristine environment against contagion and disease that afflict the northern hemisphere. Unlike Europe and Britain, as an immigrant settler nation, Australia has been a significant destination country for millions of migrants, albeit mostly from the Anglophone world. What this all means is that border control measures in the neo-colonial antipodes also have an extended and complicated genealogy, historically distinctive from the cross-border issues that regularly arise in the northern hemisphere.

In this chapter, I begin by analysing the plethora of border protection measures introduced by the Australian Government in this wider global geo-political environment. Most significantly, in an era of heightened tension

S. Pickering and L. Weber (eds.), Borders, Mobility and Technologies of Control, 179–206.
© 2006 *Springer. Printed in the Netherlands.*

fuelled by global terrorism, Australia has introduced border control technologies which, for the first time in the nation's post-federation history, disrupt the nexus between sovereignty and territory. Australia has also embarked on an aggressive policy of interventionism into the internal affairs of its Pacific island neighbours to restore 'law and order on the border'. I argue that these border protection measures are disciplinary technologies of population control that trace their genealogy to other forms of illiberal governance peculiar in some senses to Australia's history as a European outpost in the south Pacific.

1.   THE POLITICS OF BORDER CONTROL

The intense politicisation of border control has provided a ripe context for introducing measures, such as biometric testing, unreviewable mandatory detention of asylum seekers, temporary protection visas; the so-called 'Pacific solution' and the excision of thousands of islands off the Australian continent from the migration zone. In a more rational context, many of these policies imposed by a neo-liberal state would be unthinkable. Some indication of the intensity of this politicisation can be gleaned from the sheer number of regulatory and legislative changes introduced by the current Howard government prior to its re-election in 2004: at least 50 amendments to the *Migration Act 1958* since 1996, compared to 47 amendments to that the same Act over the previous four decades (that is, 1958–96); and at least 120 of the 277 changes to the Migration Regulations since 1979.

Border control issues and questions of national identity and sovereignty became paramount during the 2001 federal election campaign, which coincided with the September 11 terrorist attacks in the United States and what became known in Australia as the '*Tampa* crisis'. The tough stance taken by the Howard federal government in refusing the Norwegian freighter, the *Tampa*, with 438 rescued asylum seekers on board, to enter Australian waters just off Christmas Island created an electoral turnaround (Betts 2002: 38). The government sent in Special Air Service (SAS) troops to board the boat at gunpoint and turn it back toward Indonesia (Marr and Wilkinson 2003).

A number of other unauthorised boats carrying asylum seekers into Australian waters were politicised during the election campaign: the infamous 'children overboard' incident on 8 October and the sinking of the *SEIV X* which was carrying asylum seekers from Java, inside Australia's border protection operational zone, drowning 353 on board on 19 October 2001 (Marr and Wilkinson 2003: 194–223).[1] The climate of fear and terror fuelled by the threat of global terrorism provided an opportunistic political climate to make law and order on the border the key electoral issue during the campaign, returning a conservative government that earlier in the year looked like facing almost certain defeat. This was the first time a federal election in Australia had been fought and won on non-economic issues. Analysis of the 2001 Australian election by Ian McAllister shows that border protection cost the opposition Labor Party the election. Labor suffered a loss of 13 percent of its primary vote to two other parties, the Democrats and the Greens, over its position on refugees and asylum seekers, and seven percent to the Coalition Liberal–National parties on terrorism (McAllister 2003).

In the current geo-political context, Australia's eagerness to follow the lead of other western nations in talking up law and order on the border seems somewhat exaggerated. As an island continent, Australia's borders are nowhere near as porous as those of the United Kingdom or the United States, a point often overlooked in debates about asylum seekers and illegal immigration. Consequently, Australia has not been host to the hundreds of thousands of refugees and displaced peoples wandering the globe dispossessed of their homelands by conflict, civil war and human rights abuses. Nor has Australia experienced a lucrative black economy built upon the exploitation of thousands of illegal immigrant workers, as is the case in Europe and the United States. Yet Australia has followed the path of these western nations from the northern hemisphere in committing millions of dollars to a vast network of policies and regimes of governance aimed at policing its borders and criminalising those who cross them illegally.

The former Minister for Immigration, Phillip Ruddock, repeatedly justified his law and order rhetoric about border protection as a valid reaction to the 'assault on our border' by increasing numbers of unauthorised 'boat people'. Yet, annually, around 50,000 visa over-stayers reside illegally in Australia but do not attract the kind of adverse attention as do boat arrivals. The scale of the Australian Government's over-reaction in ushering in a plethora of reforms aimed at stemming illegal immigration certainly appears disproportionate to the size and scope of the actual problem (Mares 2001: 64). The problem, however, is not one of size, but one of politics—a politics of inclusion and exclusion which calls upon nation-states to discriminate in favour of their citizens against non-citizens.

2. CITIZENSHIP AND NON-CITIZENSHIP

Citizenship is generally understood as a universal social practice which confers civil, social, human and political rights and benefits on the citizens within a particular territory, although not always equally (Marshall 1950). Hindess (2000: 1486) argues that citizenship is also a system for classifying people as belonging or not belonging to a particular territory in 'a large, culturally diverse, and interdependent world population'. It is a dividing practice that apportions the world population into a series of manageable sub-populations which compete for prosperity in a global economic system. Consequently, the dark side of citizenship, Hindess argues, requires contemporary governments to discriminate in favour of their citizens against non-citizens, in ways which inhibit or penalise the border crossings of the non-citizen.

Naming and dividing practices are crucial markers of citizenship status, and have played a critical role in disadvantaging non-citizens who attempt to cross borders (Pickering and Lambert 2002). One of those dividing practices is to separate asylum seekers into deserving and undeserving. Australian immigration policy systematically does this in two main ways: deserving refugees are those who languish with the 19 million other displaced persons stranded in the liminal space of the refugee camp around the poorest parts of the globe, waiting for the United Nations High Commission on Refugees to either repatriate them, or find them a new home in a welcoming country. Over the last five years, Australia has taken around 12–13,000 refugees on an annual basis under its offshore humanitarian program (Department of Immigration, Multicultural and Indigenous Affairs (DIMIA) 2003a). Refugees who arrive through the offshore humanitarian program (Class XB visas, sub-classes 200–204) are entitled to immediate access to a full range of social security benefits, Medicare, public education, family reunion rights, work rights, 510 hours of English classes, the same travel rights as permanent residents and a wide range of settlement services.[2] At a symbolic level, they are represented as deserving refugees and are rewarded with immediate access to services equivalent to those enjoyed by Australian citizens. This is how the former Minister for Immigration, Phillip Ruddock (2002), describes this cohort of refugees in a ministerial statement:

> Australia contributes its fair share to the resettlement of those most in need—the principle of international burden sharing. In resettling refugees, the government devotes very considerable resources to ensuring that these people have the support they need to fully participate as members of the Australian community.

By comparison, asylum seekers who arrive in Australia unlawfully, without valid visas or travel documentation, are automatically defined as unlawful non-citizens and subject to mandatory detention while they are being processed (DIMIA 2003b). The process is often lengthy and stigmatising. They are named according to the recipe of labelling theory, as 'unlawful non-citizens',[3] and their deviant status is reinforced by other labels, such as 'boat people', 'human cargo', 'queue jumpers', 'unauthorised arrivals', 'unAustralian', 'aliens' or 'illegals', a point already made strongly by a number of criminologists (see Poynting 2002; Pickering and Lambert 2002). Their disadvantaged legal status is reinforced by a political discourse which constantly slips between people smugglers, terrorists and boat people as a group who fraudulently claim to be refugees. Take for example, this ministerial speech, delivered by Phillip Ruddock (2001b):

> Between 1 December 1999 and 3 January 2001, 3,796 people arrived unlawfully by boat from a number of Middle Eastern countries … Who are these clandestine arrivals? … Many are former terrorists, senior officers in repressive regimes, people suspected of crimes against humanity, people with criminal records, organisers of people-smuggling rackets, people who have ignored or abandoned protection already available to them elsewhere and people who have been refused migrant visas and then attempt to enter Australia unlawfully. Some destroy their documents to avoid being identified or arrive with fraudulent ones. Some claim a different nationality or to be part of a more vulnerable ethnic group. Some arrive with pre-existing health problems. Some have no legitimate protection claims.

As it turned out, most of those who arrived on the boats referred to by the Minister were subsequently determined to be refugees, not terrorists, people smugglers or criminals. Of the asylum seekers who arrived by boat in 2000, 95 percent of those who were Afghanis and 90 percent of those who were Iraqis were found to be refugees, as the former Minister has had to retrospectively acknowledge.[4]

The second way immigration policy systematically differentiates deserving from undeserving refugees is through the temporary protection visa (TPV) regime. Those who arrive unlawfully are only eligible in the first instance for temporary protection, and in reality most will never be eligible to apply for citizenship status (Marston 2003). Temporary protection visas were introduced as part of the 1999 border protection strategy, under the Migration Amendment Regulations (No 12). The federal government claims TPV holders are not punished, yet they are not entitled to the same support as offshore refugees who are granted protection visas, being excluded from most of the special settlement services that are funded by the Commonwealth to refugees who settle in Australia.[5] By denying them access to basic resettlement services such as education, accommodation, language acquisition, family reunion and secure employment opportunities, the host society is signalling the temporary and precarious nature of their stay (Marston 2003: 17). The policy is designed as a deterrent to those who arrive illegally in Australia seeking protection, for they represent, as Crock (2000: 247) notes, 'an exception of sorts to the sovereignty principle'.

On 28 August 2003, the TPV regime was broadened to encompass all onshore applicants seeking protection, regardless of whether they arrived lawfully or unlawfully.[6] Previously, TPVs were criticised as a discriminatory form of punishment for those refugees who arrived illegally and, as such, a breach of Article 31 of the *Refugee Convention 1951*. While the broader TPV regime has introduced more consistency, the new policy still discriminates against those who arrive illegally, because only those who arrive lawfully will be able to invoke the minister's new discretionary powers to apply for permanent protection. This regulation effectively gives the minister the power to decide which, if any of this class of refugee, will be eligible for Australian citizenship.

3.   BETWEEN AND BETWIXT SHIFTING BORDERS

The processes of globalisation have contributed to the upheaval, expulsion, persecution and whole-scale mass migration of people searching for security (van Hear 1998: 251). So much so, that on the one hand, asylum seekers are caught between a borderless world where persecution knows no boundary, yet on the other, a world of hard and impenetrable borders based on notions of jurisdiction, sovereignty and citizenship (McAllister 2002). Asylum seekers to Australia since September 2001 have had the added problem of being caught between and betwixt shifting borders. As the editors to this collection remind us in their introduction, borders are not fixed, impermeable or impenetrable—they are politicised, uncertain, largely symbolic and also contestable.

Following the politicisation of border control issues during the 2001 election, a new policy was introduced allowing the offshore processing of asylum seekers outside Australia's migration zone in the Manus Province of Papua New Guinea and on the Nauru islands. The *Migration Amendment (Excision from Migration Zone) Act 2001* allowed for certain parts of Australian territory to be excised from the migration zone. What this means is that asylum seekers landing on any excised part of Australia are unable to invoke protection under the United Nations Refugee Convention, for they have not technically arrived in an Australian migration territory. Their claims to asylum are assessed not by the courts but by the Department of Immigration, Multicultural and Indigenous Affairs at one of four offshore processing facilities. Should their application be unsuccessful, they may be moved to a declared country. This new measure, widely referred to as the 'Pacific solution', was part of a package of border protection measures introduced two weeks after the September 11 terrorist attacks in United States to strengthen border control amongst a flurry of law and order rhetoric during an election campaign.[7] Other measures introduced mandatory minimum sentences for people smuggling offences for the first time into the Commonwealth Criminal Code. Another sought to limit judicial review of immigration decisions.

After the establishment of these new forms of border control, most people attempting to seek asylum in Australia by boat have been intercepted at sea (Phillips and Millbank 2004). As these new measures effectively restrict Australia's protection obligations under international law, they have been criticised by the United Nations High Commission on Refugees as being at variance with the United Nations Refugee Convention (United Nations High Commission for Refugees 2003). The government has defended the measures as necessary to combat people smuggling, to prevent them from abandoning asylum seekers to an uncertain future on remote islands, and to reduce the incentives for asylum seekers to attempt the hazardous sea journey across the Pacific to one of Australia's island territories (Coombs 2005: 2).

As part of its law and order on the border campaign, the Australian Government attempted to excise up to another 3000 islands from Australia's migration zone. For almost four years these attempts faltered in a hostile Senate, but on 22 July 2005, they came into force after the Howard government took control with a majority in the Senate. In December 2002, through regulation—not legislation—the government excised four islands off the West Australian coast (Bernier, Dorre, Dirk Hartog and Faure Islands).[8] The instrument was subsequently disallowed by the Senate when the Greens and Labor parties joined forces to oppose it. The government then introduced a Bill to excise another 3000 islands from Australia's migration zone.[9] The Bill was the subject of an inquiry by the Senate, Legal and Constitutional References Committee. Most of the submissions received by that inquiry pointed out that the legislation disadvantaged asylum seekers and had little or no impact on deterring international crime or curtailing the activities of people smugglers. Not surprisingly, in December 2002 the Senate rejected the Bill. In March 2003, the government reintroduced the legislation[10] to extend the 'excision of the migration zone' to include an estimated 3000 islands across the north of Western Australia, Northern Territory and Queensland. The Bill was again rejected in the Senate by the Greens with the support of Labor. On 4 November 2003, when fourteen Kurdish asylum seekers landed on a remote island off northern Australia, the Australian Government introduced regulations to excise this island from the Australian migration zone.[11] A couple of weeks later, they were disallowed by a hostile Senate, but the regulations remained in force long enough for the asylum seekers to be placed in immigration detention on one of the Pacific islands set up as an offshore processing centre. Being an election year, the government held off reintroducing its attempt to excise thousands of islands from Australian territory until it took control of the Senate in July 2005.[12] The leader of the Democrats, Andrew Bartlett, attempted to disallow the regulations, but with the government in control of the Senate this time, the new regulations were allowed to stand (Coombs 2005).[13]

Importantly, Australia still claims sovereignty over zones excised from Australian territory, but treats these zones as extra-territorial for migration purposes, disrupting, for the first time in the history of white colonisation, the nexus between territory and sovereignty. While the excision of this territory does not otherwise affect Australia's sovereignty in relation to quarantine and fishing laws for instance (Coombs 2005: 1), at a symbolic level, this new measure represents a remarkable precedent in border control in which Australia has the dubious reputation of leading the world. It would be equivalent to the United States excising California, New Mexico or Texas, or the United Kingdom excising the Isle of Mann for migration purposes and then setting up processing centres for asylum seekers in these liminal zones for the purpose of evading or limiting their humanitarian obligations under international treaties and conventions. Evading obligations under international law is another plank in the law and order discourse to which I now turn.

4.   LEGAL BORDERS, BOUNDARIES AND BARRICADES

At the same time as migration zones have been shifted to restrict Australia's protection obligations to refugees, the Commonwealth has sought to barricade the boundaries of domestic law, not only from judicial review, but also from incursions by a human rights discourse enshrined in a number of international treaties and instruments signed and ratified by Australia. In addition to the 1951 Refugee Convention and its 1967 Protocol, Australia has protection obligations under the *Convention Against Torture and Other Cruel, Inhuman and Degrading Treatment or Punishment* (CAT), the *Convention on the Rights of the Child* (CROC) and the *International Covenant on Civil and Political Rights* (ICCPR). State signatories to these conventions and protocols undertake to cooperate in the application of these instruments. They represent the internationalisation of *non-refoulement* agreements which reinforce the boundaries of nation-states. They arose primarily in a post-World War II context as international instruments for managing the global population, by allocating citizens to a polity within a nation-state (Hindess 2000).

International treaties, such as the Refugee Convention, CAT and CROC, are instruments of international governance which confer upon individuals a legal personhood regardless of their status in any domestic legal system. Their invocation may lead to the acquisition of a new national identity by allowing stateless people or persecuted refugees a means of becoming citizens of a new state. Nevertheless, there are real limits to the power effects of international treaties, as these instruments are not legally binding or enforceable. Their efficacy is reliant on parties to the convention agreeing to implement them (Crock 1998: 30). The Australian Government has effectively barricaded the boundaries of domestic law against their systematic implementation. It has done so by interpreting these instruments within its own narrow domestic legislative and policy framework which seeks to restrict judicial review of migration decisions, and to restrict the impact of international law within domestic law. For instance, the 2001 amendments to the Migration Act tightened the definition of a refugee[14] and sought to prevent judicial review of these decisions. Currently, another Bill, the Migration Litigation Bill 2005 is before the house. The purpose of the Bill is to stem the rising tide of litigation cases by introducing a more streamlined and efficient process for handling migration litigation (Prince, Harris-Rimmer and Coombs 2005). Critics are concerned that this Bill will amount to the circumvention of the rights of asylum seekers (See Prince, Harris-Rimmer and Coombs 2005: 10).

The Australian Government has also refused to extend the refugee determination process to include asylum seekers claiming persecution under CAT or the ICCPR. Ministerial discretion provides the only policy instrument for granting protection on humanitarian grounds for applicants whose onshore claims fall outside the Refugee Convention (Paragraph 8.127, Senate Legal and Constitutional References Committee 2003: 266). A number of difficulties arise from using ministerial discretion as a de facto onshore humanitarian entry process. The reliance on the exercise of a non-reviewable, non-compellable and largely informal exercise of ministerial discretion to meet Australia's humanitarian obligations to provide protection under CAT, CROC or the ICCPR has raised widespread concerns among legal scholars, the judicial community, international lawyers and a range of refugee advocate groups (see Senate Legal and Constitutional References Committee 2003: 237–67). The main issue of concern is that a claim to protection under one of these conventions cannot be guaranteed by a discretionary power that the minister may choose not to exercise (Senate Legal and Constitutional References Committee 2003: 64).[15] At least ten submissions to the 2003 Senate inquiry into ministerial discretion argued that Australia's protection obligations under these treaties should be explicitly incorporated into domestic law, and reflected in the onshore refugee determination process, rather than left to the discretion of the minister.[16]

Some critics have argued that analysis of refugee issues couched entirely within a legalistic framework of rights overlooks the politics of globalisation and the tension around borders it generates (Green and Grewcock 2002: 89). As a discursive strategy, a human rights discourse has been marginally effective in contesting the insularity of containing refugee law within the borders of a domestic framework. Certainly, most of the debate about refugee policy invokes a human rights discourse as a form of critique (Poynting 2002; Crock 1998; Crock and Saul 2001; Hearn and Eastman 2000; Kinslor 2000). That debate has escalated, given the introduction of more and more draconian policies and laws aimed at naming, detaining, deterring, separating and evicting failed asylum seekers from Australian shores. Of particular concern is whether the temporary protection visa regime breaches the Refugee Convention by punishing those who arrive unlawfully, and by putting the onus on refugees to re-establish their refugee status. Australia is the only country in the world that does this. Also of concern has been Australia's persistent breach of CROC through its mandatory detention regime, and the arbitrary detention of asylum seekers who have protection claims under international treaties that are not recognised in domestic law. Both these latter criticisms have only recently been neutralised by changes introduced by a floundering government facing damning criticism over its detention regime.

5. BORDERS WITHIN: THE MANDATORY DETENTION REGIME

The detention of asylum seekers is a disciplinary technology that segregates unlawful non-citizens from the Australian population. Mandatory detention is justified in law and order discourse as integral to protecting Australia's borders. As Minister Phillip Ruddock (2000) is eager to point out:

An important part of effective border control is the ability to remove persons with no right to remain in Australia—immigration detention ensures those persons are available for removal.

The mandatory detention of onshore asylum seekers was introduced by a Labor government in 1992 (although the federal Labor Party no longer supports the detention of children and has softened its approach to the indefinite detention of asylum seekers who are effectively stateless). Under section 189 of the *Migration Act 1958*, unlawful non-citizens must be detained until they are either granted a valid visa or removed. As criminologists would appreciate, any form of detention is symbolically associated with banishment, exclusion, punishment and imprisonment. The detainee is consequently associated with guilt and wrong-doing (see Weber 2002).

The spatial politics of exclusion has been an important element in the mandatory detention regime, a point made by many critics (Tazreiter 2002; Crock and Saul 2001)· Roughly half the detention centre population is located in remote parts of the continent, at Baxter (Port Augusta) and Port Hedland or on one of the offshore processing centres at Christmas Island, and until recently, on Manus or Nauru, tiny islands in the Pacific region. Port Hedland is approximately 1640 kilometres from Perth, the capital of Western Australia. Baxter (at Port Augusta) is around 280 kilometres from Adelaide, the capital of South Australia. Previously, thousands of asylum seekers had been accommodated at another two remote detention centres: Woomera Detention Centre, located 470 kilometres northwest of Adelaide in the desert and Curtin Immigration Processing and Reception Centre, located about 2350 kilometres north of Perth. Both have recently been closed down, following riots, investigations and widespread condemnation of the practice of detaining asylum seekers in desert boot camps. Metropolitan detention centres located in Melbourne, Perth and Sydney tend to house short-term detainees, mostly over-stayers or illegal immigrants picked up by compliance raids on brothels, restaurants and in the building industry. The current Coalition government argues that there are sound administrative reasons justifying mandatory detention, among them,

> ensuring that unauthorised arrivals do not enter the community until their claims have been properly assessed; ensuring that unauthorised arrivals do not enter the community until after essential identity and health checks are conducted and assessments of character and security issues can be made; providing asylum seekers access to appropriate services for the processing of visa applications; and where claims to remain in Australia are unsuccessful, ensuring availability for removal. (DIMIA 2003b).

Detention centres are managed by Australian Correctional Management, a subsidiary of Wakenhut, an international provider of private prisons. Sub-contracting the responsibility for managing detention centres to a private prison company conforms to the strategy of governing at a distance, which almost inevitably leads to an accountability deficit (See Kirby 2000; Moyle 2000; Harding 1997). There have been at least 25 inquiries into Australia's detention centres, and a great deal of controversy over detention centre standards, costs, breaches of human rights, the use of chemical sedatives, the use of force, wrongful detention, the detention of children, and the arbitrary detention of failed asylum seekers who are not allowed to stay but also not permitted to leave (see Table 1).

Table 10-1. **A Non-exhaustive list of inquiries into immigration detention in Australia**

1.   Inquiry into the Circumstances of the Immigration Detention of Cornelia Rau, 'Palmer Report' (Commonwealth of Australia 2005).

2.   United Nations, Civil and Political Rights, including the Question of Torture and Detention: Report of the Working Group on Arbitrary Detention Visit to Australia (2002).

3.   *Chilout, A Report on Compliance with Detention Centre Standards in the Treatment of Children by Australasian Correctional Management (ACM) and the Australian Government in Detention Centres* (Chilout 2002).

4.   Human Rights and Equal Opportunity Commission, *Report of an Inquiry into a Complaint by Mr Mohammed Badraie on Behalf of his Son Shayan Regarding Acts of Practices of the Commonwealth of Australia* (2002).

5.   Human Rights and Equal Opportunity Commission, *Report of an Inquiry into Complaints by Five Asylum Seekers Concerning their Detention in the Separation and Management Block at the Port Hedland Immigration Reception and Processing Centre* (2002).

6.   Human Rights and Equal Opportunity Commission, *Report of an Inquiry into a Complaint by Mr Hassan Ghomwari Concerning his Immigration Detention and the Adequacy of the Medical Treatment he Received While Detained* (2002).

7.   Human Rights and Equal Opportunity Commission, *Report of an Inquiry into a Complaint by Mr XY Concerning his Continuing Detention Despite Having Completed his Criminal Sentence* (2002).

8.   Human Rights and Equal Opportunity Commission, *Report of an Inquiry into a Complaint by Six Asylum Seekers Concerning their Transfer from Immigration Detention Centres to State Prisons and their Detention in those Prisons* (2002).

9.   Human Rights and Equal Opportunity Commission, *Report of an Inquiry into a Complaint by Mr Duc Anh Ha of Acts or Practises Inconsistent with or Contrary to Human Rights Arising from Immigration Detention* (2002).

10. Human Rights and Equal Opportunity Commission, *Report of an Inquiry into a Complaint by Ms Elizabeth Ching Concerning the Cancellation of her Visa on Arrival in Australia and Subsequent Mandatory Detention* (2002).

11. Human Rights and Equal Opportunity Commission, *Report of an Inquiry into a Complaint of Acts or Practices Inconsistent with or Contrary to Human Rights in an Immigration Detention Centre* (2001).

12. Human Rights and Equal Opportunity Commission, *A Report on Visits to Immigration Detention Facilities by the Human Rights Commissioner 2001* (2001).

13. Human Rights and Equal Opportunity Commission, *National Inquiry into Children in Immigration Detention* (2001).

14. Joint Standing Committee on Foreign Affairs, Defence and Trade, *A Report on Visits to Immigration Detention Centres* (2001).

15. Phillip Flood QC, *Report of Inquiry into Immigration Detention Procedures* (Department of Immigration, Multicultural and Indigenous Affairs, 2001).

16. Commonwealth Ombudsman, *Report of an Own Motion Investigation into the Department of Immigration and Multicultural Affairs' Immigration Detention*

Table 10-1. **A Non-exhaustive list of inquiries into immigration detention in Australia**

	Centres: Report under section 35A of the Ombudsman Act 1976 (2001).
17.	Joint Standing Committee on Migration, *Not the Hilton: Immigration Detention Centres, Inspection Report* (2000).
18.	Government Response to the Recommendations from the Joint Standing Committee on Migration's report *Not the Hilton: Immigration Detention Centres, Inspection Report* (September 2000).
19.	Human Rights and Equal Opportunity Commission, *Mandatory Detention Laws in Australia: An Overview of Current Laws and Proposed Reform* (1999).
20.	Human Rights and Equal Opportunity Commission, *Those Who Come Across the Seas: Detention of Unauthorised Arrivals* (1998).
21.	Human Rights and Equal Opportunity Commission, Preliminary Report on the Detention of Boat People (1997).
22.	Joint Standing Committee on Migration, Immigration Detention Centres: Inspection Report (1998).
23.	Government Response to the Joint Standing Committee on Migration Immigration Detention Centres: Inspection Report (1999).
24.	Joint Standing Committee on Migration, Asylum, Border Control and Detention: Report (1994).
25.	Government Response to the Joint Standing Committee on Migration, Asylum, Border Control and Detention: Report (1994).

The government argues that mandatory detention is not arbitrary because detainees can leave detention by returning to their home countries. However, it is not possible for many failed asylum seekers to leave in circumstances where their home countries refuse to take them back, do not have refoulment arrangements with the deporting country, or no longer exist.

Until recently, detention practices were mandatory and non-reviewable by the courts. However, several important recent court decisions have created some cracks in the policy of non-reviewable mandatory detention. First, the High Court refused the federal government leave to appeal in the *al Masri* case.[17] Secondly, the full bench of the Family Court decided that it has the jurisdiction to make orders in relation to the welfare of children in detention.[18] Thirdly, the full bench of the Family Court recently ruled to release five children from detention, pending exhaustive attempts by the Australian Government to remove the family to Pakistan.[19] The case of the Bakhtiyari family has been well publicised. This action has now failed and the family deported; their children had spent years in detention before being deported earlier this year. Fourthly, the government's attempt to restrict the courts from making interlocutory orders for the release of people in detention, under the Migration Amendment (Duration of Detention) Bill 2002, was thwarted in the Senate by amendments pursued by Labor and the minor parties.[20] Ultimately, the government was successful in its bid before the High Court which recently decided that indefinite detention was not unlawful. This decision would have cemented unreviewable mandatory detention as a border control policy with a long-term future, if it were not for the recent revelations about unlawful detention.

Recently, the Australian Government has come under intense scrutiny following the unlawful detention of Cornelia Rau, an Australian citizen, for ten months (six months in a Brisbane correctional centre, then another four in the Baxter detention centre), and the unlawful deportation of another Australian citizen, Vivian Alvarez Solon. The cases of mistaken detention and deportation highlight the inadequacies of the mandatory detention regime (see Prince 2005 for a detailed legal analysis of the issue). The revelations sparked an inquiry headed by Mick Palmer, the former head of the Australian Federal Police, and embarrassing admissions by DIMIA that there may be many more mistakes such as these. The inquiry found: 'a serious cultural problem within DIMIA's immigration compliance and detention areas'; that DIMIA fails to deliver outcomes that respect human dignity; that DIMIA officers exercise exceptional powers and do so 'without adequate training, without proper management or oversight, with poor information systems; and with no genuine quality assurance and constraints on the exercise of these powers...' (Palmer Report 2005: ix). The Secretary for the immigration portfolio, Bill Farmer, publicly apologised before a Senate Estimates Committee for the blunder. The portfolio minister, Amanda Vanstone, announced a series of sweeping reforms to immigration detention (Vanstone 2005a), among them: a 28-day limit on immigration detention except in exceptional circumstances; establishment of a national identity verification unit; the appointment of immigration detention review managers in each state; enhancement of mental health services in immigration detention centres; and the centralisation of records that relate to individual detainees to improve information flows (Vanstone 2005a).

In response to an avalanche of criticism, the Australian Government has finally softened the mandatory detention regime. The reforms almost certainly would not have seen the light of day had it not been for the back bench revolt led by Petro Georgio, a long-term critic of mandatory detention and draconian border control measures (see Prince 2005: 4). The government has introduced a new 'removal pending visa' for long-term detainees who otherwise would have languished in detention indefinitely. The minister said the new visa was aimed at addressing the predicament of detainees who could not be removed for reasons out of their own control and who posed no security threat (Vanstone 2005b). The hitch however is that access to the visa is dependent on invitation by the Minister (Vanstone 2005c). Consequently, there are no clear and transparent guidelines for issuing the visa, and like so much refugee and immigration policy, rests on ministerial discretion as a magic bullet.

In the weeks after the Palmer report, the government introduced new legislation allowing for new community arrangements for families in detention, releasing all children from mandatory detention (Vanstone 2005d).[21] Before that, over the last few years, around 100 children had been held in immigration detention in Australia at any one time, attracting a great deal of criticism for its detrimental effects on the mental and physical health of children (Phillips and Lorrimer 2003; Ozdowski 2001; Newman et al, 2002). These are the most sweeping reforms to the mandatory detention regime since its introduction by a Labor government in 1992. They followed the release of the 2005 Palmer inquiry into Australia's immigration detention system which revealed a system that had become defensive, entrenched and deeply cynical, if not disrespecting of the asylum claims made by people categorised as 'unlawful non-citizens'. While shocking, this is hardly a surprising finding in the highly charged populist political context of law and order on the border. But now, there's a newly emergent discourse for law and order on the border taking the heat out of the controversy over the borders within. This law and order discourse is focused on the potential threats posed by the extra-territorial borders of Australia's neo-colonial neighbours.

6. POLICING THE PACIFIC: THE NEW PLANK IN BORDER CONTROL

Since decolonisation of the micro-states of the Pacific islands in the 1970s and 1980s, Australia has had little by way of bilateral relations with its Pacific neighbours. At best, Australia was indifferent. Over the last 50 years or so, Australian foreign policy has concentrated on maintaining relations with the super powers of the northern hemisphere, largely through the Australian and New Zealand and United States (ANZUS) alliance, relegating the Pacific region to the perimeter of its foreign policy agenda (Dinnen 2004). All this has recently changed and in some instances quite dramatically. In 2003, the Australian Government reversed a long history of non-intervention in the internal affairs of island states in the Pacific with a new assertive foreign policy of interventionism (Hegarty et al 2004; Dinnen 2004). This new policy followed the 11 September terrorist attacks, the 2002 Bali bombing which killed 88 Australians, and a number of high-profile people smuggling operations that went terribly wrong. The policy reversal is directly linked to the 'war on terror' by the 'coalition of the willing', led by the United Kingdom, the United States and Australia. In announcing the release of the new policy directions set out in the *Australian Foreign and*

Trade Policy White Paper, the Minister for Foreign Affairs, Alexander Downer (2003), said:

> The horrific Bali bombings last year and the threat of the proliferation of weapons of mass destruction in Iraq and North Korea remind us that we cannot take our security for granted. ... For these reasons the white paper focuses on measures we will take to counter international threats to our security, especially terrorism.

Emulating the more aggressive foreign policy stance of the United States, Australia's new assertive foreign policy in the Pacific is designed to combat what the Prime Minister, John Howard, has openly described as 'failed states that become havens for terrorists on Australia's doorstep' (Kerin 2003). The Prime Minister has also proposed that the micro-states of the South Pacific cede sovereignty by merging to form a more viable single nation-state (Vaughn 2004: 110). In a particularly non-diplomatic moment, he even went as far as to describe Australia as the United States' 'deputy' in the Asian-pacific region (Kerin 2004), upsetting many civic and political leaders from the Asian-Pacific rim.

While Australia's renewed engagement, genuine peace-keeping and nation-building efforts in partnership with Pacific neighbours is a positive turnaround of the long policy of indifference, it also raises new concerns. One of these is that the strategy of focusing on lawlessness promotes an aggressive foreign policy discourse associated with neo-colonialism. The new interventionism comes across as less designed to assist troubled island neighbours, than to protect Australia's security interests by minimising threats posed by international crime, people smuggling and terrorism in the region. The Australian Government's white paper (Department of Foreign Affairs and Trade 2003: 92) made this point abundantly clear:

> Instability in the South Pacific affects our ability to protect large and significant approaches to Australia. The Government also has a duty to protect the safety of the 13,000 Australians resident in the countries of the region—some 7000 in Papua New Guinea alone. And transnational crime in and through the region—terrorism, drug trafficking, people smuggling, illegal immigration and money laundering—is a growing threat to Australia and the South Pacific countries themselves. Cooperation with the South Pacific on such issues, particularly people smuggling, has delivered real benefits to Australia. The establishment of Australian-funded processing centres in Nauru and PNG showed how regional countries can cooperate to deal with an issue of concern to the region as a whole.

Of course, the initiatives in Nauru and Papua New Guinea referred to by the white paper are primarily about Australia protecting its borders by manipulating several Pacific islands to do the dirty work of processing asylum seekers. This is hardly 'an issue of concern to the region as a whole'. Several other new initiatives have concretised the new interventionism in foreign policy. One of these is known as the regional assistance mission to the Solomon Islands (RAMSI) and the other is officially called the enhanced cooperation (ECP) program with Papua New Guinea, a veiled guise for tied aid. Both of these initiatives reflect the new interventionism and both have been driven by a transparent law and order agenda no doubt designed to tap into populist fears and manipulate electoratal support.

The mission into the Solomon Islands to restore law and order followed the publication of an important and influential policy document, *Our Failing Neighbour: Australia and the Future of the Solomon Islands* (Australian Strategic Policy Institute 2003: 1). The document begins authoritatively, 'Solomon Islands, one of Australia's nearest neighbours, is a failing state'. It draws an analogy between rogue states like Iraq and the Solomon Islands (and points to the dire consequences of 'a failing state on our doorstep' (8). This has now become familiar sounding rhetoric justifying more law and order border control. Couching the new policy in terms similar to the United States mission to 'free Iraq' and talk about 'failed states' can be easily interpreted as 'condescending and arrogant' (Dinnen 2004: 2).

The challenge identified by the Australian Strategic Policy Institute in *Our Failing Neigbour* was how Australia could intervene more directly in the affairs of its neighbours to restore law and order and to neutralise the risk they pose to Australia's border security, while simultaneously avoiding the perils associated with neo-colonialism (2003: 9). Perhaps these are mutually exclusive policy aims. Nevertheless, considerable efforts were made to manage the intervention to at least appear as if it did not thwart the island's sovereignty. Importantly, Australia's intervention in the Solomon Islands also followed a request for assistance from its Prime Minister, Allan Kemakeza (Hegarty et al 2004: 1) and a series of protocols that ensured Australia could not be interpreted as acting in violation of the island nation's sovereignty (von Strockirch 2004). The intervention was authorised by a special Act of the Solomon Islands Government and endorsed by the Pacific Islands Forum (Vaughn 2004: 110). Just as importantly, the tiny island government had made several previous requests for Australian support, all of which were denied (Kabutaulaka 2005: 286). Previously, the Foreign Minister, Alexander Downer, had rejected requests from the Solomon Island leaders for military assistance in dealing with domestic issues as 'folly in the extreme' (Downer 2003). As Kabutaulaka argues, the remarkable turnaround in government foreign policy is really only explicable in terms of the international

Anglo-American discourses on international terrorism (Kabutaulaka 2005: 287). The preoccupation with terrorism shared by the United Kingdom, the United States and Australia has created a new found concern with 'weak' or failed states (von Strokirch 2004: 378), elevating the strategic relevance of the Melanesian micro-states of the Pacific to Australian security interests. So now, and only now, is Australia interested in the wellbeing of its closest neighbours after a long history of non-intervention in their affairs. This appears opportunist, to say the least.

The police-led mission to restore law and order in the Solomon Islands 'succeeded in restoring internal security within a relatively short time-frame' (Dinnen 2004: 2). Little wonder why. The mission involved approximately 2200 personnel, 1500 of them Australian troops, 300 military from other Pacific islands, and 350 police officers (Rixon 2003). In per capita, terms this would be equivalent to sending 88,000 foreign troops and police officers to restore law and order in Australia (Rixon 2003). While the Solomon Islands was seen as a failed state experiencing a crisis of law and order, arguably, however, the inability of its government to 'enforce its rule and maintain security' was not just a law and order crisis, but a 'crisis of economic and political development' (Sherlock 2003: 2). The problem with the metaphor of the failed state is that many of the Melanesian states like the Solomon Islands had not been built but rather simply abandoned by colonial powers (Dinnen 2004: 6). The preoccupation with the failing state metaphor represents the problem as a security threat to neighbouring countries, erasing or submerging concerns about the internal dynamics at stake, such as land rights claims in a post-colonial context, ethnic tensions, tribal and gendered violence and the conditions for enabling sustainable economic prosperity and growth essential to establishing political stability and personal security in a neo-colonial era (Sherlock 2003).

Closely aligned to the new interventionism, there has been a shift in foreign aid policy. This shift too has been sold under the guise of law and order rhetoric. Traditionally, Australian aid had been distributed in an unfettered way to buoy the underdeveloped island states in the Pacific. However, this policy was criticised for sustaining corrupt governments and ineffectual aid programs. Again, following the lead of the United States in linking aid for the developing world to 'worthy' states engaged in democratic reform and economic freedom, Australian aid to Pacific islands is now linked to a series of similar conditions (von Strokirch 2004: 376). For instance, Australian foreign aid is now directly linked with initiatives designed to promote regional stability across the South Pacific. This new strategic direction in foreign aid was particularly evident when the Foreign Affairs Minister, Alexander Downer, announced in 2003 that the annual aid package of $330 million to Papua New Guinea, a former Australian colony, was now tied to around 200 Australian police officers and a number of civilians being deployed to stabilise law and order in the country. Papua New Guinea was widely viewed in Canberra at the time as another failed state manifesting the tell-tale signs of lawlessness and dysfunction (Dinnen 2004: 8). The Prime Minister, Michael Somare, criticised the assault on his country's sovereignty brought about by this new tied aid policy, but eventually acquiesced and accepted the conditions of the enhanced cooperation program (von Strokrich 2004: 377). The main features of this program include the deployment of 230 Australian police officers; 18 Australians working in the law and justice portfolios; 36 Australian officials working in the finance sector and another ten deployed in border control, immigration and transport security (Dinnen 2004: 8). Many of the same concerns raised by the Solomon Islands rescue mission apply to this new form of interventionism: it is state-centric and short-term and may lead to long-term dependence on Australian support and intervention; it over-inflates the risk of terrorism, people smuggling and international crime; it over-simplifies domestic law and order problems; and it does not address the deeper issues of global marginalisation, economic sustainability and nation building that arise within a neo-colonial context (Dinnen 2004: 9).

It is clear that Australia's new role in policing the Pacific runs the risk of being perceived as heavy-handed, leading with 'a fist', and emulating the uncompromising diplomacy of the United States in pushing a narrow security agenda over and above issues of genuine regional strategic mutual interest. While terrorism, border control, international crime, people smuggling and illegal immigration are preoccupations of western nations in an era of global terrorism, these are hardly concerns high on the agenda of our regional neighbours. Climate change, pandemics, HIV/AIDS, land rights, the depletion of natural resources, sustainable development and economic independence, and the pressures of globalisation are issues of far greater concern. Focused squarely on a law and order agenda, the new directions manifest in policing the Pacific have hardly begun to grapple with the more fundamental issues of socio-economic development being experienced by a group of islands abandoned by their colonisers and left to 'rot' over the past several decades of foreign policy indifference.

7.   A GENEALOGY OF BORDER CONTROL

Thus far in this chapter I have analysed contemporary measures of border protection in an era of global terrorism. These technologies of population control construct onshore asylum seekers, not as refugees fleeing persecution and deserving of Australia's protection, but as threats to national security.

They also construct our Pacific island neighbours as 'failed states' that pose security threats by being susceptible to international crime syndicates, people smugglers and terrorists. It is tempting to analyse the last decade of intensification around border control in terms of an international backdrop of restrictive policy regimes in the United Kingdom and the European Union referred to as 'fortress Europe' (United Kingdom Home Office 2002). These policies too have shifted the balance from refugee protection to border control (United Nations High Commission on Refugees 2001: 161). However, being an island continent, Australia does not have the porous borders of Europe (Boeri, Hanson and McCormack 2002: vi). Nor does Australia have anything like the number of displaced persons seeking asylum as do other western nations in the northern hemisphere. Certainly, some of the border control measures discussed in this chapter are similar to the disciplinary technologies of population control which assign citizens to competing nation-states (Hindess 2000: 1486) and expel those stripped of citizenship, reducing them to bare life in a state of perpetual non-belonging (Agamben 1998). However, I want to argue in this section that in the neo-colonial antipodes, border control measures have a more extended and complicated genealogy distinctive from the cross-border issues posed in the northern hemisphere. The issues of mobility and the criminalisation of the border crossings by 'global outcasts', Roma, immigrant workers or itinerant peoples raised by the editors in the introduction to this collection pose nothing like the problem in Australia that they do in the northern hemisphere. Australia has a long and celebrated system of planned immigration making it one of the multicultural countries in the world. So why is Australian politics obsessed with border control? The answer is partly found in our history as a neo-colonial outpost of Britain.

First, the asylum seeker issue taps into deeply embedded anxieties about the fear of invasion in the sparsely populated areas of northern Australia (Mares 2001: 28). The symbolic conflation between contagion, invasion and immigration has long shaped Australian anxieties about the security of our island border. Just as rabbits, prickly pear, cane toads and carriers of infectious diseases have historically been represented as pests or threats to national health and security, successive waves of immigrants, refugees and asylum seekers have been subjected to forms of quarantine, health and character checks.[22] Such anxieties clearly underscored 70 years of the white Australia policy, lasting from 1901, under the *Immigration (Restriction Act) 1901*, to its abolition in 1973 (York 2003). Historian, Alison Bashford (2002: 345), has argued that

Over the twentieth century, the connection between contagion and immigration has been enacted in statutes and regulation, it has shaped

Australian bureaucratic structure and the organisation of its knowledge-collection and classification, it has been implemented as policy and has been publicly funded as scientific enterprise.

It is reasonable to argue therefore that the contemporary border control measures outlined above trace their genealogy to the medico-legal border controls enacted through contagious diseases legislation and quarantine regulations, which also sought to exclude, contain or decontaminate pests and persons considered threatening to the Australian island continent (Bashford 2002: 344).

Secondly, in many ways, contemporary border control technologies mirror the historical efforts deployed to contain Aboriginal populations within white-man borders, such as reserves and missions, following Britain's proclamation of sovereignty over the island continent in 1788 (Goodall 1996). Australian Indigenous people became the subjects of disciplinary technologies that, in Rowse's words, 'both succoured and regimented them' (Rowse 2002: 1514). Like detention camps, reserves and missions were spaces to which Indigenous non-citizens were exiled. The colonial government evaded its treaty obligations, not unlike the current government, by shifting borders, expunging tribal borders and rendering Indigenous peoples strangers within. Like asylum seekers, Indigenous peoples were stripped of their humanity and defined as non-citizens with few formal civil or political rights until relatively recently. These 19th and 20th century disciplinary technologies of exclusion and banishment entailed the wholesale internal migration and displacement of Aboriginal communities across tribal borders (Rowse 2002; Goodall 1996; Reynolds 1989). This strategy was later supplemented with an assimilation policy of removing 'mixed-blood' Aboriginal children to the disciplinary space of the asylum, such as the notoriously harsh Kinchella Boys Home (Human Rights and Equal Opportunity Commission 1997; Tazreiter 2002: 10).

Like the disciplining of the indigenous population, refugees are divided into sub-populations of those targeted for assimilation and those doomed to oblivion through the disciplinary technologies of containment or expulsion. Those selected for assimilation come through the offshore humanitarian program, allowed lawful entry and defined as legitimate refugees or detained indefinitely. Those who arrive without a visa seeking asylum are stigmatised as unlawful non-citizens, contained in detention centres, and, where not found to satisfy the narrow criteria of being refugees, are expelled from Australia's borders. Those who meet that criteria are further stigmatised through a regime of temporary protection, signalling their continuing status as unwelcome strangers within, with an imminent departure date. Like the white history, their status of perpetual non-belonging contains them in a state of suspended non-citizenship with no reasonable expectation of ever belonging anywhere.

Like Indigenous peoples, asylum seekers have been disenfranchised by the remapping of the Australian territory. The map of Australian migration zones embodies power effects which disenfranchise a cohort of people from claiming rights to enter and remain within Australian territory, with all sorts of other consequences for their non-citizenship status. This map manufactures Australian migration boundaries to exclude thousands of islands from Australian territory for the purposes of immigration policy. As previously explained, from 2001–5, the government introduced new laws and Regulations that effectively excised thousands of islands from Australia's migration zone (see Coombs 2005). Only those who land in a migration zone are entitled to evoke Australia's protection obligations under international law. By re-arranging the borders of these migration zones, an asylum seeker landing in an excised territory off Australia is not entitled to make an application for a valid visa, unless the minister allows it under one of her many discretionary powers. Nor are they entitled to judicial review of the determination of their refugee status. They cannot invoke Australia's protection obligations under the *Migration Act 1958* for they have not, in a narrow technical, legal sense, arrived in Australian territory for migration purposes.

The map of Australia's migration zone has an important genealogical precursor, with similar power effects. Just as the re-mapping of Australia's migration zone has disenfranchised potential asylum seekers from seeking refuge in Australia, the re-mapping of the Australian continent disenfranchised its original inhabitants of any claims to sovereignty. The map of *terra nullius Australis*, by declaring the continent empty and uninhabited, produces power effects which disenfranchised native title claims to sovereignty. Yet Tindell's anthropological tribal map of Australia reveals a dense and complex overlapping network of Aboriginal habitation across the entire continent prior to colonisation, and especially so in those areas considered by white British settlers as uninhabitable. Unlike white settlement, Aboriginal peoples did manage to occupy the entirety of the continent, not just the coastal fringes, a pattern of settlement and civilisation rendered invisible by the map of Australia as *terra nullius*. What this highlights is that maps are diagrams of power that operate as geo-political devices on a global plane to cement the boundaries around nation-states and to differentiate populations who belong from those who do not. They are instruments of government and power which draw and redraw the boundaries around sovereignty and territory.

Thirdly, the colonial practices of transportation mirror, in vital respects, the practices of deporting asylum seekers. Both entail similar disciplinary technologies of population control, forced removal, containment, expulsion, and the mass movement of people across borders on a routine bureaucratic scale (Walters 2002). Between 1787 and 1868 over 80,000 convicts, an annual average of around 1000 convicts, were transported to Australia from over-crowded British jails, to perform the forced labour tasks of nation building (Hughes 1986). In the 2001 financial year alone, 10,894 over-stayers, unauthorised persons and illegal non-citizens were removed from Australia (DIMIA 2002: 57)—ten times as many convicts transported on an average annual basis. Both policy devices entailed administrative practices that deny citizenship status to 'non-citizens'. In this sense the convict is the genealogical precursor to the asylum seeker. There are of course some differences. The transportation of convicts was about populating and building Australia through the forced migration of convict labour, while forced deportation is about expelling non-citizens and protecting the nation. Regardless, repugnant and illiberal practices of governance are deeply embedded in both these forms of population transfer and control.

8.   CONCLUSION

In this chapter, I have explored how an intensifying network of policies and regimes of governance have come to police Australian borders through regulatory techniques of socio-spatial ordering and control. I have argued that border protection measures are disciplinary technologies of population control that trace their genealogy to other forms of illiberal governance peculiar in some senses to Australia's history as a colonial outpost of Britain. First, the asylum seeker issue taps into deeply embedded anxieties about the fear of invasion. The symbolic conflation between contagion, invasion and immigration has long shaped Australian anxieties about the security of our island border, its border controls and quarantine legislation. Secondly, in many ways, contemporary border control technologies mirror the historical efforts used to contain Aboriginal populations within white man-made borders, such as reserves and missions, following Britain's proclamation of sovereignty over the island continent. And lastly, the colonial practices of convict transportation mirror in vital respects the practices of deporting of asylum seekers. Both entail disciplinary technologies of population control, such as forced removal, containment, expulsion, and the mass movement of people across borders. Neither command any respect for the dignity or human rights of global citizens.

A Machiavellian mix of sovereign laws and forms of bio-politics discursively construct asylum seekers as threats to Australian health, identity, nationhood and sovereignty, justifying overtly disciplinary forms of border control. The exercise of these powers coincides with a populist politics of intolerance for others, difference and diversity, commonly expressed as a fear of the other, fear of invasion, or white anxieties about an Asian or Middle Eastern invasion, accompanied by a collective historical memory loss about the invasion by that first unauthorised boat arrival and the population control measures that followed, through the systematic transportation of convicts and the disenfranchisement of Indigenous claims to sovereignty. On first assessment, it certainly appears as if the new interventionism in policing the 'failed states' of the Pacific, justified in terms of restoring law and order on our extra-territorial borders, has set itself on a similar strategy of illiberal governance under the familiar guise of protecting Australia's security.

In 2003, I worked as a senior researcher for the Australian Parliament and wrote a number of social policy briefs about immigration crime, border control, trafficking and the sex industry. My contribution to this book arose when I returned to academia and began to critically reflect on that unique close-up exposure to government policy making.

[1] If the same event happened today, these boats would not be determined as being inside Australia's migration zone. This is an important point to which I return later.

[2] See Department of Immigration, Multicultural and Indigenous Affairs, *Fact Sheet 66*; http://www.immi.gov.au/facts/64protection.htm#4.

[3] Australia's immigration system of strictly codified visa classes of entry and stay (as specified in the *Migration Act 1958* and its Regulations) is a system for protecting Australian sovereignty and national identity. Fundamental to the legislation is the separation of citizens from unlawful non-citizens. Section 13 defines a lawful non-citizen as a non-citizen with a valid visa within Australia's migration zone. Section 14 defines an unlawful non-citizen as '[a] non-citizen in the migration zone who is not a lawful non-citizen is an unlawful non-citizen.'

[4] The Hon. Minister Ruddock's home page, *Refugees and Asylum Seekers*; http://www. minister. immi.gov.au/faq/.

[5] See Department of Immigration, Multicultural and Indigenous Affairs, *Fact Sheet 64*, for a list of entitlements; http://www.immi.gov.au/facts/64protection.htm#4.

[6] Gazetted on 28 August 2003 as Migration Amendment Regulations 2003 No. 6 (No.224).

[7] *Migration Amendment (Excision from Migration Zone) Act 2001*; *Migration Amendment (Excision from Migration Zone) (Consequential Provisions) Act 2001*; *Migration Legislation Amendment Act (No. 5) 2001*; *Migration Amendment Act (No. 6) 2001*; *Border Protection (Validation and Enforcement Powers) Act 2001*; *Migration Legislation Amendment (Judicial Review) Act 2001*. Date of assent 27 September 2001.

[8] Under Migration Amendment Regulations 2002 (No. 4).

[9] Migration Legislation Amendment (Further Border Protection Measures) Bill 2002 [No. 2].

[10] Migration Legislation Amendment (Further Border Protection Measures) Bill 2002 [No. 2].

[11] Migration Amendment Regulations 2003 (No. 8) No. 283.

[12] Migration Amendment Regulations 2005 (No. 6) No. 171 of 2005.

[13] Motion of disallowance not allowed 18 August 2005.

[14] On 1 October 2001, the *Migration Legislation Amendment Act (No.6) 2001* introduced changes to tighten the provisions relating to persecution, as well as those relating to a particular social group. Section 91R provides that the Refugee Convention does not apply to persecution unless a convention reason is the essential and significant reason for the persecution, it amounts to serious harm, and entails systematic and discriminatory conduct. Section 91S prevents people from claiming persecution as a member of a particular social group, where there is no convention-related reason.

[15] See also submissions from Human Rights and Equal Opportunity Commission, Amnesty International Australia and the Catholic Commission for Justice, Development and Peace.

[16] Submissions from: Dr Andreas Schloenhardt, University of Adelaide; Christopher Livingston and Associates; Joanna Stratton, Australian National University Honours dissertation; Refugee Council of Australia; Human Rights and Equal Opportunity Commission; Catholic Commission for Justice, Development and Peace; Legal Aid NSW; the Uniting Church; South Brisbane Immigration and Community Legal Service and Amnesty International Australia.

[17] 'Mr al Masri had applied to return to the Gaza Strip after exhausting all avenues to be granted a protection visa. However, on the day he was to leave, Mr al Masri was told the Israeli government had refused to allow him to return. The neighbouring countries of Syria, Egypt and Jordan also refused to grant him a visa, resulting in his continued detention in the now-closed Woomera detention centre, in South Australia. Mr al Masri was released from Woomera last September after the Federal Court ruled his detention was indefinite and thus unlawful. He was deported soon after but the government continued its appeal of the Federal Court ruling in a bid to avoid a precedent that could affect its detention of hundreds of other detainees' (AAP news story, 14 August 2003).

[18] B & B & Minister for Immigration & Multicultural & Indigenous Affairs [2003] FamCA 451 (19 June 2003).

[19] B and B and The Minister for Immigration and Multicultural and Indigenous Affairs [2003] FamCA 621 (25 August 2003).

[20] See speech by Senator Sherry, Migration Amendment (Duration of Detention) Bill 2003: Second Reading Speech, Senate, *Hansard*, 8 September 2003.

[21] Migration Amendment (Detention Arrangements) 2005, date of assent 29 June 2005.

[22] For example, under regulation 785.225B, if a Medical Officer of the Commonwealth considers that the applicant has a disease or condition that is, or may result in the applicant being, a threat to public health in Australia or a danger to the Australian community, arrangements have been made, on the advice of the Medical Officer of the Commonwealth, to place the applicant under the professional supervision of a health authority in a state or territory to undergo any necessary treatment. Regulation 866.224 requires an applicant for a protection visa to undergo an examination for tuberculosis. Applicants must also satisfy the health criteria in clauses 866.223, 866.224, 866.224A and 866.224B.

REFERENCES

Agamben, G., 1998, *Homo Sacer: Sovereign Power and Bare Life*, Stanford University Press, California.

Australian Strategic Policy Institute, 2003, *Our Failing Neighbour: Australia and the Future of Solomon Islands*, The Australian Strategic Policy Institute, Canberra.

Bashford, A. 2002, Contagion, Immigration, Nation, *Australian Historical Studies*, **33(120): 334–58**.

Betts, K., 2002, Boatpeople and the 2001 election, *People and Place*, **10(2)**.

Boeri, T., Hanson, G., McCormack, B., eds., 2002, *Immigration Policy and the Welfare System,* The William Davidson Institute in association with Oxford University Press, Oxford.

Coombs, M., 2005, Excising Australia: are we really shrinking?, *Research Note No 5*, 2005-06, Department of Parliamentary Library, Canberra.

Crock, M., 1998, *Immigration and Refugee Law in Australia*, Federation Press, Sydney.

Crock, M., 2000, A sanctuary under review: where to from here for Australia's refugee and humanitarian program?, *University of New South Wales Law Journal*, **23(3): 247**.

Crock, M. and Saul, B., 2001, *Refugees and the Law*, Federation Press, Sydney.

Department of Foreign Affairs and Trade, 2003, *Advancing the National Interest: Australia's Foreign and Trade Policy White Paper,* Commonwealth of Australia, Canberra.

Department of Immigration, Multiculturalism and Indigenous Affairs (DIMIA), 2002, *Annual Report 2001–2*, Commonwealth of Australia.

Department of Immigration, Multiculturalism and Indigenous Affairs, 2003a, *Humanitarian Program Statistics*; http://www.dimia.gov.au/statistics/refugee.

Department of Immigration, Multiculturalism and Indigenous Affairs, 2003b, Unauthorised Arrivals and Detention: Information; http://www.dimia.gov.au/illegals/uad.index.htm.

Dinnen, S., 2004, Lending a fist? Australia's new interventionism in the southwest Pacific, *State Society and Governance in Melanesia Discussion Paper*, Discussion Paper 5, Research School of Pacific and Asian Studies, ANU, Canberra.

Downer, A., 2003, *Press Release* (12 February 2003); http://www.foreignminister.gov.au/releases /2003/index.html

Farmer, B., 2005, Legislation Legal and Constitutional Legislation Committee Estimates, *Senate Hansard* (25 May 2005).

For, S., 2002, Judicial review of migration decisions: ousting the *Hickman* privative clause?, *Melbourne University Law Review*, **26(3) 537–559**.

Goodall, H., 1996, *From Invasion to Embassy: Land in Aboriginal Politics in New South Wales, 1770-1972*, Allen & Unwin, Sydney.

Green, P. and Grewcock, M,, 2002, The war against illegal immigration, *Current Issues in Criminal Justice*, Special Issue: Refugee Issues and Criminology, **14(1): 87–101**.

Hage, G., 1998, *White Nation: Fantasies of White Supremacy in a Multicultural Society*, Pluto Press, Sydney.

Harding, R., 1997, *Private Prisons and Public Accountability*, Open University Press, Buckingham.

Hearn, J. and Eastman, K., 2000, Human rights issues for Australia at the United Nations: Australia's non-refoulement obligations under the Torture Convention and the ICCPR, *Australian Journal of Human Rights*, **6(1): 216–238**.

Hegarty, D, May, R., Regan, A., Dinnen, S., Nelson, H., and Duncan, R., 2004, Rebuilding state and nation in Solomon Islands, *State Society and Governance in Melanesia Discussion Paper*, Discussion Paper 2, Research School of Pacific and Asian Studies, ANU, Canberra.

Hindess, B., 2000, Citizenship in the international management of populations, *American Behavioural Scientist*, **43(9): 1486–1497**.

Home Office [UK], *Secure Borders, Safe Haven – Integration with Diversity in Modern Britain*, London, 2002.

Hughes, R., 1986, *The Fatal Shore: A History of the Transportation of Convicts to Australia 1787–1868,* Collins Harvell, London.

Human Rights and Equal Opportunity Commission, 1997, *National Inquiry into the Separation of Aboriginal and Torres Strait Islander Children from Their Families, Brining Them Home*, Commonwealth of Australia, Canberra.

Kabutqulaka, T. T., 2005, Australian foreign policy and the RAMSI intervention in the Solomon Islands, *The Contemporary Pacific,* **17(2): 283–308**.

Kerin, J., 2003, How big-stick diplomacy defused PNG rebellion, *Weekend Australian* (20 September 2003) p.17.

Kerin, J. 2004, You police the Pacific: US, *The Australian* (5 March 2004) p. 1.

Kinslor, J., 2000, Non-refoulement and torture: the adequacy of Australia's laws and practices in safe-guarding asylum-seekers from torture, *Australian Journal of Human Rights*, 6(2); http://www.austlii.edu.au/au/journals/AJHR/2000/24.html.

Kirby, P. 2000, *Report of the Independent Investigation into the Management and Operations of Victoria's Private Prisons*, Department of Justice, Melbourne.

Newman, L., Dudley, M., Gale, F., and Mares, S., 2002, Seeking refuge, losing hope: parents and children in immigration detention, *Australian Psychiatry*, **10(2): 91-96**.

McAllister, I., 2002, Border protection, the 2001 Australian election and the Coalition victory, *Australian Journal of Political Science,* **38(3): 445–463**.

Mares, P., 2001, *Borderline: Australia's treatment of Refugees and Asylum Seekers*, UNSW Press, Sydney.

Marr, D. and Wilkinson, M., 2003, *Dark Victory*, Allen & Unwin, Sydney.

Marshall, T., 1950, *Citizenship and Social Class*, Cambridge University Press, Cambridge.

Marston, G., 2003, *Temporary Protection: Permanent Uncertainty: The Experiences of Refugees Living on Temporary Protection Visas*, Centre for Applied Social Research, RMIT, Melbourne.

McMaster, D., 2002, Asylum-seekers and the insecurity of a nation, *Australian Journal of International Affairs,* **56(2):279–290**.

Ozdowski, S., 2001, *National Inquiry into Children In Detention*, Human Rights and Equal Opportunity Commission, Commonwealth of Australia, Canberra.

Palmer Report, 2005, *Inquiry into the Circumstances of the Immigration Detention of Cornelia Rau,* Commonwealth of Australia, Canberra.

Peter Moyle, 2000, *Profiting from Punishment: Private Prisons in Australia: Reform or Regression*, Pluto Press, Annandale, NSW.

Phillips, J. and Lorimer, C., 2003, Children in detention, *e-brief,* Department of Parliamentary Library, Commonwealth of Australia, Canberra.

Phillips, J. and Millbank, A., 2004, *Protecting Australia's Borders*, Research Note No. 22, Department of Parliamentary Library, Commonwealth of Australia, Canberra.

Pickering, S. and Lambert, C., 2002, Deterrence: Australia's refugee policy, *Current Issues in Criminal Justice*, **14(1):75–78**.

Prince, P., 2005, *The Detention of Cornelia Rau*, Research Brief No. 14, Department of Parliamentary Library, Canberra.

Prince, P., Harris-Rimmer, S., Coombs, M., 2005, *Migration Litigation Reform Bill 2005*, Bills Digest No. 9, Department of Parliamentary Library, Canberra.

Poynting, S., 2002, Bin Laden in the suburbs, *Current Issues in Criminal Justice*, **14(1):46–50**.

Reynolds, H., 1989, *Dispossession: Black Australians and White Invaders*, Allen & Unwin, Sydney.

Rixon, P., 2003, *Solomon Islands: One Deployment too Many?*, *Research Note*, Department of Parliamentary Library, Commonwealth of Australia, Canberra.

Rowse, T., 2002, Culturally appropriate indigenous accountability, *The American Behavioural Scientist*, **43(9):1514–1532**.

Ruddock, P. MP, Press Release 'Information on New Border Control Legislation', 7 October 2001.

Ruddock, P., 2002, Ministerial Statements: Managing Migration, *House Hansard* (13 December 2002).

Ruddock, P. *Frequently Asked Questions*, *Refugees and Asylum Seekers*; http://www.minister. immi.gov.au/faq/background/asylum_seekers.htm#1.

Ruddock, P. 2001, Ministerial Statements, *House Hansard* (27 February 2001).

Senate Legal and Constitutional References Committee, 2003, Ministerial discretion in migration matters, *Senate Hansard*, Commonwealth of Australia, Canberra.

Senate Legal and Constitutional References Committee, 2002, Migration zone excision: an examination of the Migration Legislation Amendment (Further Border Protection Measures) Bill 2002, *Senate Hansard*, Commonwealth of Australia, Canberra.

Sherlock, S., 2003, *Behind the Solomon's Crisis: A Problem of Development*, Research Note, Department of Parliamentary Library, Commonwealth of Australia, Canberra.

Tazreiter, C., 2002, History, memory and the stranger in the practice of detention in Australia, *Journal of Australian Studies*, **72:3–12**.

United Nations High Commission for Refugees, 2001, *The State of the Worlds Refugees 2000*, Oxford University Press, Oxford.

United Nations High Commission for Refugees, 2003, UNHCR criticises Australia for turning boat people away, Press Release (11 November 2003).

van Hear, N., 1998, *New Diasporas: The Mass Exodus, Dispersal and Regrouping of Migrant Communities*, UCL Press, Padstow, UK.

Vanstone, A. 2005a, Senate—Legislation Legal and Constitutional legislation Committee Estimates, *Senate Hansard* (25 May 2005).

Vanstone, A., 2005b *Press Release* (16 June 2005); http://www.minister.immi.gov.au /media_releases /media05 /index05.htm.

Vanstone, A., 2005c, *Press Release* (20 June 2005); http://www.minister.immi.gov.au /media_releases/media05/index05.htm.

Vanstone, A., 2005d, *Press Release* (28 July 2005); http://www.minister.immi.gov.au /media_releases/media05/index05.htm.

Vaughn, B., 2004, Australia's strategic identity post September 11 in context: implications for the war against terror in Southeast Asia, *Contemporary Southeast Asia*, **1: 94–115**.

von Strockirch, K., 2004, The region in review: international issues and events 2003, *The Contemporary Pacific*, **Fall: 370–382**.

Walters, W., 2002, Deportation, expulsion, and the international police of aliens, *Citizenship Studies*, **6(3): 265–292**.

Weber, L., 2002, The detention of asylum seekers: 20 reasons why criminologists should care, *Current Issues in Criminal Justice*, **14(1): 9–30**.

York, B., 2003, *Australia and refugees, 1901–2002, Chronology No. 2*, Department of Parliamentary Library, Commonwealth of Australia, Canberra.

Zwi, K., Herberg, B., Dossetor D., and Field, J., 2003, A child in detention, *Medical Journal of Australia*, **179(6): 319–322**.

Chapter 11

DE-TERRITORIALISING CRIMINOLOGY

Sharon Pickering and Leanne Weber
Monash University and University of New South Wales

In this book, we have sought to outline a new criminology of the border, however, there is much work still to be done. Criminologists are already beginning to build theories which transcend the confines of the modern state, for example, in relation to transnational policing, transnational crime, supranational forms of criminal justice, peacekeeping initiatives and restorative processes within transitional states. The contributors to this collection have addressed an as yet unexplored dimension of this project, by making state borders themselves the focus of critical analysis. In doing so, we have sought in the book to complement and extend the work done on the one hand, by scholars of transnational crime and criminal justice, who are beginning to explore de-territorialised forms of deviance and control, and, on the other, theorists of governmentality and late-modernity, who have identified worldwide trends in forms of governance which are having profound impacts on criminal justice practices within state borders.

A critical, global criminology which problematises borders will have certain distinguishing features. It will acknowledge that the state reacts differently towards citizens and non-citizens within its territory, and that this is becoming increasingly significant in the production of both criminality and of justice. It will recognise global mobility as a new basis for stratification amongst the world's populations, identify the criminalisation of border crossing as a key element in shoring up these divisions, and promote the universalisation of mobility rights as an emerging human rights objective. Such a criminology will need to concomitantly advocate new forms of constraint to counter the increasingly unaccountable exercise of de-territorialised state power. The pursuit of these objectives will take globally-aware criminologists into new literatures of citizenship, sovereignty, human rights, security, migration studies, globalisation and international law. It will

S. Pickering and L. Weber (eds.), Borders, Mobility and Technologies of Control, 207–212.

also challenge Anglophone scholars to venture beyond the intellectual boundaries of the English-speaking world.

The de-territorialised criminology we envisage must first theorise state borders before building analyses which transcend them. The contributors to this volume have individually and collectively taken the first steps towards this objective by directly tackling the elusive nature of the border. Weber has introduced the idea of the mobile border, functionally defined by the location of state border-protection activities. She has argued that, faced with the continuing failure of border protection measures to prevent unauthorised crossing, some states have turned to the manipulation of the border itself as a new technology of control, rendering the border unreachable, and effectively unknowable, to unwanted border crossers. Pickering has argued that such technologies are grounded in complex and problematic narratives of the border and borderlands and their changing social construction. Borders, and the creation of borderlands, are not only sites of unchecked violence and exception against those who cross borders in an unauthorised fashion. The borderlands that have developed have relied heavily upon security narratives and the violent counter-geographies of de-territorialised spaces, both internal and external to the state. Wonders has extended this theme using the concept of border performativity, and identified racialised, classed and gendered processes of selective inclusion and exclusion through which the border is constructed. She likens the border to a hard metal sieve, sifting and sorting travellers according to their mobility entitlements to reproduce global inequalities. Carpenter has conceptualised the United States–Mexico borderland as a militarised space where legal protections for women are effectively suspended. The victimisation of Mexican women by state agents on the one side, and by Mexican men on the other, are both examples of violent border control technologies which, on the one hand, defend a physical border, and, on the other, reinforce a social boundary which demarcates traditional gender roles.

The chapters by Danner, Wilson and Carrington, in particular, depict a border that is increasingly defined through the regulatory techniques of late-modern societies preoccupied with security and risk. Danner's chapter integrates the literatures on the war on terror, crime and drugs; mobility and immigration; civil rights, human rights, security and globalisation, in a discussion of the securitisation of United States border control. Her chapter reminds us that the criminalisation of border crossing applies not just at the border but has become, in effect, a 'status offence' which can be applied at will to those who are considered not to belong. Wilson's chapter also depicts a state preoccupied with the control of mobility in the interests of national security; employing advanced biometric techniques of identity management which apply to citizens and non-citizens alike. And Carrington's chapter extends the criminological critique of law and order policies to a review of Australian border control, drawing an historical parallel between contemporary techniques of socio-spatial ordering and the internal boundaries used to contain the movements of Indigenous Australians after European colonisation. Green has located her depiction of the border within the context of the building of an expanded European identity, envisaging the borders of Europe as a series of concentric circles intended to act as bulwarks against the spontaneous arrival of asylum seekers from Africa and the Middle East.

All these contributors have argued that the discursive construction of unauthorised border crossers as a threat to national security and well-being has been used to justify unjust policies and technologies of exclusion within the relatively secure states of the developed world. Hills, writing in the Balkan context where recent conflict and ongoing nation building make unauthorised border crossing, arguably, a more tangible threat, also problematises the border, and reports varied and fluid conceptions about the nature and function of the borders between neighbouring states. Writing from the perspective of border guards, she finds some points of agreement, but also significant divergence between European Union policy-makers, national authorities and border officials, in their conceptualisation and performance of the border.

These analyses reveal that the idea of borders cannot easily be separated from the border technologies used to defend them; that borders are, in fact, largely constituted and defined through border protection technologies. Importantly a new criminological focus on the border needs to move beyond mere documentation of these border policing or border defining measures and requires a critical re-examination of emerging state practices at and around the border. Many examples of such critiques can be found amongst the contributions to this volume. Weber has identified new expressions of administrative and executive power, such as offshore interdiction and the manipulation of borders in time and space, which go beyond traditional enforcement practices and transgress both territorial boundaries and established legal principles. Pickering has examined the ways states construct and reconstruct their actions at and around the border which may increasingly generate counter narratives of the border that go well beyond the traditional notion of a cartographic line. Moreover, she argues that a focus on the border has effectively created a policing of the frontierlands where law enforcement has become unshackled from territorial nation-states and traditional legal checks on their actions and inaction. Other examples of this extra-territorial expression of state power are Australia's 'Pacific solution', which has been discussed in the chapters by Weber and Carrington, and Green's analysis of the analogous developments in Europe, which she dubs the 'Mediterranean solution'.

These chapters have raised specific questions about the accountability of state actions at and beyond the border, involving both direct expressions of sovereign power through offshore military intervention, and the co-opting of neighbouring countries into migration control partnerships which Green has described as 'outsourcing'. These authors have criticised the abrogation of international responsibility inherent in these extra-territorial border technologies, and Green explicitly denounces as 'state crime' systematic breaches of human rights such as the *refoulement* of asylum seekers to situations of danger and the fuelling of criminal migration networks. Carpenter also has depicted the border violence perpetrated against Mexican women by border officials at the United States–Mexican border in terms of the unaccountable exercise of state power, in a militarised frontierland where state authority had become unshackled from democratic controls.

Wilson has proposed that biometric identification and surveillance technologies are constitutive of new manifestations of state power expressed at and away from borders. Presented as socially neutral and non-discriminating, but perhaps better described as indiscriminate, he argues that networks of generalised surveillance potentially reconfigure humanity itself—and not just 'outsiders'—as suspect. Thus, the power to exclude in the technologised state is not only de-territorialised, that is, extending the reach of the state beyond its physical borders, but also hyper-territorialised, through potentially ubiquitous systems of internal control. The sorting of those who belong from those who don't in post 9/11 United States is also a central theme in the chapter by Danner. She sees these internal processes of exclusion being extrapolated from 'Muslim extremists' and 'Islamic fundamentalists', to other groups of ideologically-defined dissenters. Both analyses therefore question the distinction between the protected citizen and the suspect alien, and draw attention to the hybrid category of the 'outsider within'.

Despite this growing fear of the enemy within, and the turning inward of many technologies of border control, the role of the physical border as a site of protection from external threats continues to carry enormous symbolic and political weight, as evidenced in the chapters by Carrington and Wonders. Carrington has noted that illiberal tendencies which were inherent within law and order rhetoric are intensified at the border through the politics of inclusion and exclusion, which require states to discriminate in favour of citizens. She argues that the politics of exclusion at the border draws on powerful historical discourses highlighting fear of disease, cultural destruction and invasion by sea, coupled with a particular Australian consciousness of its status as a remote and isolated island required to protect itself by repelling threats at the perimeter. Wonders has contrasted the differing construction and enforcement of borders in relation to tourists and migrants under conditions of globalisation, using categories reminiscent of the global 'tourists' and 'vagabonds' defined by Bauman, which we discuss in the introductory chapter. Wonders describes how technologies of border control in the United States and other countries of the global north operate selectively to keep out migrants perceived as risky and needy, but notes that movements of migrants and tourists both arise from similar global processes and offer similar risks and benefits for nation-states.

Writing in a different context, Hills' comparative analysis of divergent state practices at the borders of the western Balkans underlines the particular importance of physical borders as territorial markers in emerging or unstable states. In contrast to the observations by other contributors of the increasingly de-territorialised exercise of power by developed states, she concludes that security is yet to be de-territorialised in a region where this would require a level of cross-border cooperation that is currently politically unattainable. This also reminds us of the highly developed technologies of control which are necessary for the unilateral de-territorialisation of state power.

Carrington and Danner, in particular, have drawn attention to specific links between trends in criminal justice policy and emerging technologies of border control. Carrington argues that Australia has applied law and order arguments supra-nationally to justify the extra-territorial expansion of its sovereignty into the Pacific, through policing interventions in so-called 'weak states'. She critiques these developments in the context of an emergent neo-colonialism, which is firmly rooted in Antipodean history but is now taking on a new guise. Danner has drawn a parallel between the huge expenditures on the United States' wars on drugs and terrorism; connecting with arguments made by theorists of late-modernity about the increasing punitiveness of the neo-liberal state. She extends this vision to include control of the supposed enemy without, who is becoming increasingly indistinguishable from the outsider within.

The new criminology of the border that has begun to be traced in this volume has drawn extensively on literatures well beyond criminology that inform a varied approach to what might be considered the de-territorialisation of criminological inquiry. Substantively, this requires criminology to incorporate the transnational into its everyday considerations and theorisations. This task begins with inquiry that mirrors the de-territorialisation of law enforcement at and beyond the border that has both responded to and pre-empted increased mobility under conditions of globalisation. But it will quickly require criminological inquiry beyond the expanded criminal justice apparatus that has developed with the border as its *raison d'etre* and extend to the radically changing spaces of the border. Perhaps most urgent will be a criminological focus on the identity politics that inform a re-conceptualisation of sovereignty and human rights. Such de-territorialisation of criminological inquiry will develop a transversal space for criminological theory and method which is political, cultural and economic in focus. State borders will not be irrelevant in the globalised world which is now emerging, and will rather persist for some time as sites of analysis within a de-territorialised criminology. But as their role as access points to prosperity and security, and as signifiers of identity and belonging, begins to wane, their significance as sites to be defended and manipulated by states will equally diminish. In the meantime, a criminology of the border will chart the changing meanings of the border and borderlands, the emerging technologies of border control, and the impact of these technologies on those who transgress either the physical, expanded or internal borders of the nation-state. Immediately it will need to find new and increasingly complex ways to check power and violence in de-territorialised spaces and develop a criminological language for its discussion and theorisation.

Index